Lecture Notes in Computer Scie

Edited by G. Goos, J. Hartmanis and J. van Leeuwen

Springer

Berlin
Heidelberg
New York
Barcelona
Hong Kong
London
Milan
Paris
Singapore
Tokyo

Rajkumar Buyya   Mark Baker (Eds.)

Grid Computing – GRID 2000

First IEEE/ACM International Workshop
Bangalore, India, December 17, 2000
Proceedings

Springer

Series Editors

Gerhard Goos, Karlsruhe University, Germany
Juris Hartmanis, Cornell University, NY, USA
Jan van Leeuwen, Utrecht University, The Netherlands

Volume Editors

Rajkumar Buyya
Monash University
School of Computer Science and Software Engineering
C5.10, Caulfield Campus
Melbourne, VIC 3145, Australia
E-mail: rajkumar@csse.monash.edu.au

Mark Baker
University of Portsmouth
Division of Computer Science
Mercantile House, Hampshire Terrace
Portsmouth, Hants, UK, PO1 2EG, UK
E-mail: Mark.Baker@port.ac.uk

Cataloging-in-Publication Data applied for

Die Deutsche Bibliothek - CIP-Einheitsaufnahme

Grid computing : GRID 2000 ; first IEEE/ACM international workshop,
Bangalore, India, December 17, 2000 ; proceedings / Rajkumar Buyya ;
Mark Baker (ed.). - Berlin ; Heidelberg ; New York ; Barcelona ; Hong
Kong ; London ; Milan ; Paris ; Singapore ; Tokyo : Springer, 2000
 (Lecture notes in computer science ; Vol. 1971)
 ISBN 3-540-41403-7

CR Subject Classification (1998): C.2, D.1-4

ISSN 0302-9743
ISBN 3-540-41403-7 Springer-Verlag Berlin Heidelberg New York

Springer-Verlag Berlin Heidelberg New York
a member of BertelsmannSpringer Science+Business Media GmbH
© Springer-Verlag Berlin Heidelberg 2000
Printed in Germany

Typesetting: Camera-ready by author, data conversion by PTP Berlin, Stefan Sossna
Printed on acid-free paper   SPIN 10781129   06/3142   5 4 3 2 1 0

Preface

Welcome to GRID 2000, the first annual IEEE/ACM international workshop on grid computing sponsored by the IEEE Computer Society's Task Force on Cluster Computing (TFCC) and the Association for Computing Machinery (ACM). The workshop has received generous sponsorship from the European Grid Forum (eGrid), the EuroTools SIG on Metacomputing, Microsoft Research (USA), Sun Microsystems (USA), and the Centre for Development of Advanced Computing (India).

It is a sign of the current high levels of interest and activity in Grid computing that we have had contributions to the workshop from researchers and developers in Australia, Austria, Canada, France, Germany, Greece, India, Italy, Japan, Korea, The Netherlands, Spain, Switzerland, UK, and USA. It is our pleasure and honor to present the first annual international Grid computing meeting program and the proceedings.

The Grid: A New Network Computing Infrastructure

The growing popularity of the Internet along with the availability of powerful computers and high-speed networks as low-cost commodity components are helping to change the way we do computing. These new technologies are enabling the coupling of a wide variety of geographically distributed resources, such as parallel supercomputers, storage systems, data sources, and special devices, that can then be used as a unified resource and thus form what is popularly known as the "Grids". The Grid is analogous to the power (electricity) grid and aims to couple distributed resources and offer consistent and inexpensive access to these resources irrespective of their physical location. The interest in creating Grids (by pooling resources from multiple organizations) is growing due to the potential for solving large-scale problems that typically cannot be solved with local resources. Internationally there are a large number of projects actively exploring the design and development of different Grid system components, services, and applications. Pointers to these projects can be found at the following sources:

- Grid Infoware – http://www.gridcomputing.com
- IEEE Distributed Systems Online – http://computer.org/channels/ds/gc

It is projected that Grids are expected to drive the economy of the 21st century in a similar fashion to how electrical power grids drove the economy of the 20th century.

Grid systems need to hide complexities associated with the management and usage of resources across multiple administrative institutions. The following are some of the key features of Grid infrastructures:

- Flexibility and extensibility
- Domain autonomy
- Scalability
- Global name space

- Ease of use and transparent access
- Performance
- Security
- Management and exploitation of heterogeneous resources
- Interoperability between systems
- Resource allocation and co-allocation
- Fault-tolerance
- Dynamic adaptability
- Quality of Service (QoS)
- Computational Economy

The grid must be designed and created in such a way that their components (fabric, middleware, and higher-level tools) and applications handle the key design issues in a coordinated manner. For instance, Grid middleware offers services for handling heterogeneity, security, information, allocation, and so on. Higher level tools, such as resource brokers, support dynamic adaptability through automatic resource discovery, trading for economy of resources, resource acquisition, scheduling, the staging of data and programs, initiating computations, and adapting to changes in the Grid status. In addition, they also need to make sure that domain autonomy is honored but still meets user requirements such as QoS in coordination with other components. The papers accepted for inclusion in these proceedings address various issues related to the design, development, and implementation of Grid technologies and their applications.

Program Organization and Acknowledgements

The response to the workshop's call for papers has been excellent and we expect that attendance at the actual workshop will be equally impressive. The GRID 2000 program consists of a keynote speech (by Wolfgang Gentzsch on "DOT-COMing the GRID: Using Grids for Business"), an invited talk, and refereed technical paper presentations. We have accepted papers from authors of fifteen countries from among submissions from eighteen countries. We would like to thank all authors for submitting their research papers for consideration. We have grouped the contributed papers into five distinct categories, although inevitably there is some overlap:

- Network enabled server systems for the Grid (invited paper)
- Grid resource management
- Grid middleware and problem solving environments
- Grid testbeds and resource discovery
- Application-level scheduling on the Grid

The GRID 2000 meeting would not have taken place without the efforts of Viktor Prasanna, who has been the main driving force behind the international conference on High Performance Computing (HiPC). It is our pleasure to acknowledge his efforts and thank him for encouraging us to organize this annual internal meeting on Grid computing. The success of the workshop is wholly due to the hard work of the program committee members and external reviewers. They have donated their precious time for reviewing and offered their expert comments on the papers. All submitted papers have been peer reviewed by the technical program committee members and external referees. We requested four reviews for each paper and ensured that each paper received a minimum of three reviews. All highly recommended and promising works have been selected for presentation at the meeting.

We thank our keynote speaker Wolfgang Gentzsch (Director of Network Computing, Sun Microsystems) and invited speaker Satoshi Matsuoka (Tokyo Institute of Technology, Japan) for presenting their vision on Grid technologies.

We owe a debt of gratitude to all our sponsors and contributors. In particular, we would like thank R.K. Arora (C-DAC, Pune), Mohan Ram (C-DAC, Bangalore), and Wolfgang Gentzsch (Sun Microsystems) for responding to our request for financial support enthusiastically and being instrumental in obtaining generous donations from their respective organizations. Our special thanks go to Todd Needham (Microsoft Research, USA), who has voluntarily come forward to support our Task Force activities. We would also like to thank Hilda Rivera (ACM) for handling our request for ACM "in-cooperation" status. We thank Jarek Nabrzyski for his help in gathering the European Grid forum support for this workshop. Finally, we would like to thank the Springer-Verlag team, particularly Jan van Leeuwen (LNCS series editor), Alfred Hofmann (Executive Editor), Antje Endemann, and Karin Henzold. They are wonderful to work with!

We hope these proceedings serve as a useful reference on Grid computing. We wish you all the best and hope you enjoy your visit to the Silicon Valley of India!

December 2000
GRID 2000 Co-chairs
http://www.gridcomputing.org

Rajkumar Buyya   **Mark Baker**

Monash University, Australia   University of Portsmouth, UK
Http://www.buyya.com   http://www.dcs.port.ac.uk/~mab/

GRID 2000 Team

Workshop Chairs

- Rajkumar Buyya, Monash University, Australia
- Mark Baker, University of Portsmouth, England

Program Committee Members

- David Abramson, Monash University, Australia
- Ishfaq Ahmad, Hong Kong University of Science and Technology, China
- David Bader, University of New Mexico, Albuquerque, USA
- Mark Baker, University of Portsmouth, England
- Francine Berman, University of California, San Diego, USA
- Rajkumar Buyya, Monash University, Australia
- Steve Chapin, Syracuse University, New York, USA
- Jack Dongarra, University of Tennessee/ORNL, Knoxville, USA
- Wolfgang Gentzsch, Sun Microsystems, USA
- Jonathan Giddy, Distributed Systems Technology Centre, Australia
- Sergi Girona, Universitat Politecnica de Catalunya, Spain
- Ken Hawick, Adelaide University, Australia
- Hai Jin, University of Southern California, Los Angeles, USA
- William Johnston, Lawrence Berkeley National Lab. / NASA Ames., USA
- Vipin Kumar, University of Minnesota, Minneapolis, USA
- Domenico Laforenza, CNUCE (Inst. of Italian National Research Council)
- Gregor von Laszewski, Argonne National Laboratory, Chicago, USA
- Craig Lee, The Aerospace Corporation, Los Angeles, USA
- Miron Livny, University of Wisconsin, Madison, USA
- Muthucumaru Maheswaran, University of Manitoba, Canada
- Satoshi Matsuoka, Tokyo Institute of Technology, Japan
- Jarek Nabrzyski, Poznan Supercomputing and Networking Center, Poland
- Lalit Patnaik, Indian Institute of Science, Bangalore, India
- Mohan Ram, Centre for Development of Advanced Computing, India
- Alexander Reinefeld, ZIB, Berlin, Germany
- Michael Resch, High Performance Computing Center Stuttgart, Germany
- Les Robertson, European Organization for Nuclear Research, Switzerland
- Mitsuhisa Sato, Real World Computing Partnership, Japan
- Peter Sloot, University of Amsterdam, The Netherlands

GRID 2000 Additional Referees

We acknowledge the following external referees for reviewing papers (the list does not include members of the program committee, who did most of the review work):

- Achim Streit
- Antonio Lagana
- Arthur Maccabe
- Daniele Micciancio
- Dick van Albada
- Franck Cappello
- Gerd Quecke
- Heath James
- Heinz Stockinger
- Henri Casanova
- John Brooke
- Kirk Schloegel
- Mihir Bellare
- Mike Ashworth
- Omer F. Rana
- Paul Coddington
- Rafael Avila
- Spyros Lalis
- Vishwanath P. Baligar
- Walfredo Cirne
- William Leinberger
- Wolfgang Ziegler
- Yuzhong Sun

GRID 2000 Sponsors and Supporters

Institute of Electrical and Electronics Engineers (IEEE) http://www.ieee.org	
IEEE Computer Society http://www.computer.org	
IEEE Task Force on Cluster Computing (TFCC) http://www.ieeetfcc.org	
Association for Computing Machinery (ACM SIGARCH) http://www.acm.org	
EuroTools SIG on Metacomputing http://www.eurotools.org/	
European Grid Forum (eGRID) http://www.egrid.org/	
Centre for Development of Advanced Computing (C-DAC), India http://www.cdacindia.com/	
Microsoft Research, USA http://www.research.microsoft.com	
Gridware Inc., Germany/USA http://www.gridware.com	

Table of Contents

Grid Test-Beds and Resource Discovery

Application-Level Scheduling on the Grid

DOT-COMing the GRID: Using Grids for Business

Wolfgang Gentzsch

Sun Microsystems Inc, Palo Alto, California, USA

Abstract: In this presentation, a short outline of the history of past and present Grid projects in research and industry is given, followed by some near- and long-term Grid scenarios and visions on how data and compute Grids will complement current Internet services and thus change our working and living environments and habits. In essence, implementation and professional exploitation of the complex and highly sophisticated Grid technologies will still take a couple of years and give us time enough to adapt to the dramatic changes and potential opportunities Grids will create in the future.

1. Grids in Research

In the early Nineties, research groups all over the world started exploiting distributed computing resources over the Internet: scientists collected and utilized hundreds of workstations for highly parallel applications like molecular design and computer graphics rendering. Other research teams glued large supercomputers together into a virtual metacomputer, distributing subsets of a meta-application (e.g. the computer simulation of multi-physics applications) to specific vector, parallel and graphics computers, over wide-area networks.

The scope of many of these research projects was to understand and demonstrate the actual potential of the networking, computing and software infrastructure and to develop it further. This led us to Internet infrastructure projects like Globus and Legion, which enable users to combine nearly any set of distributed resources into one integrated metacomputing workbench to allow users to measure nature (e.g. with microscope or telescope), process the data according to some fundamental mathematical equations (e.g. the Navier-Stokes equations), and provide computer simulations and animations to study and understand these complex phenomena.

These projects created a new era in distributed computing, according to the book The Grid: Blueprint for a New Computing Infrastructure. Generally speaking, a computational Grid is a hardware and software infrastructure that provides dependable, consistent, pervasive, and inexpensive access to computational capabilities. These Grids, in the near future, will be used by computational engineers and scientists, associations, corporations, environment, training and education, states, consumers, etc. They will be dedicated to on-demand computing, high-throughput computing, data-intensive computing, collaborative computing, and supercomputing, potentially on an economic basis. Grid communities, among others, are national Grids (like ASCI), virtual grids (e.g. for research teams), private grids (e.g. a BMW CrashNet for the car manufacturer BMW and its suppliers, for collaborative crash simulations), and public grids (e.g. consumer networks).

R. Buyya and M. Baker (Eds.:) GRID 2000, LNCS 1971, pp. 1-3, 2000.

Today, we see the first attempts to more systematically exploit Grid computing resources over the Internet. Distributed computing projects like SETI@home, Distributed.Net, and Folderol, let Internet users download scientific data, run it on their own computers using spare processing cycles, and send the results back to a central database. Recently, Compute Power Market project has been initiated to develop software technologies that enable creating Grids where anyone can sell idle CPU cycles, or those in need can buy compute power much like electricity today.

2. Grids in Industry

Encouraged by the response of thousands of participants on these research initiatives, new Internet startup companies like Popular Power, Entropia, Distributed Science, and United Devices are trying to turn this idea into real business that resell untapped resources for a profit, hoping that computer users will be interested to donating their extra computing power to projects that crunch a lot of data, such as the search for a new cancer drug or patterns in the human genome. Other potential candidate applications are complex financial analysis and generation of intensive graphics.

While this kind of global (and 'wild') Internet computing will probably be successful in the future where privacy and security are only minor issues (i.e., mostly in research-oriented projects), global industries might have some real concerns in using this Internet computing technology for their strategic businesses. Beside security of information and data, these companies need guarantees for the availability and utilization of dedicated resources, high-level quality of services, easy, fast and authenticated computing portal access to hardware and software, and tools for accounting, reporting, monitoring, and planning.

Just recently, industry started to experiment with more commercially oriented e-business models for high-performance and data-intensive computing via the Internet. For example, debis Systemhaus, a DaimlerChrysler company in Germany, offers its NEC SX-5 supercomputer power through an Internet e-commerce gateway using a public web server, a secure web server and a discussion server. The web pages are based on JAVA applets, CGI scripting and JAVA servlets. In addition an LDAP customer database is used for the management of security and encryption certificates. A user can register using HTML forms; the secure Web site requests certificates to identify user; a hummingbird UNIX desktop from the browser redirects application to customer desktop; and Pegasus, (the application dependent job submission GUI), submits the job to the batch system.

3. Grid Resource Management

Most of the underlying sophisticated technologies are currently under development. Large research communities like the GridForum and EGrid are coordinating all kinds of Grid research, prototype Grid environments exist like public-domain Globus and Legion, research in resource management is underway in projects like EcoGrid, and the basic building block for a commercial Grid resource managers exists with Sun's Grid Engine software. Grid Engine is a new generation distributed resource management software which dynamically matches users' hardware and software requirements to the available heterogeneous resources in the network according to predefined policies usually prescribed by the management in the enterprise.

The Grid Engine acts much like our body's central nervous system (sometimes called 'The Body's Internet'). The Grid Engine Master ('the brain') with its sensors in every computer (comparable to the sensations of touch, sound, smell, taste, and sight) dynamically acts and reacts, according to set policies (comparable to move, eat, drink, sleep) to allow for full control and achieve optimum utilization and efficiency. Grid Engine has been developed as an enhancement of Codine from former Gridware Inc, according to well defined requirements from the Army Research Lab in Aberdeen, and BMW in Munich, where today Grid Engine manages over 800 powerful compute servers in each of these local Grids. Average usage increased from well under 50% to over 90%, in both environments.

4. Future Grid Economies

The next step is to enhance Grid Engine, which currently is restricted to manage local computer resources, towards 'The GRID Broker', which will be able to match the user's compute jobs with the available resources in the network, including invoicing users for the CPU power they consume, very much like todays electric power consumption, telephone usage or water supply. The Grid broker will match the user's requirements to the best fitting Application Service Provider (ASP) in the universe which optimally fulfills the user's hardware, software and service needs.

This GRID Broker belongs to the enabling technologies of the next Internet Age. The Internet, for a long time, has been used only for information. Only recently, enabled by several important improvements in hardware infrastructure, security, authentication, and ease of access, it is used for electronic commerce. And just now, the next revolutionary step complementing the Internet can be foreseen: The Grid Computing Infrastructure, i.e. all kinds of dedicated GRIDs used for collaboration and collaborative computing in industry and research, for application simulation and animation, for real-time video, on-demand virtual reality presentations, and other services for consumers and producers.

This high-quality and economically oriented usage of the Internet will be enabled by several new technologies and achievements made recently. For example, CORBA offers a standard interface definition to interconnect any distributed object in the world. JAVA provides a common platform for distributed resources and thus guarantees full cross-platform portability, and JINI allows to interconnect any electronic device in a scalable way. And the chaos which potentially can arise with this wealth of interconnected devices, clusters, subgrids, and grids, will be removed and brought into a well-organized and well-functioning 'organism', by the GRID Resource Broker, supported by intelligent agents which, through the network or wireless, report to the Central Grid Engine the details on available resources, and the consumers' habits and needs for specific resources in the GRID.

Then, eventually, in a next (and final?) step, the central Grid Engine will disappear, partly as an integrated component of the local operating systems, and partly being replaced by intelligent mobile agents, which enable a universal and self-healing environment with potentially infinite compute power available on-demand, and as easily accessible as our today's electricity, telephony, roads and water infrastructures. For URLs to projects referenced the paper see: gridcomputing.com.

Design Issues of Network Enabled Server Systems for the Grid

Satoshi Matsuoka[1,2], Hidemoto Nakada[3], Mitsuhisa Sato[4], and Satoshi Sekiguchi[3]

[1] Tokyo Institute of Technology, Tokyo, Japan
matsu@is.titech.ac.jp
[2] Japan Science and Technology Corporation, Tokyo, Japan
[3] Electrotechnical Laboratory, Tsukuba Ibaraki, Japan
nakada@etl.go.jp
sekiguchi@etl.go.jp
[4] Real World Computing Partnership, Tsukuba Ibaraki, Japan
msato@trc.rwcp.or.jp

Abstract. Network Enabled Server is considered to be a good candidate as a viable Grid middleware, offering an easy-to-use programming model. This paper clarifies design issues of Network Enabled Server systems and discusses possible choices, and their implications, namely those concerning connection methodology, protocol command representation, security methods, etc. Based on the issues, we have designed and implemented new Ninf system v.2.0. For each design decision we describe the rationale and the details of the implementation as dictated by the choices. We hope that the paper serves as a design guideline for future NES systems for the Grid.

1 Introduction

A Network Enabled Server System(NES) is an RPC-style Grid system where a client requests the service of a task to a server. There are several systems that adopt this as the basic model of computation, such as our Ninf system[1], Netsolve[2], Nimrod[3], Punch[4], and Grid efforts utilizing CORBA[5,6,7].

NES systems provides easy-to-use, intuitive, and somewhat restricted user and programming interface, This allows the potential users of Grid systems to easily make his applications "Grid enabled", lowering the threshold of acceptance. Thus, we deem it as one of the important abstractions to be layered on top of lower-level Grid services such as Globus[8] or Legion[9].

Since 1995, we have been conducting the Ninf project, whose goal has been to construct a powerful and flexible NES system [10,11], and have investigated the utility of such systems through various application and performance experiments[12]. There, we have gained precious experience on the necessary technical aspects of NES systems which distinguishes them from conventional RPC systems such as CORBA, as well as various tradeoffs involved in the design of such systems[13]. Based on such observations, we have redesigned and reimplemented version 2.0 of the Ninf system from scratch.

R. Buyya and M. Baker (Eds.): GRID 2000, LNCS 1971, pp. 4–17, 2000.

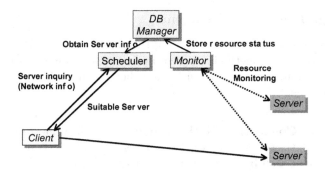

Fig. 1. General Architecture of NES Systems

The purpose of this paper is to discuss the notable technical points which led to the design decisions made for Ninf v.2.0. In particular, for the latter half of the paper we focus on the security issues, which is mostly lacking in the current generation of NES systems.

2   General Overview of NES Systems

In general, NES systems consists of the following components: (Figure 1)

- **Clients:** Requests execution of grid-enabled libraries and/or applications to the server.
- **Servers:** Receives request from clients, and executes the grid-enabled libraries and/or applications on clients' behalf.
- **Scheduler:** Selects amongst multiple servers for execution according to the information obtained from the resource database.
- **Monitors:** Monitors the status of various resources, such as computing resource, communication resource, etc., and registers the results in the resource database.
- **Resource Database:** Stores and maintains the status of monitored resources.

The Monitors periodically "monitor" the status of resources such as the server, network, etc., and registers the results in the Resource Database. The users of Grid systems modifies his applications to utilize the servers with the use of client APIs, or tools that have been constructed using the client APIs. The Client inquires the Scheduler for an appropriate Server. The Scheduler, in turn, acquires the info on computing resources, and selects the appropriate server according to some scheduling algorithm, and returns the selection to the Client. The Client then remotely invokes the library/application on the selected server by sending the appropriate argument data. The server performs the computation, and returns the result data to the client.

2.1   Design Issues in NES Systems

There are several design issues regarding the construction of NES systems, including the connection methods of client and servers, communication protocols, and security. Moreover, there is an issue of how we make the system open to future extensions.

Client-Server Connection Methodologies. The client must first establish a connection with the selected server. The sub-issues involve 1) continuous connection versus connection-by-necessity, and 2) usage of proxies.

Continuous Connection versus Connection-by-Necessity: Continuous connection maintains connection between the server and the client during the time server is performing the computation. Contrastingly, Connection-by-Necessity makes fine-grain connection/disconnection between the client and the server on demand.

Continuous connection is typically employed for standard RPC implementations; it is easy to implement under the current TCP/IP socket APIs, and furthermore, allows easy detection of server faults via stream disconnection. The drawback is the restriction on how many parallel tasks that can be invoked by a client. Since the connection to the server must be maintained, the client process is requires more file descriptors than the number of parallel tasks being invoked. However, since the number of file descriptors per process is restricted for most OSes, this limits the number of parallel tasks. Such has not been a problem for traditional RPCs, since most transactions are short-lived, and/or the number of connections were small since the user tasks are sequential.

Moreover, continuous connection requires the client to constantly be on-line, without any interruption in the communication. Thus, the client cannot go off-line, neither deliberately nor by accident; even a momentary failure in the communication will cause a fault. This again is a restriction, since some Grid-enabled libraries may take hours or even days to compute.

By contrast, in Ninf v.2.0 we have adopted Connection-by-Necessity. Basically, when the client makes an RPC request to the server, it disconnects once the necessary argument data had been sent. Once the server finishes the computation, it re-establishes a new connection with the client, and sends back the result. This overcomes the restriction of the Continuous Connection, but a) the protocol becomes more complex, due to the requirement of server-initiated and secure connection re-establishment, b) there need to be an alternative method of detecting server faults, and c) performance may suffer due to connection costs.

Direct Connection versus Proxy-based Connection. Another concern is whether to connect the client and the server directly, or assume a dedicated, mediating proxies, for various purposes including connection maintenance, performance monitoring, and firewall circumvention.

The "old" Ninf system (up to v.1.2.) employed proxy-mediated connection, for the purpose of simplifying the client libraries. All traffic was mediated by the proxy; in fact, communication with the Scheduler for server selection was performed by the proxy and not by the client itself. On the other hand, routing the communication through the proxy will result in performance overhead, which is of particular concern for Grid systems since communication of large bulk of data is typical.

Communication Protocol Commands for Grid RPC. Communication Protocol Commands, or simply Protocol Commands are a set of commands that are used to govern the communication protocol between the client and the server. They can be largely categorized into binary formats and text-based formats.

Binary formats allow easy and lightweight parsing of command sequences, but are difficult to structure, debug and extend. Contrastingly, well-designed text-based formats are well-structured, easy to understand and extent, but are less efficient and require more software efforts to parse.

Although traditionally text-based commands for communication protocols were typically simple, involving little structure such as S-expressions, there is a recent trend to employ XML for such purpose. Although XML requires more efforts on the software side for parsing etc., we can assign schema in a standard way using DTD. Since command overhead can be amortized over relative large data transfer, we believe XML is a viable option given its proliferation as well as availability of standard tools.

Security Mechanism. Security is by all means an important part of any Grid system. However, there several options for security, depending on the operating environment of the system.

If the operating environment is totally local within some administrative domain, where all the participants can be trusted, we can merely do away with security. In a slightly more wide-area and well-administered environment, such as within a University campus, it suffices to restrict access based on, say, client IP address. On the other hand, if global usage is assumed, then by all means we must guard against malicious users, and thus require authentication based on encryption. Examples are Kerberos, which employs the symmetrical key technology, and SSL, which utilizes the public key algorithm.

System Openness and Interoperability with Other Grid Systems. One important design choice is how much we make the system open to customization, especially with respect to other, more general Grid software infrastructure, and/or Grid component with some specific function. More concretely, Grid toolkits such as Globus provide low-level communication layer, security layer, directory service, heartbeat monitoring, etc. Components such as NWS(Network Weather Service[14]) provides stable monitoring and prediction services for measuring resources on the Grid, such as node CPU load and network communication performance. Conventional components which had initially not intended as a Grid services could be incorporated as well, such as LDAP, which provides a standard directory service API; Globus employs LDAP directly with its MDS(Metacomputing Directory Service), providing a Grid directory service.

By using such existing subsystems and components, we can directly utilize the functionalities which had been tried and tested, and also subject to independent improvement. On the other hand, because such subsystems are designed for generality, they have larger footprint, and could be tougher to manage. Moreover the supported platform would be the intersection of the platforms supported by individual subsystems.

3   Design and Implementation of the New Ninf System

3.1   Conceptual Design Decision Overview

We designed and implemented a new version of the Ninf system (Ninf version 2.0) with the abovementioned design issues in mind. The new system is designed to be flexible and extensible, with interoperability with existing Internet and Grid subsystems in mind. Because NES systems typically involve tasks where computation is dominant, we made design decisions that gave precedence to interoperability and flexibility over possible communication overhead if such could be amortized.

Client-Server Connections. In order to accommodate multiple, fault-tolerant, long-running calls in Grid Environments, we adopted for connection-by-necessity over continuous connections. We have also decided to employ proxy-based connections in order to simplify client structure. However, in order to avoid bandwidth bottlenecks, proxies only intervene on command negotiations between the client and server; when the actual arguments of the remote call is being transferred, the client and the server communicate directly, unless a firewall must be crossed.

Communication Protocol Commands. For flexibility, extensibility, and interoperability, we decided to adopt the usage of XML-based text commands. In the latter sections we present an overview of the DTD schema for numerical RPCs. Free parsers for C and Java are available, which simplified our implementation.

Security Mechanism. To allow Ninf to be used in a global Grid environment, we opted to construct a Globus-like, SSL-based authentication and authorization layer, which allows delegation of authentication along a security chain. Kerberos was an obvious alternative, but SSL was becoming a commercial standard, and multiple free library implementations in C and Java are available.

System Openness and Interoperability with Other Grid Systems. This was the most difficult decision, since advantages and disadvantages of employing existing Grid components could be strongly argued both ways. As a compromise, we have decided to provide default implementations of all our basic submodules;

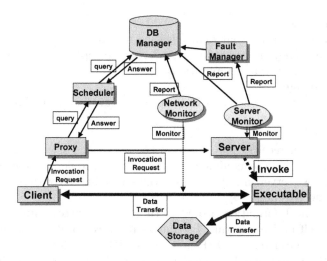

Fig. 2. Overview of the New Ninf System

however, we have designed them to have well-defined interfaces, to be pluggable with existing modules in operating environments where such services are already available. For example, although the default implementation of the resource database lookup service has its own LDAP lookup feature, it could also directly utilized Globus MDS services where they are available.

3.2   Overview of the New Ninf System V.2.0

The new Ninf system v.2.0 is composed of the following subsystems(Figure 2)

– **Client**
  A user-side component which requests (parts of) computing to be done on remote servers in the Grid. The client is "thin" in a sense that as little information as possible is retained on the client side; for example IDL of the remote call is not maintained by the client, but rather automatically shipped on demand from the server.
– **Server**
  Receives remote compute requests from the clients and invokes the appropriate executable. The server might act as a backend for invoking parallelized libraries on multiple compute nodes, such as a library written in C/Fortran+MPI served by a Cluster.
– **Proxy**
  Communicates with a Scheduler on behalf of the Client, and decides upon which server to invoke the remote computation, and forwards the request to the server. (The behavior of the proxy is similar to Netsolve Agents in this case.)

- **Executables**
  Components which actually embeds each remote applications or libraries to be invoked. They are invoked by the server, and communicate with the client to perform the actual computations.
- **Data Storage**
  Temporary storage on the Grid to store intermediate results amongst multiple servers.
- **Scheduler**
  The scheduler receives requests from the proxy, and selects an appropriate server under some scheduling algorithm. The scheduler communicates with the database server in order to drive the scheduling algorithm.
- **Database Manager**
  Manages the Information Stored in the Grid resources database. The database itself utilizes existing distributed resource database for the Internet and/or the Grid (e.g., LDAP or Globus MDS, which in turn uses LDAP itself); the resource lookup request from the client is delegated through the manager. This naturally allows other database infrastructure to be utilized.
- **Network Monitor/Server Monitor**
  Monitors the status of the network, servers, and other resources. The result is reported periodically and automatically to the database manager.
- **Fault Manager**
  Performs recovery action when some fault or error that affects the system in a global way, is detected. For example, if the server is found to be down (using heartbeat monitoring), the server is deleted from the resource database.

3.3   Client-Server Communication in the Ninf System 2.0

The new Ninf system manages the client-server communication in the following manner(Figure 3):

The client first requests the interface information of the executable to be invoked to the proxy. It then requests the invocation of the executable. The client immediately disconnects its connection with the proxy, and enters the state waiting for a callback from the proxy. The client then can proceed to issue hundreds of simultaneous requests, as there are no other pending connections.

The proxy in turn inquires the Scheduler for selection of an appropriate server (or a set of servers) to perform the invocation. The scheduler inquires the database manager for information on servers and network throughput information, as well as other resource information such as location of files used in the computation. The scheduling algorithm selects an appropriate server (or set of servers) and returns the info to the proxy. The algorithm itself is pluggable; one can employ simple algorithm as is employed with netsolve (sorting by server load), or more sophisticated algorithm such as those employed by Nimrod.

The proxy forwards the invocation request to the selected server. The server in turn invokes the executable for performing the actual computation. The executable then requests to the client the necessary arguments by sending the appropriate IDL program for marshalling. When all the arguments have been received,

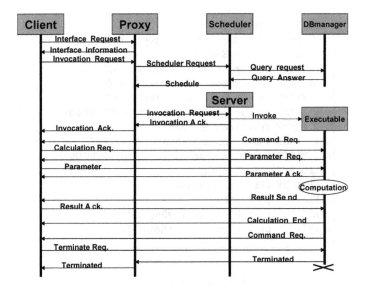

Fig. 3. Invocation Protocol

the executable notifies the client, disconnects the connection, and proceeds to compute the request. The client again enters the state to wait for callback from the executable on completion of the invocation.

When the computation is finished, the executable reconnects with the client, and transmits the result, indicating termination of the invocation. The client acknowledges the receipt with the termination command.

Finally, the executable notifies the proxy that the invocation has terminated. The proxy in turn forwards this to the client. The proxy notifies the Database Manager of the termination, allowing it to update the resource database.

3.4   Communication Protocol Commands in New Ninf

As an example of communication command protocol, we demonstrate the DTD of the protocol command for specifying and invoking on a server a remote executable, in Figure 4. Based on this DTD, here is sample invocation command in XML(Figure 5).

One may notice that the invocation command embodies two addresses, client and observer; here, client is the address used for client callbacks, where as observer is the address used to notify termination of invocation to the proxy.

3.5   Security Layer in the New Ninf System

Security in a NES system involves Authentication, Authorization, Privacy. Authentication identifies *who* is connecting to the server; authorization is *what* resources to permit to the user that has been identified; and privacy is to make

```
<!ELEMENT invoke_executable
    (issuer ,function_name, client, observer)>
<!ELEMENT issuer EMPTY>
<!ATTLIST issuer process CDATA #REQUIRED>
<!ATTLIST issuer host CDATA #REQUIRED>
<!ATTLIST issuer port CDATA #REQUIRED>
<!ATTLIST issuer session_key CDATA #REQUIRED>
<!ELEMENT function_name EMPTY>
<!ATTLIST function_name module CDATA #REQUIRED>
<!ATTLIST function_name entry CDATA #REQUIRED>
<!ELEMENT client (peer)>
<!ELEMENT observer (peer)>
<!ELEMENT peer EMPTY>
<!ATTLIST peer host CDATA #REQUIRED>
<!ATTLIST peer port CDATA #REQUIRED>
```

Fig. 4. Remote Executable Command DTD

```
<invoke_executable>
<issuer process="nsserver"
    host="hpc.etl.go.jp"
    port="30000" session_key="12345" />
<function_name module="test" entry="mmul" />
<client>
    <peer host="hpc.etl.go.jp" port="30000" />
</client>
<observer>
    <peer host="hpc.etl.go.jp" port="30001" />
</observer>
</invoke_executable>
```

Fig. 5. Example Invocation Command

communication and computation private to other users connecting to the NES system.

The new Ninf system has the client connect to the server via a shared proxy; however, server authentication and authorization must be performed with client identify, with (rather remote but still existing) possibility that the proxy may be spoofed. Another situation is when server A acts as a client and delegates part of its work to server B on another machine. There, not only that server A needs to be authenticated, but the client identity must be authenticated and authorized at server B as well. Such "delegation of identity" we deem as essential part of a NES system

The new Ninf system implements the NAA (NES Authentication Authorization) module. NAA employs SSL as the underlying encryption mechanism and implements delegation of identity and authorization on top of those. Delegation of identity is done automatically by the NAA, and the client user merely needs to specify his certificate as is done with SSL. NAA itself is relatively self-contained, and thus could be used by other NES systems such as Netsolve.

Delegation of Identity. Identity in SSL consists of a certificate certified by a CA (Certificate Authority). CA's can be made hierarchical—it is possible to sign a certificate using another (signed) certificate. In NAA, we have implemented delegation of identity by not merely directly tying in user identity with his certificate, but rather, broadened the 'identity' to include all the certificates signed using the user's certificate.

SSL employs the public key encryption algorithm, where its certificate consists of user's public key being encrypted by CA's private key. We can form a so-called *certificate chain* by generating another key pair, and encrypting them with the user's private key. On authentication, CA's public key is used to decrypt the certificate, which reveals the public key of the user. This could be used for identification (by decrypting data which had been encrypted with the private key of the user), or for a chain, could in turn be used to obtain the public key of the next element in the chain. NAA uses such a certificate chain for authentication, in that if the user's certificate appears somewhere in the chain, it is regarded as providing the user's indentity. The security layer of Globus employs a similar strategy[15].

As an example, let us consider when the client calls server A, which in turn calls server B as a client. When server A receives a connection request from the client, it generates a new key pair, and sends back its public key to the client, which is asked to create a session certificate embodying its identity. The client generates a session certificate by signing (encrypting) the public key with its own private key, and sends it back to server A. When server A connects to server B, server B must 1) authenticate the identity of the client, as well as 2) identify that the call is being made through server A. This is achieved by server A connecting with the session certificate received from the client along with the original certificate of the client. This is shown in Figure 6.

NAA Policies. We have designed NAA policies to be extensible and customizable by the system administrators.

After the client is authenticated, authorization in NAA is performed using a structure similar to Java 1.2 Policy class. A *policy* is a set of structures called *grants*, which in turn are sets of *permissions* to the user. The NAA library manages the policy structures and the identities of current clients of the system. In addition, NAA namespace is tree-structured according to the X.509 conventions. Access control is done hierarchically done along this tree using the permissions.

The server program inquires whether the certain permission is applicable to the client. The library checks the policy if there are grants that contain the

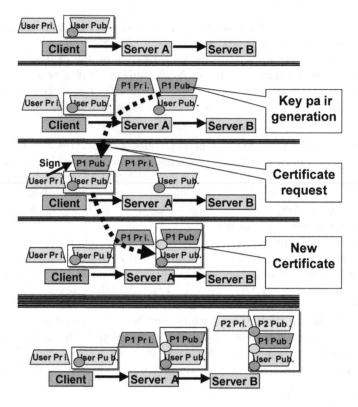

Fig. 6. Delegation of Identity

```
<!ELEMENT policy (grant)*>
<!ELEMENT grant (permission)*>
<!ATTLIST grant userid CDATA #REQUIRED>
<!ELEMENT permission EMPTY>
<!ATTLIST permission class CDATA #REQUIRED>
<!ATTLIST permission target CDATA #REQUIRED>
<!ATTLIST permission action CDATA #REQUIRED>
```

Fig. 7. Policy DTD

particular permission. Each permission consists of three attributes, *class*, *target*, and *action*. Class indicates the operation that the permission allows the client to perform. Target and action designates the subject of the operation, along with the type of the operation to be performed.

Policies are described using XML in a policy file. We illustrate the policy file DTD and an example of policy description in Figure 7 and Figure 8, respectively.

```
<policy>
  <grant userid="c=jp,o=etl">
    <permission class = "stubexec"
        target = "test/entry0" action="100 20"/>
    <permission class = "stubexec"
        target = "test/entry1" action="100 20"/>
  </grant>
  <grant userid="c=jp,o=etl,CN=nakada">
    <permission class = "stubexec"
        target = "test/entry3" action="100 20"/>
  </grant>
</policy>
```

Fig. 8. Example Policy

In the example, we have defined two grants. The first grant indicates that the user whose identity includes c=jp,o=etl (meaning the Electrotechnical Lab) can remotely execute test/entry0 and test/entry1. The second grant restricts test/entry3 to only be remotely executed by userID c=jp,o=etl,CN=nakada. Thus, the client c=jp,o=etl,CN=nakada can execute all the remote libraries (entry0, entry1, and entry3), while the client c=jp,o=etl,CN=sekiguchi can execute only (entry0 and entry1); furthermore, the client c=jp, o=titech, CN=matsuoka cannot execute any of the libraries.

We can also grant rights to specific calls made by the client through delegation of identity; for instance, in the delegation of identity scenario described earlier, we can specify a certain executable to be invoked only if a particular client was executing a library in server A which in turn had called the executable in server B. Such a case is conceivable, when a large compute server B is used as a backend for a server A, which is more subject to public usage; contrastingly, only a restricted set of jobs could be run on server B, and users are not allowed to invoke a remote library on server B directly; rather, they must do so via server A.

In this manner, the hierarchical namespace, along with the policy structure, gives fine-grained access control of resources for remote libraries in a NES system. Preliminary measurement have shown that such mechanisms do not impose significant overhead, as long as the calls granularity is large enough such that the overhead could be amortized (beyond 10s of seconds).

4 Conclusion

We have covered the technical tradeoff points of NES systems, and described how the new Ninf system v.2.0 had been designed with the tradeoffs in mind, with descriptions of why a particular choices in the tradeoffs had been made.

We hope that most of the design spaces have been covered, and will serve as a guide for designing future NES systems.

We are currently in the stage of deploying Ninf v.2.0 alongside v.1.0 to compare and verify the effectiveness of the design decisions, along with performance analysis to assess the their impact as well.

Acknowledgements. Part of this research had been performed under the sponsorship of Information Promotion Agency of Japan (IPA), under the program "The Development of Wide-Area, Distributed Computing Applications". We also would like to thank NTT Software and Computer Institute of Japan who had contributed in the design, our collaborators and users of the Ninf system, and the rest of the Ninf project team for their technical discussions and support.

References

1. Ninf: Network Infrastructure for Global Computing. http://ninf.etl.go.jp/.
2. Casanova, H. and Dongarra, J.: NetSolve: A Network Server for Solving Computational Science Problems, *Proceedings of Super Computing '96* (1996).
3. Buyya, R., Abramson, D. and Giddy, J.: Nimrod/G: An Architecture for a Resource Management and Scheduling System in a Global Computational Grid, *Proceedings of HPC Asia 2000* (2000).
4. Kapadia, N. H., Fortes, J. A. B. and Brodley, C. E.: Predictive Application-Performance Modeling in a Computational Grid Environment, *Proc. of 8th IEEE International Symposium on High Performance Distributed Computing (HPDC8)* (1999).
5. René, C. and Priol, T.: MPI Code Encapsulating using Parallel CORBA Object, *Proc. of 8th IEEE International Symposium on High Performance Distributed Computing (HPDC8)*, pp. 3–10 (1999).
6. Imai, Y., Saeki, T., Ishizaki, T. and Kishimoto, M.: CrispORB: High performance CORBA for System Area Network, *Proc. of 8th IEEE International Symposium on High Performance Distributed Computing (HPDC8)*, pp. 11–18 (1999).
7. Butler, K., Clement, M. and Snell, Q.: A Performance Broker for CORBA, *Proc. of 8th IEEE International Symposium on High Performance Distributed Computing (HPDC8)*, pp. 19–26 (1999).
8. Foster, I. and Kesselman, C.: Globus: A metacomputing infrastructure toolkit., *Proc. of Workshop on Environments and Tools, SIAM.* (1996).
9. Grimshaw, A., Wulf, W., French, J., Weaver, A. and Jr., P. R.: Legion: The Next Logincal Step Toward a Natiowide Virtual Computer, CS 94-21, University of Virginia (1994).
10. Sato, M., Nakada, H., Sekiguchi, S., Matsuoka, S., Nagashima, U. and Takagi, H.: Ninf: A Network based Information Library for a Global World-Wide Computing Infrastracture, *Proc. of HPCN'97 (LNCS-1225)*, pp. 491–502 (1997).
11. Nakada, H., Takagi, H., Matsuoka, S., Nagashima, U., Sato, M. and Sekiguchi, S.: Utilizing the Metaserver Architecture in the Ninf Global Computing System, *High-Performance Computing and Networking '98, LNCS 1401*, pp. 607–616 (1998).
12. Takefusa, A., Matsuoka, S., Ogawa, H., Nakada, H., Takagi, H., Sato, M., Sekiguchi, S. and Nagashima., U.: Multi-client LAN/WAN Performance Analysis of Ninf: a High-Performance Global Computing System, *Supercomputing '97* (1997).

13. Suzumura, T., Nakagawa, T., Matsuoka, S., Nakada, H. and Sekiguchi, S.: Are Global Computing Systems Useful? - Comparison of Client-Server Global Computing Systems Ninf, NetSolve versus CORBA, *Proc. of International Parallel and Distributed Processing Symposium* (2000).
14. Wolski, R., Spring, N. and Peterson, C.: Implementing a Performance Forecasting System for Metacomputing: The Network Weather service, *Proceedings of the 1997 ACM/IEEE Supercomputing Conference* (1997).
15. Foster, I., Kesselman, C., Tsudik, G. and Tuecke, S.: A Security Architecture for Computational Grids, *Proc. 5th ACM Conference on Computer and Communication Security* (1998).

Architectural Models for Resource Management in the Grid

Rajkumar Buyya[1], Steve Chapin[2], and David DiNucci [3]

School of Computer Science and
Software Engineering [1]
Monash University,
Melbourne, Australia
rajkumar@csse.monash.edu.au

Dept. of Electrical Engineering and
Computer Science [2]
Syracuse University,
Syracuse, NY, USA.
chapin@ecs.syr.edu

Elepar [3]
14380 N W Hunters Dr.
Beaverton, Oregon, USA
dave@elepar.com

Abstract: The concept of coupling geographically distributed (high-end) resources for solving large-scale problems is becoming increasingly popular, forming what is popularly called grid computing. The management of resources in the grid environment becomes complex as they are (geographically) distributed, heterogeneous in nature, owned by different individuals/organizations each having their own resource management policies and different access-and-cost models. In this scenario, a number of alternatives exist while creating a framework for grid resource management. In this paper, we discuss the three alternative models—hierarchical, abstract owner, and market—for grid resource management architectures. The hierarchical model exhibits the approach followed in (many) contemporary grid systems. The abstract owner model follows an order and delivery approach in job submission and result gathering. The (computational) market model captures the essentials of both hierarchical and abstract owner models and proposes the use of computational economy in the development of grid resource management systems.

1. Introduction

The growing popularity of the Internet and the availability of powerful computers and high-speed networks as low-cost commodity components are changing the way we do computing and use computers today. The interest in coupling geographically distributed (computational) resources is also growing for solving large-scale problems, leading to what is popularly known as grid computing. In this environment, a wide variety of computational resources (such as supercomputers, clusters, and SMPs including low-end systems such as PCs/workstations), visualisation devices, storage systems and databases, special class of scientific instruments (such as radio telescopes), computational kernels, and so on are logically coupled together and presented as a single integrated resource to the user (see Figure 1). The user essentially interacts with a resource broker that hides the complexities of grid computing. The broker discovers resources that the user can access through grid information server(s), negotiates with (grid-enabled) resources or their agents using middleware services, maps tasks to resources (scheduling), stages the application and data for processing (deployment) and finally gathers results. It is also responsible for

R. Buyya and M. Baker (Eds.:) GRID 2000, LNCS 1971, pp. 18-35, 2000.

monitoring application execution progress along with managing changes in the grid infrastructure and resource failures. There are a number of projects worldwide [5], which are actively exploring the development of various grid computing system components, services, and applications. They include Globus [7], Legion [9], NetSolve [10], Ninf [15], AppLes [11], Nimrod/G [3], and JaWS [16]. In [2], all these grid systems have been discussed.

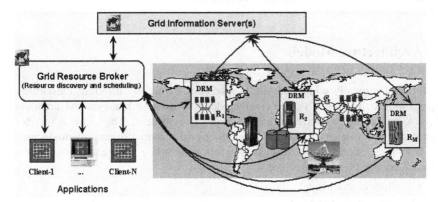

Figure 1: A Generic View of GRID System.

The current research and investment into computational grids is motivated by an assumption that coordinated access to diverse and geographically distributed resources is valuable.   In this paradigm, it is not only important to determine mechanisms and policies that allows such coordinated access, but it also seems reasonable that owners of those resources, or of mechanisms to connect and utilize them should be able to recoup some of the resulting value from users or clients. Approaches to recouping such value in the existing Internet/web infrastructure, where e-commerce sites use advertising and/or mark-ups on products sold to show revenue, do not translate well (or are unsuitable) to a computational grid framework, primarily due to the fact that the immediate user of any specific resource in a computational grid is often not a human. Instead, in a grid, many different resources, potentially controlled by diverse organizations with diverse policies in widely-distributed locations, must all be used together, and the relationship between the value provided by each resource and the value of the product or service delivered to the eventual human consumer may be very complex. In addition, it is unrealistic to assume that human-created contracts can be developed between all potential resource users and resource owners in these situations, since the potential of computational grids can only be fully exploited if similar resources owned by different owners can be used almost interchangeably.

Still, the existing real world must be acknowledged. Grid resources are largely owned and used by individuals or institutions who often provide "free" access for solving problems of common interest/public good (e.g., SETI@Home [13]), prize/fame (e.g., distributed.net [14] response to challenge for breaking RSA security algorithms), collaborative resources (GUSTO [6]), or by companies that are loathe to allow others to use them, primarily due to concerns about competition and security. The existing control over resources is subject to different policies and restrictions, as well as different software infrastructure used to schedule them. Any new approach to manage or share these resources will not be viable unless it allows a gradual layering of functionality or at least a gradual transition schedule from existing approaches to more novel ones. Even in the existing cases where money does not actually change hands, it is often important to provide a proper accounting of cross-organizational resource usage. In order to address these concerns, we propose different approaches for modeling grid resource management systems.

2. Architecture Models

As the grid logically couples multiple resources owned by different individuals or organisations, the choice of the right model for resource management architecture plays a major role in its eventual (commercial) success. There are a number of approaches that one can follow in developing grid resource management systems. In the next three sections, we discuss the following three different models for grid resource management architecture:

- Hierarchical Model
- Abstract Owner Model
- Computational Market/Economy Model

In the first, we characterize existing resource management and scheduling mechanisms by suggesting a more general view of those mechanisms. Next, we suggest a rather idealistic and extensive proposal for resource sharing and economy, which for the most part, ignores existing infrastructure in order to focus on long-term goals. Finally, we describe a more incremental architecture that is already underway to integrate some aspects of a computational economy into the existing grid infrastructure. Table 1 shows a few representative systems whose architecture complies with one of these models.

Table 1: Three Models for a Grid Resource Management Architecture.

MODEL	REMARKS	SYSTEMS
Hierarchical	It captures architecture model followed in most contemporary systems.	Globus, Legion, Ninf, NetSolve.
Abstract Owner	It follows an order and delivery model for resource sharing, which for the most part, ignores existing infrastructure in order to focus on long-term goals.	Expected to emerge.
Market/Economy	It follows economic model in resource discovery and scheduling that can co-exist or work with contemporary systems and captures the essence of both hierarchical and abstract owner models.	Nimrod/G, JaWS, Myriposa, JavaMarket.

The grid architecture models need to encourage resource owners to contribute their resources, offer a fair basis for sharing resources among users, and regulate resource demand and supply. They influence the way scheduling systems are built as they are responsible for mapping user requests to the right set of resources. The grid scheduling systems need to follow multilevel scheduling architecture as each resource has its own scheduling system and users schedule their applications on the grid using super-schedulers called resource brokers (see Figure 1).

3. Hierarchical Resource Management

The hierarchical model for grid resource management architecture (shown in Figure 2) is an outcome of the Grid Forum [20] second meeting proposed in [21]. The major components of this architecture are divided into passive and active components. The passive components are:

- *Resources* are things that can be used for a period of time, and may or may not be renewable. They have owners, who may charge others for using resources and they can be shared, or exclusive. Resources might be explicitly named, or be described parametrically. Examples of resources include disk space, network bandwidth, specialized device time, and CPU time.

- *Tasks* are consumers of resources, and include both traditional computational tasks and non-computational tasks such as file staging and communication.

- *Jobs* are hierarchical entities, and may have recursive structure; i.e., jobs can be composed of subjobs or tasks, and subjobs may themselves contain subjobs. The *leaves* of this structure are tasks. The simplest form of a job is one containing a single task.

- *Schedules* are mappings of tasks to resources over time. Note that we map tasks to resources, not jobs, because jobs are containers for tasks, and tasks are the actual resource consumers.

The active components are:

- *Schedulers* compute one or more schedules for input lists of jobs, subject to constraints that can be specified at runtime. The unit of scheduling is the job, meaning that schedulers attempt to map all the tasks in a job at once, and jobs, not tasks, are submitted to schedulers.

- *Information Services* act as databases for describing items of interest to the resource management systems, such as resources, jobs, schedulers, agents, etc. We do not require any particular access method or implementation; it could be LDAP, a commercial database, or something else entirely.

- *Domain Control Agents* can commit resources for use; as the name implies, the set of resources controlled by an agent is a control domain. This is what some people mean when they say local resource manager. We expect domain control agents to support reservations. Domain Control Agents are distinct from Schedulers, but control domains may contain internal

Schedulers. A Domain Control Agent can provide state information, either through publishing in an Information Service or via direct querying. Examples of domain control agents include the Maui Scheduler, Globus GRAM, and Legion Host Object.

- *Deployment Agents* implement schedules by negotiating with domain control agents to obtain resources and start tasks running.

- *Users* submit jobs to the Resource Management System for execution.

- *Admission Control Agents* determine whether the system can accommodate additional jobs, and reject or postpone jobs when the system is saturated.

- *Monitors* track the progress of jobs. Monitors obtain job status from the tasks comprising the job and from the Domain Control Agents where those tasks are running. Based on this status, the Monitor may perform outcalls to Job Control Agents and Schedulers to effect remapping of the job.

- *Job Control Agents* are responsible for shepherding a job through the system, and can act both as a proxy for the user and as a persistent control point for a job. It is the responsibility of the job control agent to coordinate between different components within the resource management system, e.g. to coordinate between monitors and schedulers.

We have striven to be as general as is feasible in our definitions. Many of these distinctions are logical distinctions. For example, we have divided the responsibilities of schedulers, deployment agents, and monitors, although it is entirely reasonable and expected that some scheduling systems may combine two or all three of these in a single program. Schedulers outside control domains cannot commit resources; these are known as metaschedulers or super schedulers. In our early discussions, we intentionally referred to control domains as "the box" because it connotes an important separation of "inside the box" vs. "outside the box." Actions outside the box are requests; actions inside the box may be commands. It may well be that the system is fractal in nature, and that entire grid scheduling systems may exist inside the box. Therefore, we can treat the control domain as a black box from the outside.

We have intentionally not defined any relationship between the number of users, jobs, and the major entities in the system (admission agents, schedulers, deployment agents, and monitors). Possibilities range from per-user or per-job agents to a single monolithic agent per system; each approach has strengths and weaknesses, and nothing in our definitions precludes or favors a particular use of the system. We expect to see local system defaults (e.g. a default scheduler or deployment agent) with users substituting their personal agents when they desire to do so.

One can notice that the word *queue* has not been mentioned in this model; queuing systems imply homogeneity of resources and a degree of control that simply will not be present in true grid systems. Queuing systems will most certainly exist within control domains.

Interaction of Components

The interactions between components of the resource management system are shown in Figure 2. An arrow in the figure means that communication is taking place between components. We will next describe, at a high level, what we envision these interactions to be. This is the beginning of a protocol definition. Once the high-level operations are agreed upon, we can concern ourselves with wire-level protocols.

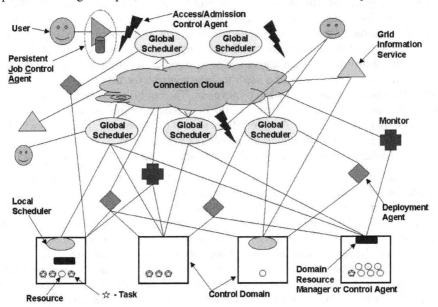

Figure 2: Hierarchical Model for Grid Resource Management.

We will begin with an example. A user submits a job to a job control agent, which calls an admission agent. The admission agent examines the resource demands of the job (perhaps consulting with a grid information system) and determines that it is safe to add the job to the current pool of work for the system. The admission agent passes the job to a scheduler, which performs resource discovery using the grid information system and then consults with domain control agents to determine the current state and availability of resources.

The scheduler then computes a set of mappings and passes these mappings to a deployment agent. The deployment agent negotiates with the domain control agents for the resources indicated in the schedule, and obtains reservations for the resources. These reservations are passed to the job control agent. At the proper time, the job control agent works with a different deployment agent, and the deployment agent coordinates with the appropriate domain control agents to start the tasks running. A monitor tracks progress of the job, and may later decide to reschedule if performance is lower than expected.

This is but one way in which these components might coordinate. Some systems will omit certain functionality (e.g. the job control agent), while others will combine multiple roles in a single agent. For example, a single process might naturally perform the roles of job control agent and monitor.

4. Abstract Owner (AO) Model

Where is the grid, and who owns it? These puzzles are not unique to the grid. When one makes a long distance phone call, who "owns" the resource being used? Who owns the generators that create the electricity to run an appliance? Who owns the Internet? Users of these resources don't care, and don't want to care. What they do want is the ability to make an agreement with some entity regarding the conditions under which the resources can be used, the mechanisms for using the resources, the cost of the resources, and the means of payment. The entity with which the user deals (the phone company, power company, or ISP) is almost certainly not the owner of the resources, but the user can think of them that way abstractly. They are actually brokers, who may in turn deal with the owners, or perhaps with more brokers. At each stage, the broker is an abstraction for all of the owners and so it is with the grid.

The grid user wants an abstraction of an entity that "owns" the grid, and to make an arrangement with that "owner" regarding the use of their resources, possibly involving a trade of something of value for the usage (which could be nothing more tangible than goodwill or the future use of their own resources). It is proposed here that each grid resource, ranging in complexity from individual processors and instruments to the grid itself, be represented by one or more "abstract owners" (abbreviated as *AOs*) that are strongly related to schedulers. For complex resources, an AO will certainly be a broker for the actual owners or other brokers, though the resource user doesn't need to be aware of this. (A resource user will hereafter be assumed to be a program, and referred to as a *client*. Human clients are assumed to use automated agents to represent him/her in negotiations with an AO.) The arrangement between the client and an AO for acquiring and using the resource can be made through a pre-existing contract (e.g. flat rate or sliding scale depending on time until resource available) or based on a dialogue between client and AO regarding the price and availability of the resource.

The remainder of this AO proposal describes what an AO looks like (externally and internally), what a resource looks like, how a client negotiates with an AO to acquire a resource, how a client interacts with a resource, and how AOs can be assembled into other constructs which may more closely resemble traditional schedulers. This work is still in the high-level design stages, in hopes that it will draw out refinements, corrections, and extensions that might help it to become viable.

General Structure of AO

At its most abstract, an AO outwardly resembles a fast-food restaurant (see Figure 3a). To acquire access to a resource from an AO that "owns" it, the prospective client (which may be another AO) negotiates with that AO through its Order Window. These negotiations may include asking how soon the resource may become available, how much it might cost, etc. If the prospective client is not happy with the results of the negotiations, it may just terminate negotiations, or might actually place an order. After being ordered, the resources are delivered from the AO to the client through the

Pickup Window. The precise protocol to be used for acquiring the resources is flexible and may also be negotiated at order time--e.g. the client may be expected to pick up the resource at a given time, or the AO may alert the client (via an interrupt or signal) when the resource is ready. Even if an order is placed (but the resource has not yet been delivered), the client may cancel the order through the order window.

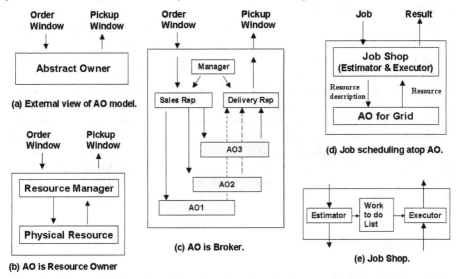

Figure 3: Abstract Owner Model for Grid Resource Management Architecture.

Little more is said here about the actual form of these "windows" except that they need to be accessible remotely, and must support a standard procedure-like interface in which values are passed to and returned from the window. Since interaction with an AO is likely to be rather infrequent and requires a relatively small amount of information flow, maximum efficiency is not necessarily required: CORBA or any number of other remote procedure invocation techniques can be used.

For the purposes of this discussion, a *resource* is roughly defined as any combination of hardware and software that helps the client to solve a problem, and a *task* is that part of a problem that is specified by the client after the resource has been delivered ("picked up") from the AO. Note that, unlike some other definitions of "task", these tasks may be very simple (e.g. a data set to be analyzed or a message to be sent), more general (e.g. a process to be executed), or very complex (e.g. a complete multi-process program and/or set of programs or processes to be executed in some order). While AOs do not specifically deal with entities called "jobs", techniques for applying the AO approach to traditional job scheduling will be addressed in the last subsection.

Resources can (and will) be regarded as objects, in the sense that they have an identity, a set of methods for initiating and controlling tasks, and attributes that serve to customize the resource. In general, the desired attributes will be determined during negotiation through the Order Window, when the client requests the resource, and will only be queried (not altered) after the resource is delivered. The methods may take many different forms, depending upon circumstances such as the type of resource, availability of hardware protections, and whether the method is to be invoked locally or remotely. For example, access to a local memory resource may have virtually no method protocol interfering with standard memory access operations, while initiating a process on a distant processor may require more substantial method invocation protocol. A resource is relinquished by invoking its "relinquish" method (or by timing out).

The external structure of an AO was formulated to allow any level of nesting. Internally, an AO will differ in structure depending on whether it is a broker or an owner (or a combination). A pure owner of a single physical resource might be very simple (see Figure 3b), where the "manager" includes the intelligence required to negotiate, keep the schedule, and deliver the resource. For a higher-level broker, it might be more complex (see Figure 3c). Here, AO1, AO2, and AO3 represent other Abstract Owners, each with an Order Window used by the Sales Representative, and a Pickup Window used by the Delivery representative. Though these subordinate AOs are shown within a single parent AO, there is no reason that this relation must be hierarchical; a single AO may provide resources to a number of different parent AOs, which may assemble these into more complex resources in different ways or for different clients sets or may support different protocols or strategies or policies.

Grid Resources

Three primary classes are proposed here to represent resources: Instruments, Channels, and Complexes. An Instrument is a resource which logically exists at some location for some specific period of time, and which creates, consumes, or transforms data or information. The term "location" may be as specific or general as the situation merits. A Channel is a resource that exists to facilitate the explicit transfer of data or information between two or more instruments, either at different locations, or in the same location at different times (acting as sort of a temporary file in that case), or instruments which share space-time coordinates but have different protection domains. A Channel connects to an Instrument through a Port (on the instrument). A Complex is nothing more than a collection of (connected) Channel and Instrument resources.

Some important sub-classes of the Instrument class are the Compute instrument, the Archival instrument, and the Personal instrument. The Compute instrument corresponds to a processor or set of processors along with associated memory, temp files, software, etc. Archival Instruments (of which a permanent file is one sub-class) correspond to persistent storage of information. Personal instruments are those that are assumed to interface directly to a human being, ranging from a simple terminal to a more complex CAVE or speech recognition/synthesis device, and its specification may include the identity of the person involved. Of course, the Instrument class is also meant to accommodate other machines and instruments such as telescopes, electron microscopes, automatic milling machines, or any other sink or source for grid data.

As stated, an instrument exists in a location, and its methods may need to be called either locally (from the instrument itself) or remotely. For example, if a (reference to

a) Compute instrument is acquired from an AO, the potentially distant process may want to invoke a "load_software" method to initiate a program on the resource. This new program may then want to invoke methods to access the temporary files or ports associated with the resource. Since the latter accesses will be local and must be efficient, it is desirable to provide separate method invocation protocols for remote and local method invocation. Moreover, remote method invocations (RMIs) may themselves require the use of intermediate communication resources between the client and the resource, perhaps with associated quality of service (QoS) constraints.

To facilitate remote method invocations, any port(s) of an instrument can be specially designated as an RMI port. Such ports will have the appropriate RMI protocol handlers assigned to them. This designation is an attribute of the port--i.e., specified at resource negotiation time, through the "order window", just as authorization and notification style are. Methods can be invoked through such a port either by connecting a channel to the port and issuing the RMI request through the channel or in a connectionless mode by specifying the object and port. The former approach is best when issuing repeated RMI calls or when QoS is desired for RMI calls, the latter is best for one-time-only calls such as initializing an instrument which has just been acquired from an AO.

Negotiating with an AO

When negotiating through the order window, the client first effectively creates a "sample" resource object of the appropriate structure and assigns each attribute either (1) a constant value, (2) a "don't care" value, or (3) a variable name (which will actually take the form of, and be interpreted as, an index into a *variable value table*). If the same variable name is used in multiple places, it has the effect of constraining those attributes to have the same value. An example of this is to use a single variable to specify the "beginning time" attribute on several Instrument objects to cause them to be co-scheduled. Another is to specify variables for Instruments' object IDs, then to use those same variables when specifying the endpoints of the channels between them. The client may also specify simple constraints on the variables in a separate constraint list.

Usually, the values in the variable value table are filled and returned by the AO when the resource is acquired, but the client can designate some subset of those variables as *negotiating variables*. For these, the AO will propose values during negotiation, which the client can then examine to decide whether or not to accept the resource. (If accepted, these values essentially become constants.) In general, it is quicker for the client to specify additional constraints instead of using negotiation variables, allowing the decision on suitability to be made wholly within the AO, but negotiating variables can help when more complex constraints are required or when a client must decide between similar resources offered by different AOs.

In all, submissions to the Order Window from the client include the sample object attributes, the variable constraint list, a Negotiation Style, a Pickup Approach, an Authorization, a Bid, and a Negotiation ID. The Negotiation Style specifies whether the AO is to schedule the resource immediately (known as "Immediate"), or is to return a specified number of sets of proposed values for the negotiation variables (known as "Pending"), or is to finish scheduling based on an earlier-returned set of negotiation variable values (known as "Confirmation"), or is to cancel an earlier Pending negotiation (known as "Cancel"). The Pickup Approach specifies the protocol to be used between the AO and client at the Pickup Window—i.e. whether the AO will alert the client with a signal, interrupt, or message when the resource becomes available, or the client will poll the Pickup Window for the resource, or the client can expect to find the resource ready at the window at a specified time. The Authorization is a capability or key which allows the AO to determine the authority of the client to access resources (and to bill the client accordingly when the resources are delivered). The Bid is a maximum price that the client is willing to pay for the resource, and may denote a pre-understood algorithm (or "contract") specifying how much the resource will cost under certain conditions. The Negotiation ID serves as a "cookie", and is passed back and forth between the client and AO to provide an identity and continuity for a multi-interaction negotiation, and continuity between the negotiation of a resource and the ultimate delivery of the resource through the Pickup Window. (A zero Negotiation ID designates the beginning of a new negotiation.)

If a Pending negotiation style is specified, the AO returns a value table containing sets of proposed values for the negotation variables, and an "Ask" price for each set. The intent of the Ask price is to inform the client of a sufficient Bid price to be used when requesting the resource, but the AO may conceivably accept even lower Bid prices depending upon the specific situation. For all negotiations, the AO returns a return code informing the client of the success of the operation, a Negotiation ID, (equal to that submitted, if it was nonzero), and an expiration date for the Negotiation ID. A single negotiation can continue until the Negotiation ID expires or a Negotiation Style other than "pending" is specified.

On a successful Immediate or Confirm request, the client can then submit the Negotiation ID to the Pickup Window, (at a time consistent with the Negotiation Style), to retrieve the resource. The Pickup Window returns the resource object, the variable value table, and a return code. Although the returned resource is logically an object, it is assumed that any attribute values that the client is concerned with are being returned in the Variable Value table, so the resource object just takes the form of a handle to access the resource object's methods.

Job Shops

AOs apparently perform only part of the standard job scheduling process—i.e. acquiring a resource—leaving the remainder to the client—i.e. assigning tasks to the resources and monitoring their completion and/or cleanup, often in sequential and dependent steps. But this is only partially true. Recall that a Compute Instrument, exclusive of the task that is eventually assigned to it by the client, may consist of both hardware and software components. While the software components often serve to create an environment in which the eventual task will execute (such as libraries or interpreters), they may also be compilers and/or complete user programs. That is, the Compute Instrument itself can be defined as a processor executing a specific program.

The task assigned to such an instrument may be a data-set or source code to be read by that program (or compiler), or even nothing at all if the resource is completely self-contained. Since the AO is responsible for preparing the instrument for delivery through the Pickup Window and recovering it after it has been relinquished, it is indeed responsible for initiating this software and cleaning up after it.

The traditional sequential nature of job steps has resulted from the prevalence of uniprocessors and traditional sequential thinking, but it is already common for parallel "make" utilities, for example, to exploit potential parallelism in job-like scripts. Similarly, in an AO resource, compute instruments running the individual "job steps" can be connected to communicate through channels, allowing them to be scheduled locally or in a distributed fashion, and scheduled sequentially or in parallel by the AO, subject to the dependences dictated by the channels and the QoS constraints assigned to those channels by the client. In this way, a job can be represented as a Complex Instrument in the AO infrastructure, where it will be scheduled.

Even with these capabilities, there is always the possibility that a more traditional job scheduler is required. In such a case, consider a new construct called a *job shop*, which uses AOs only to acquire resources, as shown in Figure 3d. See Figure 3e for an example of the internals of a standard job shop. The job shop primarily comprises "estimator" and "executor", much like an auto repair shop. The estimator deals with the customer to help determine how soon the job might be done and how much it might cost, requests the resources needed from the grid AO (through its order window), and records what needs to be done (in a job queue) when the resources are ready. The executor takes ready resources from the AO delivery window, dequeues the associated work from the job queue, builds any necessary environment for those tasks (e.g. telling message passing routines which channels to use), initiates tasks, collects answers, and notifies and returns the answer to the client.

Nesting job shops (or traditional job schedulers in general) is not as natural as nesting AOs, primarily because a job shop provides little feedback to the client until it has acquired resources *and* assigned tasks to them. This means that tasks are often assigned to some resources even before others have been allocated, and may be shipped around to where the resources are, long before they are needed there.

AO Summary

There are many remaining gaps in the above description, both in detail and in functionality. For example, little has been said about how any client, whether an end-user or another AO, will find AOs that own the desired kind of resources. Certainly, one approach is to imagine a tree of AOs (as in Figure 3c), with the client always interacting with the root AO, but it is unrealistic to consider this tree as being hardwired when residing in an environment as dynamic as a computational grid. More likely, existing Internet protocols can be adapted for this purpose, and an AO might have a third "business dealings" window to facilitate them. Before an approach like AO has any likelihood of acceptance in a large community, it must address many such challenges. Even a potentially useful and well-defined (successfully prototyped) AO protocol will not be viable unless it can coexist with other contemporary approaches. It is therefore important to understand how AOs and constructs in these other systems can build upon one another and mimic one another.

5. Market Model

The resources in the grid environment are geographically distributed and each of them is owned by a different organisation. Each of them has its own resource management mechanisms and policies and may charge different prices for different users necessitating the need for the support of computational economy in resource management. In [34], we have presented a number of arguments for the need of an economy (market) driven resource management system for the grid. It offers resource owners better "incentive" for contributing their resources and help recover cost they incur while serving grid users or finance services that they offer to users and also make some profit. This return-on-investment mechanism also helps in enhancing/expanding computational services and upgrading resources. It is important to note that an economy[1] is one of the best institutions for regulating demand and supply. Naturally, in a computational market environment, resource users want to minimise their expenses (the price they pay) and owners want to maximise their return-on-investment. This necessitates a grid resource management system that provides appropriate tools and services to allow both resource users and owners to express their requirements. For instance, users should be allowed to specify their "QoS requirements" such as minimise the computational cost (amount) that they are willing to pay and yet meet the deadline by which they need results. Resource owners should be allowed to specify their charges—that can vary from time to time and users to users—and terms of use. Systems such as Mariposa [17], Nimrod/G [3], and JaWS [16], architect their user service model based on the economy of computations and it is likely that more and more systems are going to emerge based on this concept.

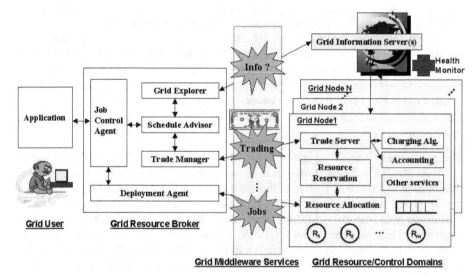

Figure 4: Market Model for Grid Resource Management Architecture.

---

[1] We use terms "economy" and "market" interchangeably.

The market model for grid resource management captures the essentials of both hierarchical and AO model presented above. Many of the contemporary grid systems fit to the hierarchical model and AO appears to be futuristic, but points out the need for economy in computation implicitly. The issues discussed in the hierarchical model apply to the market model, but it emphasizes the use of economic based resource management and scheduling. One of the possible architectures for grid resource management based on computational market model is shown in Figure 4. Resource trading model can vary depending on the method/protocol used (by trade manager) in determining the resource access cost.

The following are the key components of economy-driven resource management system:

- User Applications (sequential, parametric, parallel, or collaborative applications)
- Grid Resource Broker (a.k.a., Super/Global/Meta Scheduler)
- Grid Middleware
- Domain Resource Manager (Local Scheduler or Queuing system)

Grid Resource Broker (GRB)

The resource broker acts as a mediator between the user and grid resources using middleware services. It is responsible for resource discovery, resource selection, binding of software (application), data, and hardware resources, initiating computations, adapting to the changes in grid resources and presenting the grid to the user as a single, unified resource. The components of resource broker are the following:

- **Job Control Agent (JCA):** This component is a persistent central component responsible for shepherding a job through the system. It takes care of schedule generation, the actual creation of jobs, maintenance of job status, interacting with clients/users, schedule advisor, and dispatcher.
- **Schedule Advisor (Scheduler):** This component is responsible for resource discovery (using grid explorer), resource selection, and job assignment (schedule generation). Its key function is to select those resources that meet user requirements such as meet the deadline and minimize the cost of computation while assigning jobs to resources.
- **Grid Explorer:** This is responsible for resource discovery by interacting with grid-information server and identifying the list of authorized machines, and keeping track of resource status information.
- **Trade Manager (TM):** This works under the direction of resource selection algorithm (schedule advisor) to identify resource access costs. It interacts with trade servers (using middleware services/protocols such as those presented in [4]) and negotiates for access to resources at low cost. It can find out access cost through grid information server if owners post it.
- **Deployment Agent:** It is responsible for activating task execution on the selected resource as per the scheduler's instruction. It periodically updates the status of task execution to JCA.

Grid Middleware

The grid middleware offers services that help in coupling a grid user and (remote) resources through a resource broker or grid enabled application. It offers core services [12] such as remote process management, co-allocation of resources, storage access, information (directory), security, authentication, and Quality of Service (QoS) such as resource reservation for guaranteed availability and trading for minimising computational cost. Some of these services have already been discussed in the hierarchical model, here we point out components that are specifically responsible for helping out in offering computational economy services:

- **Trade Server (TS)**: It is a resource owner agent that negotiates with resource users and sells access to resources. It aims to maximize the resource utility and profit for its owner (earn as much money as possible). It consults pricing algorithms/models defined by the users during negotiation and directs the accounting system to record resource usage.

- **Pricing Algorithms/Methods**: These define the prices that resource owners would like to charge users. The resource owners may follow various policies to maximise profit and resource utilisation and the price they charge may vary from time to time and one user to another user and may also be driven by demand and supply like in the real market environment.

- **Accounting System:** It is responsible for recording resource usage and bills the user as per the usage agreement between resource broker (TM, user agent) and trade server (resource owner agent) [19].

Domain Resource Manager

Local resource managers are responsible for managing and scheduling computations across local resources such as workstations and clusters. They are even responsible for offering access to storage devices, databases, and special scientific instruments such as a radio telescope. Example local resource managers include, cluster operating systems such as MOSIX [18] and queuing systems such as Condor [12].

Comments

The services offered by trade server could also be accessed from or offered by grid information servers (like yellow pages/advertised services or posted prices). In this case a trade manager or broker can directly access information services to identify resource access cost and then contact resource agents for confirmation of access. The trade manager can use these advertised/posted prices (through information server) or ask/invite for competitive quotes (tenders) or bids (from trade server/resource owner agents) and choose resources that meet user requirements.

From the above discussion it is clear that there exist numerous methods for determining/knowing access cost. Therefore resource trading shown in Figure 4 is one of the possible alternatives for computational market model and it can vary depending on, particularly, trading protocols like in real world economy. Some of the real-world trading methods that can also be applied for computational economies include:

- Advertised/posted prices (classified advertisements) through information server
- Commodity exchanges
- Negotiated prices
- Call for (closed) tenders
- Call for (open) bids

Each of these methods can be applied in different situations for computational economies and they create a competitive computational market depending on the demand and supply and the quality of service. The mechanism for informing resource owners about the availability of service opportunities can vary depending on its implementation. One of the simplest mechanisms is users (buyers) or/and resource owners (sellers or their agents renting/leasing computational services) make available or post/publicise their requirements in a known location (for instance, "exchange centre, share market, or grid information service directory"). Any one or all can initiate computational service trading. Through these mechanisms one can perform the following types of actions like in real world market economies:

- Users can post their intentions/offers to buy access to resources/services (e.g., "20 cluster nodes for 2 hours for $50);
- Resource owners/grid nodes/providers/agents can post offers to sell (e.g., systems like NetSolve can announce "we solve 1000 simultaneous linear equations for $5");
- Users/resource owners can query about current opportunities including prices/bids and historical information.

The different grid systems may follow different approaches in making this happen and it will be beneficial if they are all interoperable. The interoperability standards can be evolved through grid user/developer community forums or standardization organisations such as GF [20] and eGRID [22].

6. Discussion and Conclusions

In this paper we have discussed three different models for grid resource management architecture inspired by three different philosophies. The hierarchical model captures the approach followed in many contemporary grid systems. The abstract owner shows the potential of an order and delivery approach in job submission and result gathering. The (computational) market model captures the essentials of both hierarchical and abstract owner models and uses the concept of computational economy. We have attempted to present these models in abstract high-level form as much as possible and have skipped low-level details for developers to decide (as they mostly change from one system to another). Many of the existing, upcoming and future grid systems can easily be mapped to one or more of the models discussed here (see Table 1). It is also obvious that real grid systems (as they evolve) are most likely to combine many of these ideas into a hybridized model (that captures essentials of all models) in their architecture. For instance, our Grid Economy [4] is developed as a combination of Globus and GRACE services based on a (hybridized) market model.

The importance of market models for grid computing is also reported in the journal of *Scientific American* [23]: "So far not even the most ambitious metacomputing prototypes have tackled accounting: determining a fair price for idle processor cycles. It all depends on the risk, on the speed of the machine, on the cost of communication, on the importance of the problem--on a million variables, none of them well understood. If only for that reason, metacomputing will probably arrive with a whimper, not a bang". We hope that (our proposed) computational market model for grid systems architecture along with others will help the arrival of computational grids with a big bang (not a whimper)!

References

1. Ian Foster and Carl Kesselman (editors), *The Grid: Blueprint for a Future Computing Infrastructure*, Morgan Kaufmann Publishers, USA, 1999.
2. Mark Baker, Rajkumar Buyya, Domenico Laforenza, The Grid: International Efforts in Global Computing, *Intl. Conference on Advances in Infrastructure for Electronic Business, Science, and Education on the Internet*, Italy, 2000.
3. Rajkumar Buyya, David Abramson and Jon Giddy, Nimrod/G: An Architecture for a Resource Management and Scheduling System in a Global Computational Grid, *4th Intl. Conf. on High Performance Computing in Asia-Pacific Region (HPC Asia 2000)*, China.
4. Rajkumar Buyya, David Abramson and Jon Giddy, Economy Driven Resource Management Architecture for Computational Power Grids, *Intl. Conf. on Parallel and Distributed Processing Techniques and Applications (PDPTA 2000)*, USA.
5. Rajkumar Buyya, Grid Computing Info Centre: http://www.gridcomputing.com
6. Globus Testbeds - http://www.globus.org/testbeds/
7. Ian Foster and Carl Kesselman, Globus: A Metacomputing Infrastructure Toolkit, *International Journal of Supercomputer Applications*, 11(2): 115-128, 1997.
8. Jack Dongarra, An Overview of Computational Grids and Survey of a Few Research Projects, *Symposium on Global Information Processing Technology*, Japan, 1999.
9. Steve Chapin, John Karpovich, Andrew Grimshaw, The Legion Resource Management System, *5th Workshop on Job Scheduling Strategies for Parallel Processing*, April 1999.
10. Henri Casanova and Jack Dongarra, *NetSolve:* A Network Server for Solving Computational Science Problems, *Intl. Journal of Supercomputing Applications and High Performance Computing*, Vol. 11, No. 3, 1997.
11. Fran Berman and Rich Wolski, The AppLeS Project: A Status Report, *8th NEC Research Symposium*, Berlin, Germany, May 1997. http://apples.ucsd.edu
12. Jim Basney and Miron Livny, Deploying a High Throughput Computing Cluster, *High Performance Cluster Computing*, Prentice Hall, 1999. http://www.cs.wisc.edu/condor/
13. SETI@Home – http://setiathome.ssl.berkeley.edu/
14. Distributed.Net – http://www.distributed.net/
15. Hidemoto Nakada, Mitsuhisa Sato, Satoshi Sekiguchi, Design and Implementations of Ninf: towards a Global Computing Infrastructure, *FGCS Journal*, October 1999.
16. Spyros Lalis and Alexandros Karipidis, JaWS: An Open Market-Based Framework for Distributed Computing over the Internet, *IEEE/ACM International Workshop on Grid Computing (GRID 2000)*, Dec. 2000. http://roadrunner.ics.forth.gr:8080/

17. Michael Stonebraker, Robert Devine, Marcel Kornacker, Witold Litwin, Avi Pfeffer, Adam Sah, Carl Staelin, An Economic Paradigm for Query Processing and Data Migration in Mariposa, *3rd International Conference on Parallel and Distributed Information Systems*, Sept. 1994. http://mariposa.cs.berkeley.edu:8000/mariposa/
18. Amnon Barak and Oren Laadan, The MOSIX Multicomputer Operating System for High Performance Cluster Computing, *FGCS Journal*, March 1998. www.mosix.cs.huji.ac.il
19. Bill Thigpen and Tom Hacker, Distributed Accounting on the Grid, *The Grid Forum Working Drafts*, 2000.
20. Grid Forum – http://www.gridforum.org
21. Steve Chapin, Mark Clement, and Quinn Snell, A Grid Resource Management Architecture, Strawman 1, *Grid Forum Scheduling Working Group*, November 1999.
22. European Grid Forum (eGRID) – http://www.egrid.org
23. W. Wayt Gibbs, Cyber View—World Wide Widgets, *Scientific American*, San Francisco, USA - http://www.sciam.com/0597issue/0597cyber.html

JaWS: An Open Market-Based Framework for Distributed Computing over the Internet

Spyros Lalis and Alexandros Karipidis

Computer Science Dept.,
University of Crete, Hellas
{lalis,karipid}@csd.uoc.gr
Institute of Computer Science,
Foundation for Research and Technology, Hellas
{lalis,karipid}@ics.forth.gr

Abstract. Harnessing the power of idle personal workstations remains a challenge for large scale distributed computing. In this paper, we present the Java Web-computing System (JaWS), which simpli es the connection of heterogeneous machines in a global computing grid as well as the development of applications that exploit this computing capacity. Machines are assigned to applications via a dynamic market-based mechanism that allows machine owners and clients to change their requirements even in the midst of a computation. The system takes care of the main communication issues o ering basic programming primitives that can be extended to develop class hierarchies which in turn support distributed computing paradigms. Due to the object-oriented structuring of code, development becomes as simple as implementing a few methods.

1 Introduction

The large growth of the Internet, both in the number of connected devices as well as in bandwidth, constitutes the distribution of applications over the Internet appealing. However, in order to exploit the thousands of processors that may be available at a given point in time, several issues must be addressed.

First of all, there exists the problem of machine heterogeneity, both in terms of hardware and operating system. Secondly, security considerations arise from the execution of code from untrusted parties. Programming support must also be offered through platforms that make development of distributed computations simple enough to be attractive even for inexperienced programmers. And then of course, these platforms need to be installed and maintained, a task that if proven awkward or time consuming may limit their wide deployment in practice.

Large scale distribution of computations over the Internet goes beyond dedicated server machines that are specifically set up for this purpose. It also means involving powerful yet often under-exploited machines, notably PCs, which may switch from being available to unavailable anytime. This requires a way of dynamically allocating machines to applications even in the midst of their execution. In turn, applications must be able to deal with this dynamic environment via

R. Buyya and M. Baker (Eds.): GRID 2000, LNCS 1971, pp. 36–46, 2000.

appropriate resource allocation strategies, which may depend not only on the form of the computation to be performed but also on various parameters that are supplied by the user interactively at runtime.

In this paper we present the Java Web-computing System (JaWS), which enables users to effortlessly and safely export their machines in a global market of processing capacity. Allocation of host machines to applications is dynamic and tasks can even migrate among hosts without disrupting the ongoing computation. A framework that promotes code reuse and incremental development through object-oriented extensions is offered to the programmer. Writing computations for the system can be as trivial as implementing a few routines. We feel that the ease of deploying the system and developing applications is of importance to the scientific community as most of the programming is done by scientists themselves with little support from computer experts.

The rest of the paper is organized as follows. Section 2 gives an overview of the system architecture. Details about the resource allocation mechanism are given in Sect. 3. In Sect. 4 we show how our system can be used to develop distributed computations in a straightforward way. A comparison with related work is given in Sect. 5. Section 6 discusses the advantages of our approach. Finally, future directions of this work are mentioned in the last section.

2   System Architecture

In order to guarantee maximal cross-platform operability the system is implemented in Java. Due to Java's large scale deployment, the system can span across many architectures and operating systems. Low administrative cost and an acceptable degree of security for the providers of host machines is achieved by having the host runtime system implemented as an applet that is downloaded over the Internet via a Java enabled web browser.

On the programmer's side we provide an open, extensible architecture for developing distributed computations. Basic primitives are provided which can be used to implement diverse, specialized processing models. Through such models it is possible to hide the internals of the system and/or offer advanced support in order to simplify application development.

2.1   Overview of System Components

An overview of the system's architecture is depicted in Fig. 1. The basic components of our system are the market server, hosts, the host agent, schedulers, tasks and client applications.

The *Market Server* is the meeting place for trading processing power. Based on the orders issued by hosts (sellers) and distributed computations (buyers), the market server produces matches and thus allocates resources.

A *Host* is a machine made available to be used by clients. A host participates in the market through the *Host Agent*, a Java applet that takes care of the communication with the rest of system in a transparent way. To install the host

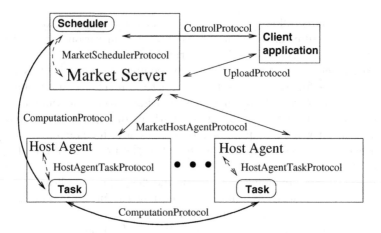

Fig. 1. Overview of architecture

agent, the owner of a host machine simply visits a URL with a Java enabled web browser. From that point onwards, the host agent computes the benchmark scores needed for the host's profile and takes care of placing orders in the market server on behalf of the user. The host agent also downloads, initializes and runs tasks assigned to the machine, thus acting as a runtime kernel for task execution.

The *Client Application* is an application which needs to perform computations that require considerable processing power. Through the system, a computation may either be distributed as a set of mobile tasks across many machines or come as a single task to be scheduled on fast machines speeding up its execution.

A computation consists of a *Scheduler* and one or more *Tasks*. The scheduler essentially implements the resource allocation strategy for a given application by placing respective orders in the market for acquiring machines to complete the computation. New orders can be issued at any time in order to adapt to fluid market conditions. When a host is allocated to the application scheduler, a task is launched in that machine to assist in completing the computation. Notably, the number of tasks to be created need not be specified a priori; it can be determined at runtime, as a function of available machines in the system and/or parameters supplied to the scheduler. Tasks can move between different machines (host agents) while preserving their state.

2.2   Basic System Protocols

There are six protocols used for communication by the system. The *UploadProtocol* is a fixed, published Remote Method Invocation (RMI) interface used by the client application to upload a computation to the market server and to instantiate it's scheduler. A client application may instantiate multiple schedulers to simultaneously launch the same code with multiple data.

The *ControlProtocol* is a published RMI interface for the client application to control a scheduler. Through this interface it is possible to start a computation with new parameters, alter the computation's budget for acquiring hosts, instruct the scheduler to kill all tasks and exit, etc. The basic functions are implemented in the system classes. The programmer can introduce computation specific control functions by extending this interface.

The *ComputationProtocol* is used within the bounds of a single computation for communication among tasks and the scheduler. It is application dependent and thus unknown to the system. We do, however, provide message passing support, which is not further discussed in this paper.

The *MarketSchedulerProtocol* is used for local communication between the market server and schedulers. The market server implements a standard published interface for servicing requests from schedulers such as placing orders and retrieving host and market status information. Respectively, schedulers provide methods for being notified by the market of events such as the opportunity to acquire a new lease, a change in the client's account balance, the completion of a task's work and the failure of a host that was leased to them. Similarly, the *HostAgentTaskProtocol* provides local communication among a host agent and the task it is hosting. The agent implements a published interface for servicing requests from tasks, such as retrieving information about a host's performance.

The *MarketHostAgentProtocol* is a proprietary protocol used by the market server and the host agent. It allows orders to be placed in the market by the host. It is also used to retrieve tasks from the market, ask for "payment" when tasks complete and to post benchmarking data to the market server.

3   Resource Allocation

Host allocation is based on machine profiles. Both hosts (sellers) and clients (buyers) submit orders to the market server, specifying their actual and desired machine profile respectively. The parameters of an order are listed in table 1. The *performance vectors* include the host's mean score and variance for a set of benchmarks over key performance characteristics such as integer and floating point arithmetic, network connection speed to the market server etc. The host *abort ratio* is the ratio of computations killed by the host versus computations initiated on that host (a "kill" happens when a host abruptly leaves the market). The host performance vectors and abort ratio are automatically produced by the system. Host profiles can easily be extended to include additional information that could be of importance for host selection.

A credit based [1] mechanism is used for charging. Credit can be translated into anything that makes sense in the context where the system is deployed. Within a non-profit institution, it may represent time units to facilitate quotas. Service-oriented organizations could charge clients for using hosts by converting credit to actual currency.

An economy-based mechanism is employed to match the orders that are put in the market. For each match, the market produces a lease, which is a contract between a host and a client containing their respective orders and the price of use agreed upon. Leases are produced periodically using continuous double auction

Table 1. Parameters specified in orders

Parameter	Description	
	Sell Orders	Buy Orders
price/sec	The minimum amount of credit required per second of use of the host.	The maximum amount of credit offered per second of use of the host.
lease duration	The maximum amount of usage time without renegotiation.	The minimum amount of usage time without renegotiation.
granted/demanded compensation	Credit granted/demanded for not honoring the lease duration.	
performance statistics vectors	The host's average score and variance for each of the benchmarks (measured).	The average performance score and variance a buyer is willing to accept.
abort ratio	The host's measured abort ratio.	The abort ratio a buyer is willing to accept.

[8]. A lease entitles the client to utilize the host for a specific amount of time. If the client's task completes within the lease duration, then the buyer transfers an amount of credit to the seller as a reward, calculated by multiplying actual duration with the lease's price per second. If the lease duration is not honored, an amount of credit is transfered from the dishonoring party to the other.

4   Supporting Distributed Computing Paradigms

Through the set of protocols offered by the system, it is possible to develop a wide range of applications. More importantly generic support can be provided for entire classes of distributed computations. Applications can then be developed by extending these classes to introduce specific functionality. Figure 2 shows schematically how the various issues of distributed computing are dealt with, in a layered fashion, in JaWS. Different implementations may exist for each layer, depending on the desired functionality. Application programmers may either rely on existing implementations or choose to develop their own solutions based on more basic primitives. They can also make their implementations available to others by registering the corresponding archives on the public JaWS web site.

One of our goals in creating the system was to provide APIs allowing for quick development of classes of computations. As an example, in the following we briefly indicate how support for embarrassingly parallel computations can be implemented in JaWS. Other distributed computation paradigms, or even different approaches to the same problem, can be supported in similar way.

4.1   The Generic Master – Slave Model

In the "Master - Slave" model work is distributed among many processors by a distinguished processor referred to as the "master". The other processors,

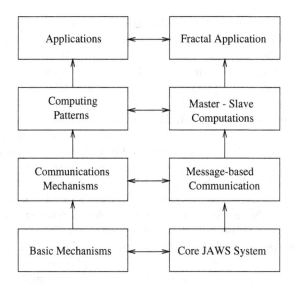

Fig. 2. Overview of architecture

referred to as "slaves", complete the work assigned to them and return the results to the master. In order to process its workload a slave does not need to communicate with any other slave. This model is used in image processing, genetics algorithms, brute force search and game tree evaluation. One possible implementation of this model is sketched below. For brevity, only the methods a programmer has to be aware of are shown.

```
public interface MSControl extends gr.jaws.SchedulerControl {
  public void startComputation( Object partitionParams,
    Object orderParams ) throws java.rmi.RemoteException,
    AlreadyStartedException, ExitingException;
  public void stopComputation() throws java.rmi.RemoteException,
    NotStartedException, AlreadyStoppingException;
  public Object[] getResults() throws java.rmi.RemoteException;
  public void stopScheduler() throws java.rmi.RemoteException;
}
public abstract class MSScheduler
extends gr.jaws.models.msg.MsgScheduler implements MSControl {
  public abstract Object[]
    createPartitions( Object partitionParams );
  public abstract void placeOrder( Object orderParams );
}
public abstract class MSTask
extends gr.jaws.models.msg.MsgTask {
  protected abstract Object processPartition( Object partition );
}
```

A computation is initiated using the *MS_Control.startComputation* method. The scheduler can execute several computations during its lifetime. An ongoing computation can be aborted at any time by calling *MS_Control.stopComputation*. If there is no more need for the scheduler, i.e. the application does not need to perform any other computations on JaWS, a call to *MS_Control.stopScheduler* will cause the scheduler to exit releasing all associated resources.

When a computation is started, *MS_Scheduler.createPartitions* produces the partitions of the computation. These are forwarded to *MS_Task* instances, residing on hosts allocated to the computation. Once the data arrives an invocation to *MS_Task.processPartition* is triggered for processing the data. The results are returned to the scheduler to be retrieved by *MS_Scheduler.getResults*.

The resource allocation strategy employed in this case is simple. The scheduler places a bid in the market using *MS_Scheduler.placeOrder*, as long as there are still partitions to be processed and all of the hosts allocated so far are busy. Bid parameters are provided by the programmer to take into account application specific allocation parameters and may also be supplied by the user at runtime.

It is important to notice that programmers need to implement just three methods in order to complete a computation following this model. All other implementation issues, including the resource allocation strategy of the scheduler, remain hidden. The *MS_Control* interface, which defines the primitives for controlling and retrieving the results of the computation, is implemented by the base *MS_Scheduler* class and thus does not concern the programmer. This master/slave model could be further extended to introduce additional functionality such as check-pointing and restarting of tasks for fault tolerance. Programmers would exploit this functionality without effort.

4.2   A Sample Client Application

On top of this framework, we have developed a fractal generator application, which calculates the Mandelbrot, and Julia sets. It was adopted, within a few days, from a fractal generation program created by Peter Walser [14].

The fractal generation application consists of two major parts: the application interface and the computation. The computation is further constituted of two modules, the scheduler and the task. A scheduler is instantiated for each fractal requested and tasks are installed on hosts acquired, carrying out the actual work.

For each fractal a distinct control thread is launched in the client application along with a new scheduler on the market server's side. The control thread instructs the scheduler to create the desired fractal and retrieves the results in order to draw them on screen. Evidently, several computations may be running concurrently and competing with each other for resources.

When launching the application, the scheduler and task classes are uploaded and registered to the JaWS server using the corresponding *Upload* protocol call (a RMI invocation):

```
upIf = (gr.jaws.UploadInterface)
   java.rmi.Naming.lookup( "//host.domain.gr:1200/" +
```

```
      gr.jaws.UploadInterface.upIfName );
  upIf.uploadCode( user, passwd, "fractalApp", "fractalApp.jar",
    jarContents, "FractalScheduler", false );
```

After uploading the appropriate classes, it is possible to instantiate several schedulers in a similar manner, again through the JaWS *Upload* protocol:

```
  controlInterface = (FractalControl)
    upIf.instantiateScheduler( user, passwd, "fractalApp" );
```

Once a scheduler is instantiated and a handle to its remote interface is received, computations can be started and controled as already described via calls to methods *startComputation*, *stopComputation*, and *getResults*.

The process of implementing the scheduler was straightforward. Only two methods were necessary: one for creating partitions and one for bidding in the market. The number of partitions created, as well as the bid, are determined by parameters passed to each method that stem from user input from the client application. Analogously, the task implementation merely required the programming of a single method. An implementation sketch is given below:

```
public class FractalScheduler
extends gr.jaws.models.ms.MSScheduler {
  public Object[] createPartitions( Object pars ) {
    FractalPartitionsDef fp = (FractalPartitionsDef) pars;
    Object[] partitions =
      new FractalPartition[ pars.totalPartitions];
    for( int i=0; i<partitions.length; i++ )
      partitions[i] = /* Code for calculating partition i */
    return partitions;
  }
  public void placeOrder( Object orderPars ) {
    FractalOrderParams p = (FractalOrderParams) orderPars;
    placeBuyOrder( p.units, p.price, p.duration,
      0,0, null,null, 0.0 );
  }
}
public class FractalTask extends gr.jaws.models.ms.MSTask {
  public Object processPartition( Object partition ) {
    FractalPartition p = (FractalPartition) partition;
    /* Code for calculating fractal partition p */
    return myPart;
  }
}
```

It is evident that the amount of work required for creating the computation was minimal. Using the "Master - Slave" framework, one can develop any computation that falls under this computation pattern by implementing just 3 methods and thus the goal of ease of programmability is therefore achieved.

5   Related Work

Popular distributed programming environments such as PVM [9] and MPI [9] lack advanced resource allocation support. PVM allows applications to be notified when machines join/leave the system, but the programmer must provide code that investigates hosts' properties and decide on proper allocation. MPI, using a static node setup, prohibits dynamic host allocation: such decisions are taken a priori. Both systems require explicit installation of their runtime system on hosts. A user must therefore have access to them, as she must be able to login in order to spawn tasks. This is impractical and may result in only a few hosts being utilized, even within a single organization. Finally, the choice of C as the main programming language, compared to Java, is an advantage when speed is concerned, but to be able to exploit different architectures, the user must provide and compile code for each one of them, adding to the complexity and increasing development time due to porting considerations. The maturation of Java technology ("just in time" compilation, Java processors, etc.) could soon bridge the performance gap with C. Notably, a Java PVM implementation is underway [6], which will positively impact the portability of the PVM platform.

Condor is a system that has been around for several years. It provides a comparative "matchmaking" process for resource allocation through its "classified advertisement" matchmaking framework [11]. A credit-based mechanism could be implemented using this framework, but is currently unavailable. Condor too requires extensive administration and lacks support for easy development.

Systems such as Legion [10] and Globus [7] address the issues of resource allocation and security. They provide mechanisms for locating hosts and signing code. However, both require administration such as compiling and installing the system and thus require administrative access to the host computer. They do not support the widely popular Windows platform (though Legion supports NT) and do little to facilitate application development for non-experts. Globus merely offers an MPI implementation whereas Legion provides the "Mentat" language extensions. Legion's solution is more complete but also complicated for inexperienced programmers. It requires using a preprocessor, an "XDR" style serialization process and introduces error-prone situations since virtual method calls will not work as expected in all cases. Stateful and stateless objects are also handled differently. Finally, adding hosts to a running computation is done from the command line and additional hosts are assigned to the computation at random – there is no matching of criteria.

Several other systems using Java as the "native" programming language have been designed for supporting globally distributed computations, such as Charlotte [3], Javelin [4] and Challenger [5]. These systems automatically distribute computations over machines. However, they do not employ market-based principles to allocate hosts and do not maintain information about hosts' performance.

The market paradigm has received considerable attention in distributed systems aiming for flexible and efficient resource allocation. A system operating on the same principles as ours is Popcorn [12]. Popcorn also uses auction mechanisms to allocate hosts to client computations and exploits Java applet technology to achieve portability, inter-operability and safety. However it does not provide "host profiling", nor promotes incremental development.

6   Discussion

Besides the fact that the allocation strategies used in most systems don't take into account "behavioral patterns" of hosts, there is also virtually no support for leasing. We argue that both are invaluable for efficient resource allocation in open computational environments.

Providing information about the statistical behavior of participating hosts can assist schedulers in task placement decisions, avoiding hosts that degrade performance (and waste credit). For example, assume a scheduler has two tasks to allocate. Blind allocation on two hosts is not a good idea; unless two machines exhibit comparable performance, the faster machine will be wasted since the computation will be delayed by the slower one. Similarly, using the abort ratio, unstable hosts can be avoided when placing critical parts of a computation. Those can be assigned to more "expensive" but stable hosts. Computations implementing check-pointing and crash-recovery could utilize less credible hosts.

The lack of leasing is also a drawback in open environments: a client could obtain many processors when there is no contention and continue to hold them when demand rises. This is unacceptable in a real world scenario where credit reflects priorities or money. This would imply that prioritized or wealthy computations can be blocked by "lesser" ones. To guarantee quality of service, some form of leasing or preemption must be adopted. Leases are also practical in non-competitive environments. The lease duration allows users to indicate the time during which hosts are under-utilized. Based on this knowledge, tasks can be placed on hosts that will be idle for enough time, and checkpoints can be accurately scheduled, right before a host is about to become unavailable.

Finally, it is generally acknowledged that incremental development increases productivity by separation of concerns and modular design. Distributed computing can benefit from such an approach. Modern object-oriented programming environments are a step towards this direction, but significant programming experience and discipline are still required. We feel that with our system's design, it is possible even for inexperienced programmers to write computations rapidly.

7   Future Directions

New versions of the Java platform will offer more fine grained control in the security system. Using the new mechanisms we expect to be able to provide more efficient services, such as access to local storage for task checkpoints, invocation of native calls to exploit local, tuned libraries such as [2] [13]. Logging mechanisms along with the signing of classes, will further increase security.

We also wish to experiment with schedulers capable of recording the performance of previous allocations. Accumulated information can perhaps be converted into "experience", leading towards more efficient allocation strategies.

Lastly the issue of scalability needs to be addressed. The current architecture is limited by the market server. A single server could not handle the millions or billions of hosts connecting to a truly world-wide version of this service. It would also be impossible to have all schedulers running on the machine. We intend to overcome this problem by introducing multiple market servers that will allow traffic to be shared among several geographically distributed servers.

References

[1] Y. Amir, B. Awerbuch, and R. S. Borgstrom. A cost-bene t framework for online management of a metacomputing system. In *Proceedings of the First International Conference on Information and Computation Economies*, pages 140-147, October 1998.

[2] M. Baker, B. Carpenter, G. Fox, S. H. Ko, and S. Lim. mpiJava: An Object-Oriented Java Interface to MPI. Presented at International Workshop on Java for Parallel and Distributed Computing, IPPS/SPDP 1999, April 1999.

[3] A. Baratloo, M. Karaul, Z. M. Kedem, and P. Wycko . Charlotte: Metacomputing on the web. In Ninth *International Conference on Parallel and Distributed Computing Systems*, September 1996.

[4] P. Cappello, B. Christiansen, M. F. Ionescu, M. O. Neary, K. E. Schauser, and D. Wu. Javelin: Internet-based parallel computing using java. In *Proceedings of the ACM Workshop on Java for Science and Engineering Computation*, June 1997.

[5] A. Chavez, A. Moukas, and P. Maes. Challenger: A multiagent system for distributed resource allocation. In *Proceedings of the First International Conference on Autonomous Agents '97*, 1997.

[6] A. Ferrari. JPVM   The Java Parallel Virtual Machine. *Journal of Concurrency: Practice and Experience*, 10(11), November 1998.

[7] I. Foster and C. Kesselman. Globus: A metacomputing infrastructure toolkit. *Intl J. Supercomputer Applications*, 11(2), 1997.

[8] D. Friedman. The double auction market institution: A survey. In D. Friedman and J. Rust, editors, *Proceedings of the Workshop in Double Auction Markets, Theories and Evidence*, June 1991.

[9] G. A. Geist, J. A. Kohl, and P. M. Papadopoulos. PVM and MPI: a Comparison of Features. *Calculateurs Paralleles*, 8(2):137-150, June 1996.

[10] A. S. Grimshaw and W. A. Wulf. The legion vision of a worldwide computer. *CACM*, 40(1):39-45, 1997.

[11] R. Raman, M. Livny, and M. Solomon. Matchmaking: Distributed resource management for high throughput computing. In *Proceedings of the Seventh IEEE International Symposium on High Performance Distributed Computing*, July 1998.

[12] O. Regev and N. Nisan. The POPCORN Market   an Online Market for Computational Resources. In *Proceedings of the First International Conference on Information and Computation Economies*, pages 148-157, October 1998.

[13] The Java Grande Working Group. Recent Progress of the Java Grande Numerics Working Group. http://math.nist.gov/javanumerics/ reports/jgfnwg-02.html.

[14] P. Walser. idx fract home page. http://www2.active.ch/ pro xima/java/-idxfract/idxfract.htm.

MeSch - An Approach to Resource Management in a Distributed Environment

Gerd Quecke [1] and Wolfgang Ziegler [1]

[1] GMD - German National Research Center for Information Technology
SCAI - Institute for Scientific Computing and Algorithms
Sankt Augustin, Germany
{Gerd.Quecke, Wolfgang.Ziegler}@gmd.de

Abstract. Resource management in the typical Grid environment based on multi-MPP systems or clusters today still is one of the challenging problems. We will present MeSch, a solution for the problem of resource allocation and job scheduling in a distributed heterogeneous environment. MeSch has been implemented and tested successfully in the heterogeneous multi-MPP environment of GMD's Institute for Scientific Computing and Algorithms. MeSch allows users to access simultaneously, through a single request, heterogeneous resources distributed across the linked systems. This is possible either through explicit demands for different resources or through implicit scheduling of resources resulting from interpretation of requests. The scheduling system is available for both batch and interactive usage of resources. MeSch is implemented based on locally available scheduling facilities thus respecting the different scheduling systems and policies of the computing centers in the Grid.

1 Introduction

Resource management and job scheduling in the typical Grid environment based on multi-MPP systems or clusters today still is one of the challenging problems. Especially in a geographically distributed and heterogeneous environment it turns out, that although scheduling tools and policies are available for each subsystem, there is a lack of global resource management and thus, resource allocation is far away from being performed automatically. On the contrary: a substantial amount of human communication on all levels is necessary to partition the application, locate resources, and observe the behavior of distributed modules.

We will present MeSch, a light-weight solution for the problem of resource allocation and job scheduling in a distributed heterogeneous environment. The same way, a Grid application uses the Grid resources as a metacomputing environment allowing to make use of more than one MPP system or cluster, MeSch leads to the idea of building a metascheduler, which takes the burden of resource allocation for a metajob. The approach here is to build the metascheduler such, that it can use schedulers of all subsystems involved for all co-ordination and resource allocation tasks.

We will discuss the requirements, a local scheduler should have in order to be suitable for global scheduling. In addition, we describe the basic algorithm of a

R. Buyya and M. Baker (Eds.:) GRID 2000, LNCS 1971, pp. 47-54, 2000.

prototype MeSch metascheduler which allows co-ordination of the whole scheduling process during the application lifetime including resource allocation. The algorithm was especially designed to allow simultaneous access to the requested resources, a requirement typically needed by parallel applications.

2 State of the Art

Until now, the only solution to overcome these problems is to use scheduling systems that are able to completely handle resource management for all resources involved. However, trying to use heterogeneous environments as they are becomes difficult if such attempts will be based on a single task approach as a regular service, without any need to change local administration rules and policies. Or, for example, to introduce local components like the GRAMs of the Globus [6] system building an additional encapsulating layer that interfaces to local resource management systems. However, this approach implies an "overhead" which may not be desirable for smaller computing centers.

We are well aware that there are other powerful systems like Globus, Legion or Unicore [6,7,5] providing a broader range of integrated tools. These projects are part of the foundations of the Grid and will be propagated more and more as the Grid evolves.

MeSch, however, is directed to a simple and efficient way of bundling distributed computing resources for the "bigger" parallel jobs of a user without the need to install one of the systems mentioned above.

3 Requirements for Global Resource Management

3.1 MeSch Scheduler Hierarchy

The MeSch approach handles resource allocation as a global task which can be divided into subtasks that may be delegated to co-operating schedulers of the subcomponents of a Grid environment. Ideally, we won't discard local schedulers; instead, we build the metascheduler on top of the local ones. This allows us to build a hierarchy of schedulers.

In the same sense as a traditional scheduler maintains the nodes/processors as allocatable resources, the metascheduler does with systems (or partitions of systems). The advantage is, that all subsystems can act in their usual way with their own policy. Moreover, allocation of processors remains in the responsibility at the local system level and is not explicitly done by the metascheduler. As subsystems remain responsible for allocation, the local use of subsystems is not affected. No restriction is imposed on local scheduling strategies and administrative policies.

The MeSch approach does not impose any restrictions on the type of Grid system: they may be homogeneous or heterogeneous, geographically distributed, any combination of MPP, cluster, and dedicated systems.

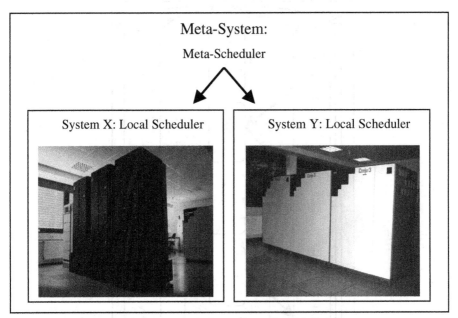

Fig. 1. Meta-Scheduler as a Hierarchy of Schedulers

3.2 Requirements for Local Schedulers

However, MeSch requires some local scheduler attributes in order to be able to take over the burden of the overall scheduling task's global synchronization

In order to provide simultaneous access to required resources, methods of getting reliable information about suitable time slots must be available. This information enables MeSch to determine a common time slot on all Grid components that are required for a Grid application. First subscheduler suggestions about available time slots in general will not lead to a solution for the complete metajob. Thus, we must be able to ask for alternative time slots to have a chance to determine a commonly agreed time slot for simultaneous access.

If a commonly suitable time slot can be determined, the MeSch metascheduler must be able to inform each subscheduler to fix the time slot and to guarantee that it will allocate required resources at the agreed start time for the agreed time interval.

MeSch synchronization management requires several iterations of interaction with subschedulers to find a solution for a suitable time slot. Obviously, offered time slots must be (pre-)reserved by subschedulers, while they are under consideration for suitability. An allocation agreement protocol eases the synchronization process by defining a set of states a job may have from an scheduling request to its final execution.

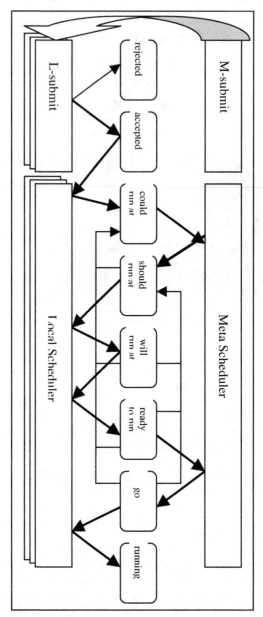

Fig. 2. Time Agreement Protocol

Each subscheduler, that can be modified to follow the allocation agreement protocol for metajob scheduling requests, is usable in a MeSch controlled Grid environment. Of course, if the local scheduler may not be modified to handle the allocation agreement protocol this may be implemented in a wrapper, given the local scheduler at least provides mandatory attributes like the ability to start jobs at a given time and to do estimation of future resource allocation.

3.3 Allocation Agreement Protocol

The goal of the allocation agreement protocol is to agree with all local schedulers in the allocation of local resources simultaneously for the same time interval.

We assume a specialized L-submit operation for each local scheduler, which accepts requests from the meta M-submit. L-submit knows that incoming requests are for a metajob, and thus it enables the time agreement protocol. This essentially means, that some additional information such as state, meta-identifier, etc. are to be maintained, and that the local scheduler knows about the time agreement protocol for this job.

M-submit calls the L-submit operation which sets the initial Accepted/Rejected state. A local preview will calculate a proposed CouldRun time, which the metascheduler will change to ShouldRun as a result of analyzing all meta components. The local scheduler will agree with a WillRun answer.

The ReadyToRun state, set by the local scheduler, indicates that local allocation is being prepared. The local resources are allocated, once the metascheduler has found common agreement by indicating the Go state.

If the analysis of offered time slots does not yield a solution, the metascheduler will go back in the protocol line and make better proposals. For the local schedulers: if they cannot fulfill a metascheduler request for a dedicated time slot, they make new proposals due to their local schedule policy.

4   A Prototype Implementation

4.1 Using EASY as a Modeling Tool

MeSch has been implemented and tested successfully in the heterogeneous multi-MPP environment of GMD's Institute for Scientific Computing and Algorithms. The available MPP environment allowed to attack the problem in a heterogeneous environment without having to deal with the problem of geographical distribution. Our prototype environment consists of an IBM SP2 with 34 nodes and NEC Cenju-4 with 64 processors.

Both systems use an enhanced EASY scheduler [1,2], which has been modified to fulfill the time agreement protocol.

The EASY concept is basically built on a "backfill" strategy. Our enhancements ensure, that even if a job has low precedence, it will be started, if its requirements do not have any implications for jobs of higher priority. The idea is to optimize system throughput by avoiding idle resources. As a side effect of this full backfill strategy, for all skipped jobs an estimated start time is available. This allowed us to provide a complete job estimation list, which is available to users and informs them about worst case start/stop times.

With this preview feature for each job, we have one basic property necessary to build MeSch: it enables MeSch to get actual information about scheduled time slots. In addition, an EASY job may be scheduled with a StartAt option.

For our prototype MeSch, EASY as a local scheduler fulfills the basic requirements for information gathering. The allocation algorithm had to be changed to support the time allocation algorithm. For the MeSch, in addition to new submit and release operations, only a previewer had to be implemented, which keeps control of the states of all local schedulers involved. The prototype allows submission of jobs in an EASY-like way.

5   An Example

In our prototype implementation, Meta components of the environment are specified explicitly by referencing the number of nodes of the respective systems, as in the example

```
msubmit -n70 -t300 -rSysA[30],SysB[40] -bmyjob
```

The batch job myjob requires 300 minutes of CPU time, 30 nodes of the SysA, as well as 40 nodes of SysB system. The command above will be separated by MeSch into the partial submissions

```
SysA: lsubmit -n30 -t300 -bmyjob
SysB: lsubmit -n40 -t300 -bmyjob
```

Each of the local systems will handle the respective request according to its local policy. Backfilling allows to find worst case time slot. According to the time agreement protocol MeSch is able to accept proposals from the local schedulers or to make new proposals until all schedulers involved agree to a common time slot.

As an example of the time agreement protocol, assume SysB accepting the metajob request. Refer to figure 2 for an overview of the state names and sequence.

With the EASY internal preview facility, the local scheduler of SysB signals a CouldRunAt time interval starting at time ts. The scheduler assures availability of requested resources to the metasystem. With the ts information from all local schedulers, the MeSch scheduler can determine the max(tsi) start time. A ShouldRunAt proposal to the local scheduler in general signals that for the reason of simultaneous access a later time than ts is favored by MeSch. A local scheduler may reject the request, proposing a new time slot and signalling the CouldRunAt state; it may accept the new time and signal a WillRunAt state for the respective part of the metajob. This iterative procedure leads to a commonly accepted WillRunAt state for each part of the metajob.

At arrival of the agreed time slot, the local scheduler will signal a ReadyToRun to MeSch, which - if everything is right - will allow local scheduling to allocate the required resources immediately by signalling a Go state.

Each of these states may be rejected: Whenever the metascheduler is not able to accept a local scheduler proposal, it resets to the WillRunAt proposing an optimal time slot up to its knowledge about all local scheduler proposals. Whenever a local scheduler is not able to accept a MeSch proposal, it resets to the CouldRunAt state proposing the next available time slot for the metajob part, that can be guaranteed according to the local scheduling strategy and administrative policy.

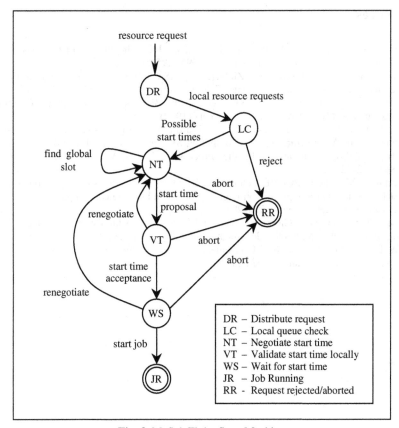

Fig. 3. MeSch Finite State Machine

6 Conclusion

The MeSch approach is a prototype metajob scheduler approach for a Grid environment. Its main advantage is that local scheduling policies are not affected by Grid jobs. The meta job scheduling can be viewed as using local schedulers as resource managers in a scheduler hierarchy. However, for an easy to implement allocation agreement protocol, local schedulers must provide a run time estimation facility for submitted jobs and accept and guarantee dedicated start time specification.

The practicability of the approach has been demonstrated by a prototype implementation based on an enhanced EASY scheduler version.

Currently we are investigating how to implement scheduling for visualization devices such as a workbench for applications with real-time visualization demand.

References

1. Lifka, D.: The ANL/IBM SP scheduling system. Job Scheduling Strategies for Parallel Processing, Lect. Notes Comput. Sci. 949 (1995) 295–303
2. Grund, H., Link, P., Quecke, G., Ziegler, W. EASY Job Scheduler for Cenju-3. Proc. of the First Cenju Workshop, HPC Asia '97, Seoul, Korea (1997) 20–34
3. Foster, I., Kesselman, C., (eds): The Grid: Blueprint for a Future Computing Infrastructure. Morgan-Kaufmann Publishers (1999)
4. Czajkowski, K., Foster, I., Kesselman, C., Martin, S., Smith, W., Tuecke, S.: A Resource Management Architecture for Metacomputing Systems. In Proc. of The 4th Workshop on Job Scheduling Strategies for Parallel Processing. LNCS, Vol. 1459, Springer Verlag, (1998), 62-82
5. Romberg, M.: The UNICORE architecture: Seamless access to distributed resources. In 8th IEEE International Symposium on High Performance Distributed Computing. LNCS, Vol. 949, Springer Verlag, (1999), 287-293
6. The Globus project: Globus Toolkit 1.1.3 System Administration Guide. (2000), http://www.globus.org/toolkit/documentation/globus_sag1.1.3.pdf
7. The Legion Project: Resource Management in Legion. (1998), http://legion.virginia.edu/papers/legionrm.pdf

Resource Management Method for Cooperative Web Computing on Computational Grid

Hye-Seon Maeng[1], Tack-Don Han[1], and Shin-Dug Kim[2]

[1] Media System Lab., Dept. of Computer Science,
Yonsei University, Seoul, Korea
{carchi, hantack}@kurene.yonsei.ac.kr
[2] Parallel Processing Lab., Dept. of Computer Science,
Yonsei University, Seoul, Korea
sdkim@kurene.yonsei.ac.kr

Abstract. Web computing only requires connection to a certain URL via Java applet supported web browser. Existing Web computing research has assumed that the application program can be partitioned into a lot of independent modules. In this paper a scalable communication method among distributed processes are proposed. And an analytic model is devised for Web computing communication time according to the characteristics of application programs and computing environment based on this method. It also provides a decision function to determine the degree of hierarchy for managing resources. With this function, the users can determine how the Web computing hierarchy architectures should be constructed to reduce the communication overhead and achieve the performance improvement.

1 Introduction

As the computing methods suggested in meta computing [10], clustering computing [11], and etc. require user account and installation of a certain program to use the other's computer as computing resources. Web computing only requires connection to a certain URL via Java applet supported web browser [1], [2], [3].

Existing Web computing research has assumed that the application program can be partitioned into a lot of independent modules [2], [3]. So eager scheduling method has been adapted as a robust scheduling method. Under this assumption and with this scheduling algorithm, communications among distributed modules cannot be performed. Though some approaches suggested the communication method among distributed modules in Web computing, these methods cannot be scalable to a huge computational environment [1].

In fact, any communication intensive applications cannot be executed with performance gain on the computational grid. But the applications that consist of much ratio of computation time to communication time can be effectively executed in parallel on these environments. So the support for communications among distributed processes can widen the applicable areas in Web computing.

R. Buyya and M. Baker (Eds.): GRID 2000, LNCS 1971, pp. 55–64, 2000.

In this paper a scalable communication method among distributed processes are proposed. And an analytic model is devised for Web computing communication time according to the characteristics of application programs and computing environment based on this method. It also provides a decision function to determine the degree of hierarchy for managing resources. With this function, the users can determine how the Web computing hierarchy architectures should be constructed to reduce the communication overhead and achieve the performance improvement.

In Section 2, Web computing hierarchy structure is proposed for cooperative Web computing environment. In Section 3, shared memory mechanism and operating methods for proposed hierarchy structure are explained. Section 4 provides an analytic model for the Web computing execution time and communication time. And also a decision function to determine the degree of hierarchy is introduced. Some real application is analyzed with the analytic communication model and experiment is performed with this application to show the usefulness of suggested method.

2   Web Computing Virtual Environment

When application program can be partitioned into the independent jobs, a manager computer has only a role for job distribution and result gathering. When it should be partitioned into the cooperative jobs, the manager computer should have a responsibility of communication among distributed processes in addition to above roles.

In the latter case, one process assumes a certain process is working normally and tries to communicate with it. So worker computers cannot be added or deleted during execution time and Web computing environment should be managed with stationary method.

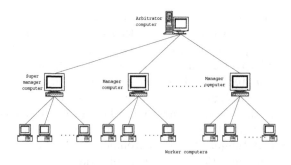

Fig. 1. Web computing hierarchy structure.

In the proposed method, worker computers should be registered to Web computing virtual environment via connecting to an arbitrator computer. When a client computer requires a group of worker computers, an arbitrator selects worker computers in the pool according to network distance and availability. The numbers of worker computers and manager computers should be determined by a client computer. The decision function for the number of manager computers according to the application characteristics is suggested in next section.

When the needed numbers are fixed, the arbitrator computer constructs virtual computing environment with registered worker computers. As worker computer can open connection to the manager computer under security restriction, the communication among worker computers is performed through communication among manager computers. So the connection between worker-manager and manager-manager is established. The hierarchy structure for proposed Web computing environment is as Figure 1. The super-manager computer is the computer that is in charge of executing a sequential part for application.

3   Shared Memory Mechanism

In this section, a shared memory system model for communication among worker computers and manager computers for cooperative work is proposed. The shared memory space is allocated within the manager computers. As there exist more than one manager computers, a portion of shared memory distributed to each manager computer should form a global shared memory, to be managed with distributed shared memory (DSM) mechanism.

The proposed shared memory mechanism provides two kinds of shared data types to reduce communication overhead and a shared datum can be declared as one of these types. The programmers can select a shared data type according to the access pattern of any data. One shared data type uses data replication algorithm and is called the multiple copied (MC) type. This type is managed with full-replication algorithm [7]. For this type of data, all manager computers have their own copies of data. A read request can be served at its parent manager computer of a worker computer that raises this read request but a write request requires data updates for all the manager computers. This writing policy is from the cache managing method, write-update.

Another data type doesn't replicate data and is called the single copied (SC) type. This type is managed with distributed-central algorithm [7]. When a datum is declared as the SC type, all manager computers create the object for the data but the latest value of that data is maintained in only one manager computer as an owner manager computer of that data. Read/write requests can be served locally in the parent manager computer when the owner manager computer and the parent manager computer are the same computer. This type of accesses is called as local accesses. But in another case, these requests should be served remotely from the owner manager computer and this type of accesses is called as remote accesses. Figure 2 shows the shared data access mechanism according to the data types and locations.

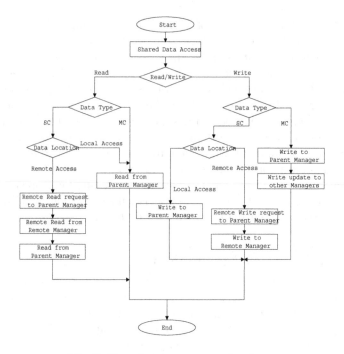

Fig. 2. Shared data access mechanism.

4   The Analytic Model for Execution Time and Hierarchy Level

Parallel execution time is composed of computation time and communication time. The computation time shows little variation when the computer and program are fixed, and it is not shared by any other program. But the communication time can cause much variation according to the circumference status. In this section, the application execution time is analyzed in terms of the computation time and communication time, and then the communication time is analyzed according to various factors. With the analyzed result, a decision function for the degree of hierarchy is introduced. This function can be used to determine the degree of hierarchy to reduce the communication overhead.

4.1   Application Execution Time

The execution time for parallel computing in the Web computing is divided into the execution time of sequential parts and that of parallel parts. In the proposed environment, the sequential part is executed on a super-manager computer and the parallel parts are executed on all the worker computers. The number of parallel parts can be determined according to any given application program. When the execution time of the i-th sequential part is denoted as TS_i and the execution time of the i-th parallel part is denoted as TP_i, and the execution time of an application program A is defined as follow.

$$T(A) = TS_0 + \sum_{i=0}^{m} (Max_k(TP_i^k) + TS_i), \tag{1}$$

In this model, m is assumed to be one for simplicity. This model can be easily expanded by repetition of a code pair of one parallel part and one sequential part. When the jobs are well load balanced, $Max_k(TP_i^k)$ can be written as TP_i of any worker computer. Now the execution time of A is redefined as follow;

$$T(A) = TS_0 + TP + TS_r, \tag{2}$$

where TS_0 is the execution time for the front sequential part and is the same as in previous definition. TS_r is that for the rear sequential part and then can be represented as follow;

$$TP = T_{CP} + T_{CM}. \tag{3}$$

As the number of communications is varied according to the application, the computation time and the communication time are denoted as follow;

$$T_{CP} = \sum_{j=1}^{t} T_{CP}^j \text{ and } T_{CM} = \sum_{j=1}^{t} T_{CM}^j, \tag{4}$$

where T_{CM}^j is the j-th communication time for a given parallel part and T_{CP}^j is the j-th computation time which happens just before T_{CM}^j. The number of communications, t, can be more than or equal to one. The communication time is heavily influenced by a specific computing environment and the communication overhead can vary depending upon the factors to configure the environment.

4.2 Shared Memory Access Time

In the proposed Web computing environment, communication time is the time to access any shared data. With one manager computer, i.e. under single managing, MC type and SC type are managed with the same mechanism and may involve the same amount of access time. But with more than one manager computers in hierachy, i.e. with multi-managing, the shared data access time is varied according to the type of shared data and their locations as indicated in Figure 2. Cost factors involved in accessing the shared data are defined in Table 1.

With single-managing, the time to access a shared datum from a worker computer to its manager computer, T^{W-M} can be calculated as follow;

$$T^{W-M} = |D| \cdot U_t \tag{5}$$

. To read a shared datum, it is required to send a read request signal. After sending this signal, the shared datum read is transferred. To write a shared datum,

Table 1. The cost factors for accessing shared data.

Factor	De nition	Factor	De nition
U_t	Unit data transfer time	P	Number of worker computers
$|D|$	Size of transferred data in unit words	M	Number of manager computers

it is required to send the datum to be written first and then an acknowledgement signal is transferred. The shared data access time should include both the signal and the datum transfer times but the amount of signal transfer time is relatively small when the size of the actual data is big. So the signal transfer time is omitted in Eq. (5).

The condition that there is no communication request simultaneously caused in this application is assumed. When assuming the existence of each communication request from n worker computers, the shared data access time should be redefined as n times of T^{W-M} [4] to represent the worst case. The redefinition of T^{W-M} with an argument as the number of the worker computers that can simultaneously cause any communication request is as follow;

$$T^{W-M}(n) = n \cdot |D| \cdot U_t. \tag{6}$$

When all the worker computers send the requests to access the shared data simultaneously, the time to complete all these requests can be $T^{W-M}(P)$. With Eq.(6), the shared data access time with single-managing can be calculated as Table 2.

Table 2. Shared data access time with single-managing.

Sync. purpose	Access time	Ratio
Yes	$T^{W-M}(P)$	ρ
No	$T^{W-M}(1 + \lfloor (P-1) \cdot c \rfloor)$	μ

A shared data access can be performed for the purpose of synchronization, where simultaneous communication requests from all other worker computers should be reflected in the shared data access time. A shared data access without the purpose of synchronization is not interfered by all other worker computers but by some other worker computers. If a communication request ratio,c, is defined as the ratio of communication time to computation time for any given application, the value of $\lfloor (p-1) \cdot c \rfloor$ means the number of worker computers that can request their respective shared data accesses simlutaneously. The values of ρ and μ are the ratios of data accesses with synchronization purpose and without synchronization purpose respectively. The sum of them becomes always one.

Though an application program may have a large number of shared data accesses, the average access time for any single access can be calculated. The time to access a single shared datum with single-managing,$T_C M^1 M$ is obtained as follow;

$$T_{CM}^{1M} = T^{W-M}(P) \cdot \rho + T^{W-M}(1 + \lfloor (P-1) \cdot c \rfloor) \cdot \mu. \tag{7}$$

To calculate the shared data accesss time with multi-managing, a new cost factor should be introduced. With Eq.(6), the shared data access time to the parent manager computer from a worker computer can be claculated. With multi-managing, the owner manager computer and the parent manager computer can be different. In that case, any handling time occurred from a particular parent manager computer to its owner manager computer should be added to the shared data access time. When there exist n communication requests caused simultaneously from a parent manager computer to some owner manager computers, the completion time of these requests is as follow;

$$T^{M-M}(n) = 2n \cdot |D| \cdot U_t. \tag{8}$$

$T^{M-M}(n)$ shows twice as much as $T^{W-M}(n)$ because a parent manager computer and an owner manager computer are located at different subnets when requesting any communication. When transfering a datum between two different manager computers, the datum should be passed from the sourcing subnet to the target subnet via main network. The transfer time in a subnet is usually longer than ten times of the transfer time in the main network. So the transfer time in the main network is omitted in this equation. With multi-managing, the average number of worker computers is P/M in one subnet. Thus the shared data access time can be classified according to the data types and the locations as obtained as Table 3.

Table 3. Shared data access time with multi-managing.

Sync. purpose	Type	Access	Access time	Ratio
Yes	SC	Read/write	$T^{W-M}(\frac{P}{M}) + q_S \cdot T^{M-M}(\frac{P}{M})$	ρ
No	MC	Read	$T^{W-M}(1 + \lfloor (\frac{P}{M} - 1) \cdot c \rfloor)$	μ_{MR}
		Write	$T^{W-M}(1 + \lfloor (\frac{P}{M} - 1) \cdot c \rfloor)$ $+T^{M-M}(M - 1 + \lfloor (\frac{P}{M} - 1) \cdot c \rfloor)$	μ_{MW}
	SC	Read/Write	$T^{W-M}(1 + \lfloor (\frac{P}{M} - 1) \cdot c \rfloor)$ $+q_N \cdot T^{M-M}(1 + \lfloor (\frac{P}{M} - 1) \cdot c \rfloor)$	μ_S

A shared datum in SC type can be accessed by a local access or a remote access depending on its location and the computer requesting that datum. The values of q_S and q_N are the ratios of remote accesses over the overall shared data accesses with synchronization purpose and without synchronization purpose respectively.

The values of ρ, μ_{MR}, μ_{MW}, and mu_S are the ratios of data accesses for each type and the sum of them is always equal to one. The time to access a single shared datum under multi-managing with M manager computers, $T_{CM}^{MM}(M)$ is represented as follow;

$$T_{CM}^{MM}(M) = \{T^{W-M}(\frac{P}{M}) + q_S \cdot T^{M-M}(\frac{P}{M})\} \cdot \rho\mu$$
$$+T^{W-M}(1 + \lfloor(\frac{P}{M} - 1) \cdot c\rfloor) \cdot \mu$$
$$+T^{W-M}(M - 1 + \lfloor(\frac{P}{M} - 1) \cdot c\rfloor) \cdot (\mu + q_N \cdot \mu_S). \qquad (9)$$

From Eq.(7) and Eq.(9), the average reduced overhead for a single shared data access time with M manager computers, $R(M)$ can be calculated as $T_{CM}^{1M} - T_{CM}^{MM}(M)$. From the factors of $R(M)$, is always positive and does not influence any change of the direction curve of $R(M)$, so we can omit this term from the equation. By this, a decision function for the degree of multi-managing, $L(M)$ is defined as follow;

$$L(M) = \frac{R(M)}{U_t \cdot |D|} = \rho \cdot P(1 - \frac{1 + 2q_S}{M}) + \mu \cdot \lfloor(P - 1) \cdot c\rfloor$$
$$-(\mu_{MR} + 3\mu_{MW} + (1 + 2q_N) \cdot \mu_S) \cdot \lfloor(\frac{P}{M} - 1) \cdot c\rfloor$$
$$-2((M - 1)\mu_{MW} + q_M \cdot \mu_S), \qquad (10)$$

assuming that M is more than or equal to two.

To obtain the most reduced communication overhead, the degree of multi-managing can be determined when $L(M)$ has a maximum value. But the more manager computers mean the high costs so the degree of multi-managing can be obtained according to a trade-off between the reduced communication overhead and the cost of multi-managing.

5   Application Program Analysis and Experiment

An application is analyzed in terms of parameters by using the analytic communication model and the degree of multi-managing is determined. And then experiments are performed with these applications to show the effectiveness of multi-managing. The experiment is performed in the Ethernet simulation environment with SMPL [Mac87]'s Ether model.

The Jacobi algorithm [8] is an iterative method for solving the linear system $Ax = B$ for the unknown vector x. As this program involves a lot of data parallelism, both the computation and communication loads can be well balanced among the worker computers.

Let an application program A be the probem on which Jacobi algorithm is applied to $K \cdot K$ grid to determine the next temperation. Figure 3 shows the shared data portion among the manager computers when using P worker

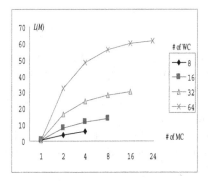

Fig. 3. Value of L(M) function.

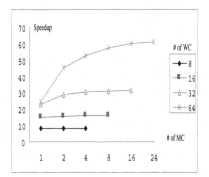

Fig. 4. Execution speedup.

computers ($WC_1 - WC_P$) and M manager computers ($MC_1 - MC_M$). All the worker computers except the both side worker computers have two $1 \cdot K$ data in their shared memory. Each of worker computers located at both sides has only one $1 \cdot K$ data. The whole size of shared data is $1(P-1) \cdot K$. All data accesses are performed for synchronization purpose and so all shared data are declared as SC type. When using M manager computers, $a(M - 1) \cdot K$ elements are shared by each of two manager computers. As all SC type data should be located within one of two manager computers, the ratio of remote accesses to the whole SC type data, q_s can be calculated as follow;

$$q_s = 0.5 \cdot \frac{2(M - 1)K}{2(P - 1)K} = \frac{M - 1}{2(P - 1)}$$

As all shared data are declared as SC type, the value of ρ is one and the ratios of other factors are all zero. With these factors, $L(M)$ function shows the the result as in Figure 3. It shows that the value of $L(M)$ function increases much more when the number of worker computers increases because in that case the overhead of communication becomes much significant. The value of $L(M)$ increases when the number of manager computers increases because multi-managing can reduce the communication overhead. The value of $L(M)$ will converge when the number of manager computers increases much more and the user should determine the number of manager computers according to a trade-off between the reduced communication overhead and the cost of multi-managing.

The experiment with $10^5 \cdot 10^5$ area and 500 iterations is executed. Figure 4 shows the variation of speedup when the number of manager computers varies. The result of the speedup graph looks similar to the result of $L(M)$. When the number of worker computers is quite big, the speedup is far from the linear speedup with single-managing but it becomes near the linear speedup with multi-managing. High degree of multi-managing can help avoiding this network contention much more in such an application with high data parallelism especially when there are a large number of worker computers.

6   Conclusion

In this paper a scalable communication method among distributed processes are proposed. And an analytic model is devised for Web computing communication time according to the characteristics of application programs and computing environment based on this method. It also provides a decision function to determine the degree of hierarchy for managing resources. With this function, the users can determine how the Web computing hierarchy architectures should be constructed to reduce the communication overhead and achieve the performance improvement.

References

1. Arash B., Mehmet K., Zvi K., and Peter W.: Charlotte: Metacomputing on the Web, International Conference on Parallel and Distributed Computing Systems, (1996) 151-159.
2. Bernd O. C., Peter C., Mihai F. Ionescu,: Javelin: Internet-Based Parallel Computing Using Java, ACM Workshop on Java for Science and Engineering Computation, (1997) 30-40.
3. Sarmenta, L.,: Bayanihan: Web-Based Volunteer Computing Using Java, Int'l. Conference on World-Wide Computing and its Applications (WWCA'98), Springer-Verlag Lecture Notes in Computer Science, (1368), (1998) 444-461..
4. M. J. Clement, M. R. Steed, P. E. Crandall: Network Performance Modeling for PVM Clusters, Supercomputing, (1996).
5. M. H. MacDougall: Simulating Computer Systems: Techniques and Tools, The MIT Press, (1987).
6. Holger Karl: Bridging the Gap between Distributed Shared Memory and Message Passing, Concurrency: Practice and Experience (10), (1998) 1-14.
7. Michael S. and Songnian Z.: Algorithms Implementing Distributed Shared Memory, IEEE Computer, (1990) 54-64..
8. M.J. Quinn: Parallel Computing:Theory and Practice, McGraw-Hill Book Company, (1994).
9. D. Zwillinger: Handbook of Integration, Jones and Bartlett, (1992).
10. A. S. Grimshaw and W. A. Wulf: The legion vision of a worldwide virtual computer, Communication of the ACM, 40(1), (1997).
11. Chungmin C., Kenneth S., Miron L.: The DBC: Processing Scienti c Data Over the Internet, International Conference on Distributed Computing Systems, (1996).

Architecture for a Grid Operating System

Klaus Krauter and Muthucumaru Maheswaran

Advanced Networking Research Laboratory
Department of Computer Science
University of Manitoba
Winnipeg, MB R3T 2N2, Canada
krauter@cs.umanitoba.ca masheswar@cs.umanitoba.ca

Abstract. A Grid architecture is proposed that is motivated by the large-scale routing principles in the Internet to provide an extensible, high-performance, scalable, and secure Grid. Central to the proposed architecture is middleware called the Grid operating system (GridOS). This paper describes the components of the GridOS. The GridOS includes several novel ideas including (i) a flexible naming scheme called Gridspaces , (ii) a service mobility protocol, and (iii) a highly decentralized Grid scheduling mechanism called the router-allocator.

1   Introduction

A Grid is a computing and data handling virtual system formed by aggregating the diverse services provided by distributed resources to synthesize problem solving environments. Some of the issues in Grid architecture are: (a) supporting adaptability, extensibility, and scalability, (b) allowing systems with different administrative policies to inter-operate while preserving site autonomy, (c) co-allocating resources, and (d) supporting quality of service.

In this paper we present a novel, highly decentralized, architecture for Grid computing that borrows features from Internet routing architectures. The central component of the architecture is the Grid operating system (GridOS). The GridOS is middleware that runs on all machines constituting the Grid. Because a Grid can have machines that range from high-performance supercomputers to handheld personal digital assistants and networks that range from gigabit-rate fiber networks to low-speed wireless LANs, it is necessary for the GridOS to be adaptable. The GridOS is designed in a modular fashion around a kernel so that the resident functionality can be changed on the fly. This design naturally supports extensibility and adaptability.

The GridOS design includes several novel ideas including (i) a flexible naming scheme called the "Gridspaces", (ii) a service mobility protocol, and (iii) a highly decentralized Grid scheduling mechanism called a router-allocator. The Gridspaces concept supports aggregation of resource names based on attributes. This enables a hierarchical resource discovery scheme that is more scalable than a flat scheme. In our architecture, the GridOS runs on each node that participates in the Grid. Therefore, it is essential that the GridOS is lightweight so

R. Buyya and M. Baker (Eds.:) GRID 2000, LNCS 1971, pp. 65–76, 2000.

that the overhead is minimal and at the same time powerful enough to support different services. One way of achieving this requirement is to dynamically instantiate services on demand. Our GridOS provides a service mobility protocol to migrate/replicate services depending on the demand. Another innovation of the GridOS is the use of request routing to decentralize resource allocation.

Section 2 describes the major features of our Grid architecture. Section 3 presents our approach to naming in the Grid. In Section 4, we examine some approaches for resource management for our architecture. Section 5 describes the architecture of the fundamental building block in our GridOS, the Grid Kernel. Section 6 presents related work.

2   Grid Architecture

In our architecture, the Grid consists of endsystems that provide resources to the Grid. Heterogeneous networks may connect the endsystems. Endsystems can range from a wireless PDA to a large cluster of supercomputers. The non-bandwidth resources such as disk capacity, computing cycles, and database services are provided by endsystems. Clients on other endsystems may use these resources The network links that interconnect the endsystems provide bandwidth resources. The Grid is responsible for managing endsystem resources, bandwidth resources, and meeting quality of service levels. Endsystems compose a series of resource requests that are routed to other endsystems that fulfill the resource requests. Specialized nodes called router-allocators examine resource requests and route them either directly to another endsystem or to another router-allocator.

Because the Grid in envisioned to scale up to Internet proportions, it is essential for the Grid to have a scalable architecture. This issue is addressed in our architecture by leveraging some important concepts from Internet routing [14]. The nodes (endsystems and router-allocators) are grouped into "autonomous systems" called Grid Domains. The nodes in a Grid domain have common resource management polices and are under the same administrative authority.

The resource management protocols are based on a datagram model. Similar to Internet routers the router-allocators do not maintain state for any resource requests that pass through them. Resource state and scheduling information is maintained on endsystems rather than on the router-allocators. Router-allocators route requests to likely endsystems but endsystems are free to reject the resource request. Resource information from endsystems and bandwidth utilization on links is periodically transmitted from the endsystems to the router-allocators. The router-allocators use this information to construct a soft state database [21] on resources so they can adapt to resource utilization and link congestion. This approach provides fault tolerance and self-healing capabilities for the Grid. In addition to this database which is contains short-lived information the router-allocators also maintain a long-lived resource capability database. Border router-allocators provide resource aggregation facilities and implement inter Grid domain resource management polices.

Router-allocators apply policy rules to resource management and the distribution of resource management information. Border router-allocators implement inter domain policies and all router-allocators within a domain implement intra domain policies.o

The endsystems and router-allocators run the GridOS which is middleware with a modular architecture. The central component of the GridOS is the Grid Kernel. The GridOS has a base set of components including the Grid Kernel and additional modules plug into the base environment to provide added functionality. This approach is similar to the extendable router architecture described in [5]. The GridOS is not a full-fledged operating system rather it is a set of processes that runs on each machine to form the middleware. The Grid Kernel is small and lightweight providing basic services for the extension modules. The Grid Kernel provides protocol processing, module management and coordination framework. The modules provide resource management functions such as scheduling policies, resource monitoring, resource accounting, and specialized resource discovery functions. The set of modules that is attached to the Grid Kernel determines the level of functionality of the corresponding GridOS. Thus the GridOS for an endsystem differs from the GridOS for a router-allocator. The security and integrity of the GridOS must be ensured so the loading and migration mechanisms will be integrated with the security management features.

3   Naming in a Grid System

In distributed systems, a name space is defined as a set of names that conform to the syntactic and semantic rules of the naming system [23]. This section, describes generalized name space for Grids called a Gridspace.

The Grid manages a widely distributed set of resources across multiple administrative domains. The naming of the objects it manages is important to the overall scalability and reliability of the Grid. The Gridspace must interoperate with or extend schemes such as DNS or LDAP. The management of Gridspace content will be specific to the objects that are being managed, thus the Gridspace management must be as extensible as the rest of the Grid architecture. The approaches described in [1] and [24] motivate our approach.

A Gridname is assigned to each object that is managed by a router-allocator. A Gridname is a set of name specifiers. A name specifier may be either an attribute-value pair or a hierarchy of attribute-value pairs. When the name specifier is a hierarchy, the upper level attribute-value pair sets up the context for the lower level attribute-value pairs. A Gridname reference is a pointer that refers to an object that is managed by another router-allocator, i.e., a reference to a Gridname in another Gridspace. A summary of the name specifiers associated with the corresponding Gridname may be associated with the Gridname reference.

A Gridspace is defined as a set consisting of Gridnames for managed objects, Gridname references to objects in other Gridspaces, and references to other Gridspaces. Gridnames within a Gridspace must be unique to that Gridspace.

Thus all objects in the Grid can be uniquely named using a hierarchical naming scheme. Each router-allocator has a Gridspace and a Gridspace manager associated with it. The Gridspace manager is responsible for effecting operations on the Gridspace.

A Gridspace manager manages the content and consistency of a Gridspace. The Gridspace manager enforces no semantics on the contents of a Gridspace or the operations on those contents other than naming constraints and common operations on Gridnames. The GridOS on the managed objects will have Gridspace agents that are responsible for sending management messages to the Gridspace managers. These agent-manager transactions may be performed on detecting a change on the managed object or at predefined intervals. The predefined time intervals may be much larger for these transactions compared to the ones used for status information updates. The agent-manager model we use in the Gridspaces is similar to the model used in the simple network management protocol.

At startup, a router-allocator has an associated Gridspace and Gridspace manager. The Gridspace will be initialized to contain Gridnames for the objects managed by the router-allocator, i.e., the Gridspace would not have references to other Gridnames or references to other Gridspaces at startup. Then the router-allocators exchange the Gridnames between them. When a router-allocator receives a foreign Gridspace it will create reference entries to each of the Gridnames found in the foreign Gridspace. This is only true if the foreign Gridspace is in the same Grid domain as the receiving router-allocator. At the convergence of this process, each router-allocator within a Grid domain will have the complete knowledge of the managed objects within the domain in their Gridspace. Because the Gridnames describe objects using long-lived attributes frequent update messages are not needed to keep the Gridspace consistent.

The border router-allocators summarize their Gridspaces and advertise it to the border router-allocators of the other domains. The summarization process virtualizes the Gridnames, i.e., the Gridnames in the exported Gridspace may not have corresponding physical objects. The virtual Gridnames in the exported Gridspace reference indicate the "capability" of the managed objects to the other Gridspaces.

The Gridspace can be considered as a persistent distributed database that is weakly consistent. Suppose a resource is no longer available at an endsystem it takes the endsystem some time before Gridname entry in the associated Gridspace is updated. Although other Gridspaces have references to they may have stale summary of the name specifiers associated with the Gridname references. This makes the database weakly consistent. The weak consistency is handled by the resource management protocol that uses the Gridspace information as shown in the next section.

The approaches described in [1], [18], and [24] are being examined for potential mechanisms that can be used to efficiently implement our notion of Gridspaces. We are also investigating how to interface the Gridspaces to existing namespaces and databases in an efficient and high performance way.

4 Resource Management in a Grid System

Resource management in our architecture extends the query routing approach in [17] to the general resource management problem. The resource management protocols are based on datagrams that are exchanged between nodes. The protocols can be functionally split into resource dissemination, resource discovery and resource scheduling. Dissemination pushes information about resources from endsystems that have resources to other nodes. Resource discovery pulls resource information from other nodes to an endsystem. Resource scheduling protocols are used to assign resources to requests including co-allocation of resources across different nodes.

The resource management protocols are extensible with extensions provided by the modules that are loaded on top of the kernel. Extensibility is a problem for nodes that receive extended message content and do not have the extension modules. Possible solutions are to dynamically load extensions into the node across the network or ignore the content altogether.

The endsystems are the sources and sinks of all resource management protocol datagrams in the Grid. Resource requests are generated by endsystems that other endsystems fulfill by providing their resources. Router-allocators route resource messages between endsystems and other router-allocators. Border router-allocators apply domain resource management policies for inter domain resource messages. The scheduling of resources is performed by the endsystems. All resource management information is maintained as soft state.

Figure 1 illustrates the request routing and data dissemination processes inside a router-allocator. The two processes while sharing common data structures are functionally split. The shaded region indicates the components involved in request routing and allocation and the unshaded region indicates the components involved in data dissemination.

4.1 Resource Status Dissemination

A large number of nodes may make uniform status dissemination too costly. Heterogeneity in resource characteristics and resource requests may make it unnecessary to uniformly disseminate the status [19].

One of the major overheads of dissemination are messages that keep the distributed status database consistent. We can use different properties of the Grid environment to minimize update messages. Resource attributes are split into two classes: short-lived attributes and long-lived attributes. Short-lived attributes are disseminated through the Grid status registry mechanism shown in Figure 1. Long-lived attributes are disseminated via Gridspaces. Consequently, it is possible to have different update policies for Gridspaces and Grid status registries. One approach is to use frequent update messages for the Grid status registry but to restrict the update message propagation area. Alternatively, Gridspaces may be updated less frequently but on a larger propagation area. The extent of update message propagation for the Grid status registry may be

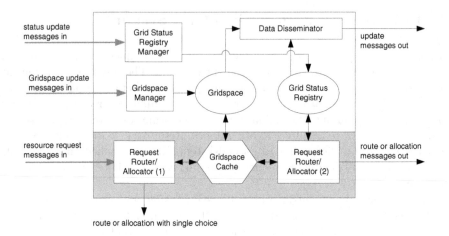

Fig. 1. Request routing and data dissemination in a router-allocator

decided based on the importance and uniqueness of the resource or based on administrative policies [19].

In addition to disseminating resource status information it is also necessary to disseminate information regarding the services offered by the different Grid nodes. Including the Gridnames that describe the services in the respective Gridspaces performs a transparent dissemination of service information. This feature aids the service mobility that is described below.

To enhance scalability , our architecture divides the overall system into Grid domains. Border router-allocators are responsible for connecting domains to form the Grid and disseminating data between domains. Administrative policies are used to restrict the content of the data dissemination messages. Border router-allocators also aggregate the Gridspace update messages using the Gridspace aggregation policies. Updating the Grid status registry dependents on the policy. One policy may update status only within a Grid domain and another policy would update based on a dynamically chosen network distance.

4.2   Resource Discovery

Resource discovery in distributed systems is typically based on a distributed database approach or a mobile agent approach. In our architecture, we use a hybrid approach. For example, the Gridspace is maintained as a weakly consistent distributed database. Because of the way Gridspaces aggregate the attributes of the managed objects there may not be detailed information for a remote object. Once a resource discovery query walks through the aggregated Gridspace that entry is cached in the Gridspace cache. This can be considered as an agent based approach. However, the benefit of this approach over the agent based approach is that the subsequent queries that may be interested in the same object need not incur the full overhead until the cached entries are timed out.

4.3   Resource Scheduling

Resource scheduling is done in a distributed way using both the router-allocators and endsystems. Endsystems are responsible for the scheduling of the resources on their node. Endsystems also generate requests for resources elsewhere in the Grid. When a resource request arrives at a router-allocator, the router-allocator consults the Gridspace to determine the best way to handle the resource request.

The router-allocator may process the request in several ways. If it determines that a remote resource is best for handling the request it will forward the request to the corresponding router-allocator. Alternatively, the router-allocator may find a loaded Grid scheduling service and delegate the request processing. This scheduling service may be implemented using wide-area schedulers such as Globus, Gallop, or MSHN. The scheduling services are registered with the Gridspace at the router-allocator and the request routing mechanism will find the service when it queries the Gridspace. In some situations, it may be necessary to schedule a request over several different resources (referred to as co-allocation or multi-scheduling in [8]).

Scheduling uses a three-phase protocol between the endsystems providing the resources and the endsystems requesting the resources. The protocol also follows an end-to-end allocation model rather than following an in-core allocation model. More specifically, the router-allocators just facilitate the resource scheduling by guiding the resource requests to the most appropriate endsystem. They do not keep any state information that keep track of the request-to-resource mappings and make any binding decisions.

When a resource request arrives at a router-allocator, it consults its Gridspace and Grid status registry as shown in Figure 1 and may decided to split the original request into a number of smaller requests and route the request fragments on to other endsystems and other router-allocators. This is a recursive process that can cross Grid domains. The endsystems then send a response indicating if the resource can be scheduled. The responses then return to the originating endsystem, which then sends out a scheduling request to the endsystems that responded to the resource request. This completes the three-way handshake for scheduling resources.

There are different ways of routing the acknowledgements and scheduling request messages. The request acknowledgements could be sent directly to the originating system or via the router-allocators. Sending the messages via the router-allocators allows the dynamic updating of Grid status registries without waiting for the periodic resource dissemination messages. There are two different options for the message flow when scheduling resources. The first option is directly send scheduling messages from the requesting endsystem to the endsystem providing the resources. The second option is to route the messages along the router-allocators. The first option does not inform the router-allocators of resource allocation. The second option enables the router-allocator to update the Grid status registry entries.

4.4   Service Mobility Protocol

The purpose of the service mobility protocol is to provide extensibility and ad-aptability to the GridOS while maintaining the lightweight nature of the Grid Kernel so that the Grid can execute on a wide variety of platforms. Consider a Grid domain with several endsystems and a single router-allocator. This router-allocator also acts as the border router-allocator because it is the sole router-allocator for the domain. As the load on the node increases it may be necessary to off-load some of the work by migrating the router-allocator to another node or replicating the router-allocator functionality to another node and sharing the load.

The GridOS provides service mobility as a built-in service at each node. This service is responsible for monitoring the mobility-enabled services and deciding when and where they should be replicated or migrated. Although our design does not allow new migration or replication policies to be added to the system it allows the Grid domain administrator to set the values of fine-tuning parameters for the migration and replication logic. In the simplest case, the mobility protocol module monitors the CPU load at the local node and when a threshold set by the domain administrator is reached, it will initiate the replication and/or migration process. It requests other potential nodes for bids for hosting the service that needs to be moved. Other considerations such as network vicinity may be considered in deciding the set of potential nodes. All nodes, i.e., the current node and the potential nodes are in the same administrative domain.

After receiving the bids, the mobility service needs to decide which node it is going to choose and whether it is going to replicate or migrate. Of it replicates the service to another node it will need to modify the Gridspaces in the local node as well as the remote node to reflect this replication. The data dissemination protocol is used to inform the Gridspaces in the other nodes about the new instance of the service. Instead of simply monitoring the CPU load at the node, it may be beneficial to use a combination of fraction of the CPU cycles delivered to the service under consideration and the demand for the service. The replication may be made further efficient if the service is replicated to a location closer to the region where the service is in high demand [25].

5   Grid Kernel Architecture

The GridOS runs on all nodes that are part of the Grid. The GridOS is organized in a modular fashion with Grid Kernel as the central component. The Grid Kernel is designed to be small, efficient and lightweight. The Grid Kernel provides only functions that are absolutely required to have a node be part of the Grid. The extension modules provide all other functions.

The kernel provides basic functions such as the processing of the resource management protocols, the module management of the extension modules, and the Grid security on a node. It is run as a user mode application using the services of the host operating system to execute and monitor jobs. The Grid kernel does not require system mode operating systems privileges but some of the extension modules may be interfacing with native operating system services that require extended privileges. The kernel does not require that the module be written in a particular language only that it provides a standard binary interface so that the proper functions can be invoked.

The kernel is structured in layers. The bottom layer, the kernel to native operating system interface is responsible for providing a uniform interface to native functions. The second layer consists of the resource protocol processing component, module management component, and a security manager component. The top layer, the module to kernel interface layer provides a uniform interface for extension modules to the services provided by the kernel and the loaded modules.

The resource protocol processing component is responsible for processing the protocol messages and protocol events. The processing involves dispatching the extension modules that handle message content. The module management component keeps track of the modules that are currently loaded on top of the kernel. It also provides the services to dynamically load and unload the modules. The Grid security manager authenticates the modules that may be loaded dynamically. The security manager implements the generic security mechanisms used by the modules. There may be a number of different security authorization and authentication modules specific to the resources used by the node but the security manager manages the overall access and control in conjunction with these modules.

The use of modules and Gridspaces on top of a common kernel provides the ability to have Grid software that is customized to the needs of individual nodes. Thus each node in the Grid only runs the modules that are required to manage the resources specific to the node. This approach reduces the overhead required for a node to be part of the Grid. For example, a workstation, supercomputer, and bandwidth broker would have very few modules in common since the resources provided by these nodes to the Grid vary widely.

The module structure for an endsystem and a router-allocator node are somewhat different. The Grid kernel and Grid Manager module are common but the router-allocator would contain routing and resource routing policy manager modules whereas the endsystem would contain resource specific manager modules. The Grid Manager module is a mandatory on all nodes since it provides the basic functions for the node to be part of the Grid.

The endsystem node would have a number of different resource managers that manage requests for a specific resource such as a specialized database or computational resource. The request routing and allocation module in the router-allocator is responsible for handling the resource requests coming in to the router-allocator. Based on the information it finds in the Gridspace and the Grid status registry, it may either send the request to another router-allocator or to an endsystem. Any administrative policies that may determine the outcome of the resource request processing are also implemented by this module.

The Grid manager module consists of a Gridspace naming module, a node monitoring module, and a service mobility module. The naming module enforces the local and global Gridspace naming rules. The node monitoring module monitors the state of the local node and notifies other modules or the kernel of state changes. The service mobility module implements the moving of modules and their associated Gridspaces from one node to another node.

Resource specific manager modules typically consists of a resource management component, a Gridspace management agent component, a resource monitoring component, and a resource specific security component. The resource management component interfaces with the native resource management functions to perform the actual scheduling of the resource. The Gridspace management agent is very similar to the simple network management protocol agent. The Gridspace management agent is responsible for tracking that status of the managed object and notifying the Gridspace manager about the relevant changes. The resource monitoring component is used to track resource utilization rates and important events for that resource. The resource specific security component interfaces to the authentication and authorization module that this resource uses to authenticate and authorize resource requests from another Grid node.

The kernel structure, module management, resource monitoring facilities, and service mobility make it possible to dynamically change the resources and behavior of the Grid. For example, there is no significant difference between a router-allocator and an endsystem node other than the modules that are loaded on top of the Grid kernel. The node that is hosting different Grid modules to make up a router-allocator may become heavily loaded. This will prompt the service mobility protocol to replicate/migrate the router-allocator functionality to other nodes thus shedding some of the load on the node. Further, the failure of a router-allocator could be detected by an endsystem and it could then load the required modules to provide this service. Endsystems may also migrate some services to other nodes within the Grid.

6   Related Work

Existing Grid computing systems can be divided into two categories, application enabling systems and user access systems. The application enabling systems provide application programmers with tools that allow applications to access globally distributed resources in an integrated fashion. Examples of such systems include ATLAS [2], Globe [13], Globus/GUSTO [6], [7], Legion [10], and ParaWeb [3]. The user access systems provide the end users of the Grid with transparent access to geographically distributed resources in a location independent manner. Examples of such systems include CCS [20], MOL [22], NetSolve [4], and PUNCH [15].

The Grid Integrated Architecture [9], an extension of the Globus/GUSTO effort, intends to provide a globally distributed uniform infrastructure. Our GridOS corresponds to part of the Grid services layer in the architecture. The major difference between our GridOS architecture and the architecture in [9] is that our architecture features a Grid with fine grain adaptability. With the service mobility protocol and the extensible Grid Kernel design, it is possible to adapt the different nodes of the Grid according to the usage requirements and the node's capacity. The Ninja project [11], [12] is building a network computing structure centered on "network documents" and implemented using Java. There are similarities between their multispaces and our Gridspaces but we focus on using Gridspaces as a weakly consistent capability database and they use multispaces as function repository. Their use of XML in network document is for dynamic application loading rather than for resource specific management extensions.

7 Conclusions

This paper presents a Grid architecture that is motivated by the large-scale routing principles in the Internet to provide an extensible, high-performance, scalable, and secure Grid. The central idea of the proposed architecture is to layer a Grid operating system on top of the resources to construct a Grid. The resources may have their own schedulers, accounting mechanisms, and security mechanisms. The GridOS interfaces with the services provided by the local resources and exports them to the Grid level. This paper describes the components of the GridOS.

The GridOS includes several novel ideas including (i) a flexible naming scheme called the "Gridspaces", (ii) a service mobility protocol, and (iii) a highly decentralized Grid scheduling mechanism called the router-allocator. The combination of flexible naming, service adaptability, service extensibility, and highly decentralized resource management results in a novel Grid architecture. A Grid system based on this architecture can execute across a widely varying resource set that may include wireless PDAs and powerful supercomputers.

References

1. W. Adjie-Winoto, E. Schwartz, H. Balakrishnan, and J. Lilley, The design and implementation of an intentional naming system , Operating Systems Review, Vol. 34, No. 5, Dec. 1999, pp. 186-201.
2. J. E. Baldeschwieler, R. D. Blumofe, and E. A. Brewer, ATLAS: An infrastructure for global computing , 7th ACM SIGOPS European Workshop, 1996.
3. T. Brecht, H. Sandhu, M. Shan, and J. Talbot, ParaWeb: Towards world-wide supercomputing , 7th ACM SIGOPS European Workshop, 1996.
4. H. Casanova and J. Dongarra, Netsolve: A network solver for solving computational science problems , Supercomputing, 1996.
5. D. Decasper, Z. Dittia, G. Parulkar, and B. Plattner, Router plugins: A software architecture for next-generation routers , IEEE/ACM Transactions on Networking, Vol. 8, No. 1, Feb. 2000, pp. 2-15.
6. I. Foster and C. Kesselman, Globus: A metacomputing infrastructure toolkit , Int'l Journal of Supercomputer Application, Vol. 11, 1997.
7. I. Foster and C. Kesselman, The Globus project: A status report , 1998 IEEE Heterogeneous Computing Workshop (HCW '98), 1998, pp. 4-18.

8. I. Foster and C. Kesselman, eds., The Grid: Blueprint for a new computing infrastructure, Morgan Kaufmann, San Francisco, CA, 1999.

9. I. Foster, Building the Grid: Integrated services and toolkit architecture for next generation networked applications , www.Gridforum.org/building_the_Grid.htm, 1999.

10. A. S. Grimshaw, W. A. Wulf, and et. al., The Legion vision of a world-wide virtual computer , Communications of the ACM, Vol. 40, 1997.

11. S. Gribble, M. Welsh, E, Brewer, and D. Culler, The MultiSpace: an evolutionary platform for infrastructural services , 1999 Usenix Annual Technical Conference, 1999.

12. T. Hodes and R. Katz, A document-based framework for Internet application control , 2nd USENIX Symposium on Internet Technologies and Systems, 1999.

13. P. Homburg, M. v. Steen, and A. S. Tennanbaum, An architecture for a wide area distributed system , 7th ACM SIGOPS European Workshop, 1996.

14. C. Huitema, Routing in the Internet , 2nd Edition, Prentice-Hall, Upper Saddle River, NJ, 2000.

15. N. Kapadia and J. Fortes, PUNCH: An architecture for web-enabled wide-area network-computing , Cluster Computing: The Journal of Networks, Software Tools and Applications; Special Issue on High Performance Distributed Computing. 1999.

16. K. Krauter and M. Maheswaran, Towards a High Performance Extensible Grid Architecture , HPCS 2000, June 2000

17. P. Leach and C. Wieder, Query routing: Applying systems thinking to Internet search , 6th Workshop in Hot Topics in Operating Systems, 1997, pp. 82-86.

18. J. Ordville and B. P. Miller, Distributed active catalogs and meta-data caching in descriptive name services , IEEE Int'l Conference on Distributed Computing Systems, May 1993, pp. 120-129.

19. M. Maheswaran and K. Krauter, A Parameter-based Approach to Resource Discovery in Grid Computing Systems, TR-CS, Computer Science, University of Manitoba, under preparation.

20. F. Ramme, Building a virtual machine-room a focal point in metacomputing , Future Generation Computer Systems, Vol. 11, 1995.

21. S. Raman and S. McCanne, A model, analysis, and protocol framework for soft state-based communication , ACM SIGCOMM, 1999, pp. 15-25.

22. A. Reinefeld, R. Baraglia, T. Decker, J. Gehring, D. Laforenza, F. Ramme, T. Romke, and J. Simon, The MOL project: An open, extensible metacomputer , 1997 IEEE Heterogeneous Computing Workshop (HCW '97), 1997, pp. 17-31.

23. P. K. Sinha, Distributed Operating Systems: Concepts and Design, IEEE Press, New York, NY, 1997.

24. A. Vahdat, M. Dahlin, T. Anderson and A. Aggarwal, Active names: flexible location and transport of wide-area resources , USENIX Symposium on Internet Technologies and Systems, 1999.

25. T. Vaseeharan and M. Maheswaran, Towards a novel architecture for wide-area data caching and replication , First International Conference on Internet Computing (IC 2000), June 2000

Data Management in an International Data Grid Project

Wolfgang Hoschek[1,3], Javier Jaen-Martinez[1], Asad Samar[1,4],
Heinz Stockinger[1,2], and Kurt Stockinger[1,2]

[1] CERN, European Organization for Nuclear Research, Geneva, Switzerland
[2] Inst. for Computer Science and Business Informatics, University of Vienna, Austria
[3] Inst. of Applied Computer Science, University of Linz, Austria
[4] California Institute of Technology, Pasadena, CA, USA

Abstract. In this paper we report on preliminary work and architectural design carried out in the Data Management work package in the International Data Grid project. Our aim within a time scale of three years is to provide Grid middleware services supporting the I/O-intensive world-wide distributed next generation experiments in High-Energy Physics, Earth Observation and Bioinformatics. The goal is to specify, develop, integrate and test tools and middleware infrastructure to coherently manage and share Petabyte-range information volumes in high-throughput production-quality Grid environments. The middleware will allow secure access to massive amounts of data in a universal namespace, to move and replicate data at high speed from one geographical site to another, and to manage synchronisation of remote copies. We put much attention on clearly specifying and categorising existing work on the Grid, especially in data management in Grid related projects. Challenging use cases are described and how they map to architectural decisions concerning data access, replication, meta data management, security and query optimisation.

1 Introduction

In the year 2005 a new particle accelerator, the Large Hadron Collider (LHC), is scheduled to be in operation at CERN, the European Organization for Nuclear Research. Four High Energy Physics (HEP) experiments will start to produce several Petabytes of data per year over a life time of 15 to 20 years. Since this amount of data was never produced before, special efforts concerning data management and data storage are required.

One characteristic of these data is that most of it is read-only. In general, data are written by the experiment, stored at very high data rates (from 100 MB/sec to 1GB/sec) and are normally not changed any more afterwards. This is true for about 90% of the total amount of data. Furthermore, since CERN experiments are collaborations of over a thousand physicists from many different universities and institutes, the experiment's data are not only stored locally at CERN but there is also an intention to store parts of the data at world-wide

R. Buyya and M. Baker (Eds.:) GRID 2000, LNCS 1971, pp. 77–90, 2000.

distributed sites in so-called Regional Centres (RCs) and also in some institutes and universities. The computing model of a typical LHC experiment is shown in Figure 1.

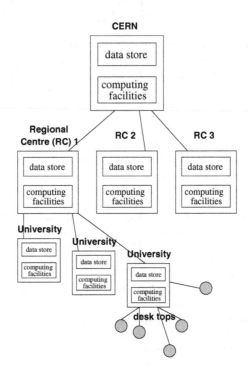

Fig. 1. Example of the network of one experiment's computing model

These RCs are part of the distributed computing model and should complement the functionality of the CERN Centre. The aim is to use computing power and data storage in these Regional Centres and allow physicists to do their analysis work outside of CERN with a reasonable response time rather than accessing all the data at CERN. This should also help the collaboration to have many scientists working spread around the world. Regional Centres will be set up for instance in Italy, France, Great Britain, USA and Japan.

By its nature, this is a typical Grid application which combines two aspects of today's Grid technology: Computational and Data Grids. In order to meet this challenge, the HEP community has established a project called "Research and Technological Development for an International Data Grid". The objectives of this project are the following. Firstly, establish a Research Network which will enable the development of the technology components essential for the implementation of a new world-wide Data Grid on a scale not previously attempted. Secondly, demonstrate the effectiveness of this new technology through the large scale deployment of end-to-end application experiments involving real users. Finally, demonstrate the ability to build, connect and effectively manage large general-purpose, data intensive computer clusters constructed from low-cost commodity components. Furthermore, the project does not only cover HEP but also other scientific communities like Earth Observation and Bioinformatics.

The entire project consists of several work packages for middleware development, computing fabric and mass storage management, testbeds and applications. In this paper we present the data management aspects of the project. The objectives are to implement and compare different distributed data management approaches including caching, file replication and file migration. Such middleware is critical for the success of heterogeneous Data Grids, since they rely on efficient, uniform and transparent access methods. Issues to be tackled within three years include:

- the management of a universal namespace
- efficient data transfer between sites
- synchronisation of remote copies
- wide-area data access/caching
- interfacing to mass storage management systems.

A major aim of the project is to build on existing experience and available software systems. For the startup phase we have chosen the Globus toolkit as the starting point for our middleware research and development. Globus is a promising toolkit and has already proved several times that it is applicable for large Grid projects [12].

The paper is organised in the following way. The section on related work gives an overview of data management in current data Grid projects and discusses related issues of distributed database management systems and distributed file systems. Section 3 emphases the challenging requirements of data-intensive Grid applications. In sections 4 and 5 we present the overall architecture of the data management middleware components and give details on the individual components. Finally, conclusions and future work are presented.

2   Survey and Discussion of Related Work

Traditional distributed file systems like Network File System (NFS) [18] and Andrew File System (AFS) [15] provide a convenient interface for remote I/O with a uniform file name space. However, this approach does not support multisite replication issues and also cannot achieve good performance due to a lack of collective I/O functionalities, i.e. batch I/O and scheduled I/O. In contrast, parallel file systems like Vesta [5] and Galley [16], provide collective I/O but do not address complex configurations, unique performance trade-offs and security problems that arise in wide area environments. Finally, remote execution systems enable location-independent execution of tasks scheduled to remote computers, but do not support parallel I/O interfaces or access to parallel file systems.

In distributed database research replication becomes more and more important. However, the research emphasis is on update synchronisation of single transactions on replicas [1] rather than considering the problem of transferring large amounts of data, which is an issue in our case.

None of these legacy systems are able to satisfy the stringent requirements, posed by both the scientific community and the industry, of having geographically distributed users and resources, accessing Petabyte-scale data and performing computationally intensive analysis of this data.

The notion of the "Grid" has been related to having access to distributed computational resources, resulting in being able to run computation intensive applications. The concept of having a Grid infrastructure which can support data intensive applications is new to the Grid community. There are a few projects, like Globus [4] and Legion [13], which were initially directed towards computational Grids but are now also adding support for distributed data management and integrating this with the computational Grid infrastructure. There is yet another class of on-going projects which have directed their efforts to support the distributed-data intensive applications from the very beginning. These mainly include Particle Physics Data Grid (PPDG)[17], Grid Physics Network (GriPhyN)[8], Storage Request Broker (SRB)[21] and the China Clipper[11] project.

The Global Access to Secondary Storage (GASS) API provided by Globus is the only component in the latest version of the toolkit which performs tasks related to data management. The scope of GASS API, however, is limited to providing remote file I/O operations, management of local file caches and file transfers in a client-server model with support for multiple protocols [3]. The Globus group is currently working on some of the data management issues including replica management and optimising file transfers over wide area networks [4]. The Globus philosophy is not to provide high level functionality, but to develop middleware which can be used as the base for developing a more complicated infrastructure on top.

The Legion project does not have any explicit modules working on data management issues. However, it does provide very basic data management functionality, implicitly, using the backing store "vault" mechanism [13]. High level issues like replica management, optimised file transfers and data load management are not addressed.

The Particle Physics Data Grid (PPDG) project is focussed on developing a Grid infrastructure which can support high speed data transfers and transparent access. This project addresses replica management, high performance networking and interfacing with different storage brokers [17]. This is a one year project and so the intentions are not to have very high level deliverables but to develop a basic infrastructure which can fulfill the needs of physicists.

The Grid Physics Network (GriPhyN) project is a new project whose proposal has been sent to NSF for approval in April 2000. The main goal of the project is to pursue an aggressive programme of fundamental IT research focussed on realising the concept of "virtual data" [8].

Storage Request Broker (SRB) addresses issues related to providing a uniform interface to heterogenous storage systems and accessing replicated data over wide area. SRB also provides ways to access data sets based on their attributes rather than physical location, using the Metadata Catalog (MCAT) [21]. MCAT is a meta data repository system, which provides a mechanism for storing and querying system level and domain independant meta data using a uniform interface [14]. The China Clipper project has its high level goals to support high speed access to, and integrated views of, multiple data archives; resource discovery and automated brokering; comprehensive real-time monitoring of networks and flexible and distributed management of access control and policy enforcement for multi-administrative domain resources [11]. The project goals cover most aspects of a Grid infrastructure and also addresses the middleware development and not only the high level services.

These are the main initiatives which are looking at data management issues in a distributed environment. One of the main goals of our project is to work in collaboration with these on-going efforts, and use the middleware developed by them if it satisfies our requirements. Our final work aims at a system which would integrate or interact with these projects so that end-users can benefit from the efforts being put in, from all over the globe.

3   Use Cases

In our Data Grid initiative three different real-world application areas are included:

- High Energy Physics (HEP)
- Earth Observation
- Bioinformatics

Common to all these areas is the sharing of data in terms of information and databases, which are distributed across Europe and even further afield. The main aim is to improve the efficiency and the speed of the data analysis by integrating widely distributed processing power and data storage systems. However, the applications offer complementary data models, which allow us to assess how well a given solution can be applied to a general-purpose computing environment.

HEP is organised as large collaborations where some 2,000 researchers distributed all over the globe analyse the same data, which are generated by a single, local accelerator. The data access itself is characterised by the generalised dynamic distribution of data across the Grid including replica and cache management. As for Earth Observation, data are collected at distributed stations and are also maintained in geographically distributed databases. In molecular biology and genetics research a large number of independent databases are used, which need to be integrated in one logical system.

In order to get a better understanding of some of the requirements for the Data Grid, let us briefly outline the general characteristics of HEP computing. Experiments are designed to try to understand the physical laws of nature and to test the existing models by studying the results of the collisions of fundamental particles, which are produced after acceleration to very high energies in large particle accelerators. For example, beams of protons are accelerated in opposite directions and are forced to collide in all detectors along the accelerator. Each of these collisions is called an *event*. The detectors track the passage of produced particles. Moreover, the analysis of physical contraints of the produced particles implies computationally intensive reconstruction procedures.

Typical uses in HEP fall into two main categories, namely data production and end-user analysis:

1. Data production
   - central experimental data production at CERN (these data come directly from the on-line data acquisition system of the detector)
   - distributed event simulation
   - reconstruction of event data
   - partial re-reconstruction of event data
2. End-user analysis
   - interactive analysis
   - batch analysis on fully reconstructed data
   - analysis on full event data including "detector studies"

A typical interactive end-user analysis job starts with selecting a large initial collection of independent events. This means that the physics result obtained by processing the event collection is independent of the sequence of processing each single event. During the analysis jobs physicists apply some "cuts" on the data and thereby reduce the number of events in the event collection. In other words, a cut predicate is developed which is applied to the event collection in order to sieve out "interesting" events.

The process of constructing single cut predicates, i.e. optimisations of physics selections, can take several weeks or months, where the current version of the cut predicate is applied to the whole event collection or to subsets of it. One obvious optimisation for such an analysis job is to keep the most frequently used subset of events on the fastest storage (for example, in the disk cache).

An analysis job can possibly compute some very CPU intensive functions of all events, for example, a reconstruction algorithm could create a complex new event object which has to be stored for later analysis. This new object can be regarded as some additional information for this particular event.

Other jobs could apply multiple functions to every event. However, a considerable amount of time is spent on reading the objects, i.e. fetching the objects from the disk cache or from tape. Since all events are independent, a coarse grained parallelism based on the event level allows for a high degree of freedom in I/O scheduling and thus the events can be processed on different CPUs in parallel.

The Data Management tasks are to handle uniform and fast file transfer from one storage system to another. What is more, by studying the access patterns, meta data and file copies need to be managed in a distributed and hierarchical cache. In addition, security issues and access rights of the particular users must be considered.

4   Architecture

The Data Grid is a large and complex project involving many organisations, software engineers and scientists. Its decomposition must meet a number of challenges. The architecture must

- be easy to understand in order to be maintainable over time. Complex and fragile components are discouraged.
- be flexible so that different organisations can plug-in their own packages. A model based on a layered set of interfaces enables multiple implementations to coexist. Each implementation of an interface may focus on different characteristics such as performance or maintainability.
- allow for rapid prototyping. Thus it should leverage previous work as much as possible.
- be scalable to massive high throughput use cases. Careful design and layering is necessary to achieve this.
- respect the nature of distributed development. Effort is split between multiple teams, each working on a substantial component. Therefore components must be well defined and loosely coupled.

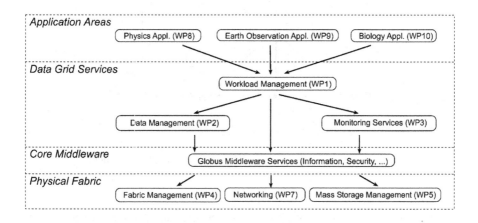

Fig. 2. Overall interaction of project work packages

We now sketch the overall architecture of the Data Grid as depicted in Figure 2. WP indicates the work package within the entire project. *High Energy Physics*, *Earth Observation*, and *Biology* exploit the developments of the project to offer transparent access to distributed data and high performance computing facilities to their respective geographically distributed community. *Workload Management* defines and implements components for distributed scheduling and resource management. *Data Management* develops and integrates tools and middle-ware infrastructure to coherently manage and share Petabyte-scale information volumes in high-throughput production-quality Grid environments. *Monitoring* provides infrastructure to enable end-user and administrator access to status and error information in a Grid environment. *Globus* services form the core middleware. *Fabric Management* delivers all the necessary tools to manage a computing centre providing Grid services on clusters of thousands of nodes. The management functions must uniformly encompass support for everything from the compute and network hardware up through the operating system, workload and application software. The *Networking* work package uses the European and national research network infrastructures to provide a virtual private network between the computational and data resources forming Data Grid testbeds. *Mass Storage Management* interfaces existing Mass Storage Management Systems (MSMS) to the wide area Grid data management system.

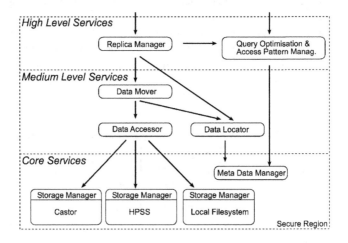

Fig. 3. Overall interaction of data management components

The Data Management work package which is our primary concern in this paper consists of a layered set of services as shown in Figure 3. Arrows indicate "use" relationships. Component A uses component B to accomplish its responsibilities. The *Replica Manager* manages file and meta data copies in a distributed and hierarchical cache. It uses and is driven by plugg-able and customisable replication policies. It further uses the *Data Mover* to accomplish its tasks. The data mover transfers files from one storage system to another one. To implement its functionality, it uses the *Data Accessor* and the *Data Locator*, which maps location independent identifiers to location dependent identifiers. The Data Accessor is an interface encapsulating the details of the local file system and mass storage systems such as Castor [2], HPSS [10] and others. Several implementations of this generic interface may exist, the so-called *Storage Managers*. They typically delegate requests to a particular kind of storage system. Storage Managers are outside the scope of this work package. The Data Locator makes use of the generic *Meta Data Manager*, which is responsible for efficient publishing and management of a distributed and hierarchical set of objects. *Query Optimisation and Access Pattern Management* ensures that for a given query an optimal migration and replication execution plan is produced. Such plans are generated on the basis of published meta data including dynamic monitoring and configuration information. All components provide appropriate *Security* mechanisms that transparently span worldwide independent organisational institutions.

5   Data Management Components

5.1   Data Accessor

One of the core problems that any data management system has to address is the heterogeneity of repositories where data are stored. This is even more of a critical aspect when data management has to be targeted in a wide area network environment. The main problem to be solved is the variety of possible storage systems. These can be either mass storage management systems like HPSS, Castor, UniTree, and Enstore [7], multiple disk storage systems like DPSS [6], distributed file systems like AFS, NFS [18], or even databases. This diversity is made explicit in terms of how data sets are named and accessed in all these different systems. For instance, in some cases data are identified through a file name whereas other systems use catalogues where data are identified and selected by iterating over a collection of attributes or by using an object identifier.

To limit the scope of our initial work we will concentrate on data collections that are stored in either Hierarchical Storage Management (HSM) or local file sytems, leaving aside the extremely complex case of homogeneous access to data stored in different database systems. We are targeting specially HSMs because they provide an automatic and transparent way of managing and distributing data across a storage hierarchy that may consist of tapes, compressed disk and high-performance disk. This type of storage system is vital for HEP applications where the volume of data generated requires the use of tapes as a cost-effective media, and where data access requirements range from accessing it many times an hour during analysis to accessing it very infrequently ("cold" data).

Having these assumptions in mind, the problem to be solved within this component of our system is the definition of a single interface that can be used by higher level modules to access data located in different underlying repositories. Thus, this module will have to make the appropriate conversions for Grid data access requests to be processed by the underlying storage system and to prepare the underlying storage system to be in the best condition to deliver data in a Grid environment. For HSMs, strategies like when data should be staged to a local disk cache before a Grid transfer is triggered, what requests are queued together to get the best performance in terms of tape mounts, and when files in the local cache are released to free space for new incoming requests will be performed by this subsystem in close coordination with the facilities provided by the storage system (existing internal catalogues, mechanisms for data transfer between tapes and local disks, etc).

In summary, this subsystem will hide from higher layers the complexities and specific mechanisms for data access which are particular to every storage system manipulating the performance factors which are proprietary for each system.

5.2   Replication

Replication can, on the one hand, be regarded as the process of managing copies of data. On the other hand, replication is a caching strategy where identical files are available at multiple places in a Grid environment. The main purpose of replication is to gain better response times for user applications by accessing data from locally "cached" data stores rather than to transfer each single requested file over the wide area network to the client application. Fault tolerance, and hence the availability of data, are key items of replication. Replication yields performance gains for read operations since a client application can read data from the closest copy of a file. Update and hence write operations need to be synchronised with other replicas and thus have a worse performance than updates on single copies. The performance loss of replication depends on the update protocols and network parameters of the Grid.

The problem of data replication not only involves the physical transfer of data among sites and the update synchronisation among the different available copies, but is also related to the more complex problem of deciding which are the policies or strategies that should trigger a replica creation. In a Grid environment replication policies are clearly not enforced by a single entity. As an example, system administrators can decide for production requirements to distribute data according to some specific layout, schedulers may require a particular data replication schema to speedup execution of jobs, and even space constraints or local disk allocation policies may force certain replicas to be purged. Therefore, the replication subsystem needs to provide adequate services for task schedulers, Grid administrators, and even local resource managers within clusters to be able to replicate, maintain consistency, and obtain information about replicas to be able to enforce any required policies.

The replication domain includes data and meta data to be replicated. These impose different requirements on the underlying communication system in the Grid. Since we are dealing with Petabytes of data that have to be transferred over the network to Regional Centres, there is an essential requirement for fast point-to-point file replication mechanisms for bulk data transfer. However, in case of limited available bandwidth and limited efficiency (not all the theoretical bandwith is available) a solution that replicates everything everywhere may not be feasible.

The meta data replication requires a client-server communication mechanism at each Grid site. The Globus toolkit offers two possibilities: sockets and a more high level communication library called *Nexus*. The communication subsystem is required to implement different replication protocols like synchronous and asynchronous update methods. An important input factor for the decision of the underlying update mechanism is data consistency. A detailed survey of replica updates can be found in [19].

Once data are in place, the Data Locator is responsible for accessing physical files, mapping location independent to location dependent identifiers. This mapping is required in order to enable transparent access to files within a uniform namespace.

User requests are not directly handed to the Data Accessor, but are routed through the Replica Manager. The Replica Manager provides high level access services and optimises wide-area throughput via a *Grid cache*. It is an "intelligent" service that knows about the wide-area distribution of files. It analyses user access patterns in order to find out where and how files are to be accessed in optimal ways. As a consequence of these access pattern analysis, replicas are created and purged at remote sites.

The Data Accessor simply accesses files which are selected by the Replica Manager. With the Replica Manager taking care of wide-area caching, the mass storage system at each site is responsible for the *local caching* of files.

5.3   Meta Data

The glue for components takes the shape of a Meta Data Management Service. Particularly interesting types of meta data are:

- Catalogues comprising names and locations of unique and replicated files, as well as indexes.
- Monitoring information such as error status, current and historical throughput and query access patterns.
- Grid configuration information describing networks, switches, clusters, nodes and software.
- Policies enabling flexible and dynamic steering.

The key challenge of this service is to integrate diversity, decentralisation and heterogeneity. Meta data from distributed autonomous sites can turn into information only if straightforward mechanisms for using it are in place.

The service manages a large number of objects referred to by identifiers. Respecting the loosely coupled nature of the Grid, it must allow for maintainance of autonomous partitions *and* good performance, both over the LAN and WAN. Thus, the service is build on a fully distributed hierarchical model and a versatile and uniform protocol, such as Lightweight Directory Access Protocol (LDAP) [22]. Multiple implementations of the protocol will be used as required, each focussing on different trade-offs in the space spanned by write/read/update/search-performance and consistency.

5.4   Security

Certain security aspects of a Grid infrastructure are tightly coupled to Data Management. Identifying these issues, and adapting the Data Management components accordingly, is of vital importance. Some of these issues are discussed here.

An important global security issue is to deal with the Grid cache. The site which owns the data has to make sure that the remote sites hosting its data caches provide the same level of security as the owner requires for their data. This will be a serious issue when dealing with sensitive data where human or intellectual property rights exist. The fact that different sites will probably be using different security infrastructures will result in more complications. It is, therefore, required to evaluate strategies and develop tools which can be used to ensure the same level of security with heterogenous underlying security infrastructures.

Synchronous replication strategies, instead of using an on-demand or time scheduled approach, raise a lot of security concerns for the participating sites. A synchronous solution would involve giving time indefinite write permissions to other nodes in the Grid, so that whenever a replica is updated or deleted, the same operation can be propagated to all the remote replicas. An on-demand or time scheduled solution (asynchronous) is more secure and less consistent, though not as responsive.

The replica selection will depend on many factors, including the security policies of the nodes which contain these replicas. We may want to select a replica from a node which is more "friendly" as compared to one which forces more access restrictions.

The sensitivity levels associated with data and meta data might be different. The actual data might be more sensitive for some sites than their meta data or vice versa. This difference has to be incorporated in the overall design of the Data Management as well as the security system.

Several policy matters which are expected to vary from site to site include

- the usage of a synchronous replication strategy or something more secure,
- the importance of meta data as compared to real data in terms of security
- how much weight to be given to security when selecting a replica.

The intention is not to force all the sites in the Grid to agree on a common policy, but to design a system which is flexible enough to absorb heterogeneity of policies and present a consistent yet easy-to-adapt solution.

5.5   Query Optimisation

Queries are one way for an application user to access a data store. In a distributed and replicated data store a query is optimised by considering multiple copies of a file. A set of application queries is considered to be optimally executed if it minimises a cost model such as a mixture of response time and throughput.

The aim of a query execution plan is to determine which replicated files to access in order to have minimal access costs. We do not want to elaborate much further on a cost model here. However, the optimal query execution plan is based on static and dynamic influences like the following [9]:

- size of the file to be accessed

- load on the data server to serve the requested file
- method/protocol by which files are accessed and transferred
- network bandwidth, distance and traffic in the Grid
- policies governing remote access

The outcome of a query can be either the result of the query itself or a time estimate of how long it takes to satisfy a query. The Meta Data Management service will be used to keep track of what data sets are requested by users, so that the information can be made available for this task.

Query optimisation can be done at different levels of granularity. The method stated above is only based on files and also requires a set of files as an input parameter to the query execution plan. Often files have a certain schema and users query single objects of a file. This requires an additional instance that does the mapping between object identifiers (OID) and files by using a particular index [20] which satisfies the expected access patterns. This introduces another level of complexity for the query optimisation because objects can be available in multiple copies of files and the optimal set of files has to be determined to satisfy the query. Note that the OID file mapping is not an explicit task of the Data Management work package and needs additional information from Workload Management and Application Monitoring.

6   Conclusion and Future Work

In this paper we reported on preliminary work and architectural design which has been carried out in the work package "Data Management" in an International Data Grid project which has been proposed recently. We motivated our Data Grid approach by a detailed discussion and categorisation of existing work on the Grid, especially of data management in Grid related projects. The aim of our three year project is to provide Grid middleware services for the scientific community dealing with huge amounts of data in the Petabyte range, whereas the essential goal is to support world-wide distributed real-world applications for the next generation experiments in High Energy Physics, Earth Observation and Bioinformatics.

Basing the initial work on Globus, we have a Globus test bed running and preliminary promising prototypes are being implemented and tested. First results will be available by the end of the year. Furthermore, we are in close contact with the Globus developers concerning evolving Data Grid ideas and implementations.

Acknowledgements. We would like to thank Les Robertson for bootstrapping this interesting work, and Ben Segal for valuable feedback and contributions to the paper. Thank you to all Data Grid members for their interesting discussions.

References

1. T. Anderson, Y. Breitbart, H. Korth, A. Wool. Replication, Consistency, and Practicality: Are These Mutually Exclusive? Proc. SIGMOD International Conference on the Management of Data, pp. 484-495 1998.
2. O. Barring, J. Baud, J. Durand. CASTOR Project Status, Proc. of Computing in High Energy Physics 2000, Padova, Febr. 2000.
3. J. Bester, I. Foster, C. Kesselman, J. Tedesco, S. Tuecke. GASS: A Data Movement and Access Service for Wide Area Computing Systems. In Proceedings of the Sixth Workshop on I/O in Parallel and Distributed Systems, May 1999.
4. A. Chervenak, I. Foster, C. Kesselman, C. Salisbury, S. Tuecke. The Data Grid: Towards an Architecture for the Distributed Management and Analysis of Large Scienti c DataSets. Network Storage Symposium, Seattle 1999.
5. P. Corbett and D. Feitelson. Design and Implementation of the Vesta Parallel File System. In Proceedings of the Scalable High-Performance Computing Conference, pages 63-70, 1994.
6. DPSS: Distributed Parallel Storage System, http://www-itg.lbl.gov/DPSS/
7. Enstore: http://www-isd.fnal.gov/enstore/design.html
8. GriPhyN: Grid Physics Network, http://griphyn.org/
9. K. Holtman, H. Stockinger. Building a Large Location Table to Find Replicas of Physics Objects. Proc. of Computing in High Energy Physics 2000, Padova, Febr. 2000.
10. HPSS: High Performance Storage System, http://hpcf.nersc.gov/storage/hpss/
11. W. Johnston, J. Lee, B. Tierney, C. Tull, D. Millsom. The China Clipper Project: A Data Intensive Grid Support for Dynamically Con gured, Adaptive, Distributed, High-Performance Data and Computing Environments. Proc. of Computing in High Energy Physics 1998, Chicago 1998.
12. W. Johnston, D. Gannon, B. Nitzberg. Grids as Production Computing Environments: The Engineering Aspects of NASA's Information Power Grid. Eighth IEEE International Symposium on High Performance Distributed Computing, Redondo 1999.
13. LEGION: http://www.cs.virginia.edu/ ∼ legion/
14. MCAT: A Meta Information Catalog, http://www.npaci.edu/DICE/SRB/mcat.html
15. J. Morris, et al. Andrew: A Distributed Personal Computing Evironment. Comms. ACM, vol 29, no. 3, pp. 184-201, 1996.
16. N. Nieuwejaar, D. Kotz. The Galley Parallele File System. In Proceedings of the 10th ACM International Conference on Supercomputing, pages 374-381, Philadelphia, ACM Press, May 1996.
17. PPDG: Particle Physics Data Grid, http://www.cacr.caltech.edu/ppdg/
18. R. Sandberg. The Sun Network File System: Design, Implementation and Experience, Tech. Report, Mountain View CA: Sun Microsystems, 1987.
19. H. Stockinger, Data Replication in Distributed Database Systems, CMS Note 1999/046, Geneva, July 1999.
20. K. Stockinger, D. Duellmann, W. Hoschek, E. Schikuta. Improving the Performance of High Energy Physics Analysis through Bitmap Indices. To appear in DEXA'200, Springer Verlag, Sept. 2000.
21. SRB: Storage Request Broker, http://www.npaci.edu/DICE/SRB/
22. W. Yeong, T. Howes, S. Kille. Lightweight Directory Access Protocol, RFC 1777. Performance Systems International, University of Michigan, ISODE Consortium, March 1995.

XtremWeb: Building an Experimental Platform for Global Computing

Cécile Germain, Vincent Néri, Gilles Fedak, and Franck Cappello

Laboratoire de Recherche en Informatique.
Universite Paris Sud
http://www.XtremWeb.net

Abstract. Global Computing achieves highly distributed computations by harvesting a very large number of unused computing resources connected to the Internet. Although the basic techniques for Global Computing are well understood, several issues remain unadressed, such as the ability to run a large variety of applications, economical models for resource management, performance models accounting for WAN and machine components, and nally new parallel algorithms based on true massive parallelism, with very limited, if any, communication capability. The main purpose of XtremWeb is to build a platform to explore the potential of Global Computing. This paper presents the design decisions of the rst implementation of XtremWeb. We also present some early performance measurement, mostly to highlight that even some basic performance features are not well understood yet.

1 Introduction

The XtremWeb project is dedicated to the study of a particular execution model in the general framework of Global (or Meta) Computing. In this model, all the computing power is provided by volunteer computers. These computers offer some of their time to execute a piece of a very large application, under more or less severe restrictions on the use of this time.

The XtremWeb environment and the other related ones like Entropia.com, Distributed.net, Seti@home [3] are Web extensions of cycle stealing concepts originally intended for networks of workstations. Condor [6], Globus [10], Atlas [5], Nimrod/G [1] and some other systems have addressed the issues of cycle stealing in the context of LAN environments. The main characteristics of a LAN and a Web environment drastically diverge.

- *Number of connected machines*: hundreds for a LAN; millions for the Web.
- *Security and protection*: stations inside a LAN are well identified; machines on the Web could be very malicious.
- *Stability* : the Mean Time Between Failure (MTBF) on a LAN is several days, versus several minutes on the Web. Moreover, the LAN stations are permanently attached to the network and belong to the institutions that may steal their cycles, while the machines on the Web do not belong to the project that wants to borrow them. In particular, the owner of a machine may unplug its machine, either physically, or from the project at any time.

R. Buyya and M. Baker (Eds.:) GRID 2000, LNCS 1971, pp. 91–101, 2000.

These differences make cycle stealing on Internet much more challenging than the simple adaptation of existing systems to the Web. However, cycle stealing on the web may provide unprecedented computing and storage power. It may also provide a new framework for the study of parallel algorithms, mostly because an application may use a nearly unlimited number of processors poorly coupled.

The XtremWeb project aims at building a platform for experimenting with global computing capabilities. The Global computing platform is designed to be a substrate for plug-in experiments. Some issues to be addressed are: sizing of the environment components (servers, network, workers) according to applications features; high performance and secure execution (relies on program isolation); modeling resource and workload management as inputs for scheduling algorithms; and the impact of the application characteristics, either compute- or data-intensive.

The next section presents main issues of global computing systems. The XtremWeb architecture is detailed in section 3. The first implementation is presented in section 4. Section 5 displays some early experiments. The next section exemplifies a typical application. The last section concludes.

2   Global Computing Issues

All Global Computing systems must exhibit a set of desirable properties. We quote them and discuss how they specialize in the XtremWeb case.

- *Scalability*. It must scale to hundreds of thousands nodes, with corresponding performance improvement. The target performance is throughput, not latency of individual computations.
- *Heterogeneity*. Target machines are personal computers and workstations. Load-sharing facilities (LFS, Condor), or batch systems, such as the IBM Load-Leveler are not considered as a part of the chain of contribution: the workstations will decide on an individual basis if and when they are willing to contribute.
- *Availability*. The owner of a computing resource must be able to define a policy which limits the contribution of the resource.
  The policy is defined by a type of activity at the workstation level, and is binary: when this type of activity makes a transition from "off" to "on", the workstation is immediately released, whatever loss in the global computation this may imply.
- *Fault tolerance*. True hardware or software faults, including unplugged laptops, and unexpected computation aborts due to the availability policy, must be managed identically, as an interrupted computation does not have the right to use local computer resource to save any of its state or to signal the event to the global system.
- *Security*. All participating computers should be protected against malicious or erroneous manipulations, and the global computation result should not be exposed to be tampered with.
- *Usability*. The system should be easy to deploy and to use.

3 The XtremWeb Design

3.1 Application Scope

XtremWeb focuses on an important class of applications : the *embarrassingly parallel* ones, also coined as *multi-parameter*. These applications consist of a large number of instances of the same computation applied to varying input parameters. In this case, each computation completes independently of the others, and the information flows only between the worker and the dispatcher. If one computation fails, because the worker has been preempted, other ongoing computations will not be affected.

3.2 The Pull and Steal Model

The XtremWeb execution model combines a pull model and a cycle-stealing scheme. In the pull model, workstations (*workers*) withdraw work from a central agent (*the dispatcher*), in opposite to a push model, where workstations are borrowed by an external agent. The cycle-stealing scheme is characterized by constraints that can prevent the computation to complete, even without any computer or network failure.

The paradigm of the pull-and-steal model is the screen-saver scheme, as exemplified by the popular SETI@home project [3] and Nimrod/G [1]. When a participating workstation is not interactively used, as detected by a screen saver utility, the workstation participates in the global computation. As soon as the user comes back to the workstation, the screen saver vanishes and so does the ongoing computation; all unfinished work is lost.

The pull model is not limited to the screen saver scheme, and not even to cycle-stealing. It can be extended to a strategy for dynamic load balancing on a large set of workstations, each of them with a variable level of commitment to the solution of the global application. For instance, some of them may be willing to contribute only if their activity is not above a certain, locally determined, threshold, while other ones may be fully devoted to the application. One of the objectives of the XtremWeb architecture is to accommodate these various contributing policies, including the screen-saver one, in an unified framework.

3.3 One-Sided Communication

In the framework of Massively Parallel Processing, one-sided communication has been exemplified by various implementation of *get* and *put* primitives. The main idea is that one participant can perform all information transfer, either put, (i.e. writing to a remote partner), or get, (i.e. reading from a remote partner). The cooperation of the accessed remote partner is not required at the programming level, even if an underlying infrastructure must ensure the actual access. This contrasts with message-passing schemes, where both partners must collaborate through paired send/receive calls. In the distributed computing framework, one-sided communication is provided by RPC (Remote Procedure Call) or RMI (Remote Method Invocation), following the programming model.

All XtremWeb information transfers are controlled by the workers. They perform RMI calls to the dispatcher, and no provision is made for the contrary. The first motivation for this choice is security: with one-sided communication, the workers security is guaranteed by server authentication and protection of the data transmission from the server.

Another motivation is ease of deployment. The security policy of the dispatcher is configurable, while the one of the worker is not. Callbacks from the dispatcher to a worker depend on the last one, and can thus be blocked by firewalls, or require the adoption of very slow protocols such as http.

With this scheme, the dispatcher performance becomes even more critical. While one part of the communication overhead is distributed across the workers, all the control cost is centralized on the dispatcher. The abstract dispatcher must then be instantiated in as many actual dispatchers as necessary to sustain the throughput required by the expected number of workers.

3.4 Native Code Execution

XtremWeb targets high performance. Thus, although the workers protection suggests execution in a virtual environment, typically sand-boxed Java bytecode, performance dictates that the end-user code should remain native.

Like most of the other Global Computing system XtremWeb uses native code execution. However, in contrary to them, XtremWeb allows any workers to execute different and downloadable applications.

New applications are made downloadable following a verification process that is more complicated than the byte code verification of Java virtual machines but less secure. First, only trusted institutions can propose codes to integrate in XtremWeb. Second, the code is executed on dedicated workers. Third the code is encrypted before downloading to workers. Fourth, the code download procedure uses a private-public key to secure the transaction. This verification process cannot prevent from any fault case because testing (second phase) may not execute all code sections with all possible parameters sets. So there is still a risk of execution error, which is not the case, in principle, with bytecodes and virtual machines.

A more flexible way to allow downloadable high performance native code execution is the technique known as Software Fault Isolation [4]. This kind of approach is necessary to allow the execution of any application without deeply checking the application before execution. We plan to evaluate this approach in future version of XtremWeb.

4 Implementation

4.1 Java Based Coordination and Coupling

The first implementation of the XtremWeb infrastructure is completely written in Java. The Java language and APIs provide portability (related to the ease of deployment issue). It also provides language-level constructs for concurrency through the Java Threads, and parallelism through Java RMI. Integrating binary high performance code is straightforward through Java Native Interface. Finally, special-purpose APIs are available for nearly any special functionality required, in particular authentication and encryption through the Secure Socket Layer (SSL) system and vendor-neutral database access through Java DataBase Connectivity (JDBC).

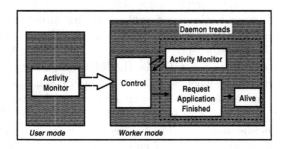

Fig. 1. The worker

Figure 1 shows the worker architecture. In user state, a background process running at low priority monitors the computer activity, following the availability policy, and also the CPU activity for performance prediction service (see below). When the computer becomes available, a new process is launched. This process starts with a control thread, that creates a monitoring thread and a compute thread, and waits forever for the monitoring thread to terminate. The compute thread invokes *WorkRequest* and *getWork*. This calls register the worker to the dispatcher and returns a description of the work to be done as well as the needed work input. Then the compute thread runs the actual computation and invokes *WorkFinished* and *WorkResult* for transferring back the results to the dispatcher. It also launches a thread that periodically invokes *WorkAlive* to signal its activity to the dispatcher. The dispatcher continuously monitors these calls. When a worker has not called for a sufficient long time, the worker computation is considered lost and rescheduled for another worker.

When the monitoring thread detects an increase of the machine load or an external device activation, it terminates immediately, causing the other threads to die. The compute and alive threads run as Java daemon threads. This implementation ensures that whatever synchronization is implied in the invocation of remote methods on the dispatcher, threads cannot become deadlocked.

5   Early Experiments on Server Throughput

One of the main parameter of the performance for XtremWeb application is the ability of the server to answer to work requests. Most transactions between the server and the workers are implemented in terms of Java RMI. RMI overhead for an empty call is more than 500 μs on a 200MHz Pentium, and increases with the complexity of the objects passed back and forth [11]. This high overhead comes from the underlying TCP protocol, and from the design of the serialization procedure, which allows for dynamic class loading. However, the main performance concern for XtremWeb is throughput, not latency since workers are supposed to be spread across a very large geographic area.

XtremWeb throughput has two components: the dispatcher throughput and the aggregate workers throughput. The first one is related to the dispatcher capability for concurrently handling multiple RMIs, while the second one is related to the scheduling policy. Early experiments deal with dispatcher throughput.

The XtremWeb architecture requires a large number of short RMI, corresponding to *WorkAlive* calls. The required RMI throughput is the product of the number of workstations controlled by the RMI call frequency. Predicting the actual RMI call frequency when WAN congestion is taken into account will be the subject of further research. In this section, we report three experiments which measure the dispatcher capacity in terms of RMI throughput. All experiments were conducted on idle machines. The Solaris machine is an UltraSparcII biprocessor at 400MHz, running Solaris 2.7 and Solaris_JDK1.2.1; the Linux machine is a Pentium III biprocessor at 500MHz, running Linux 2.2.13 and jdk 1.2.2 from Blackdown.

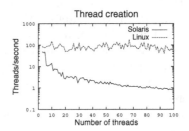

Fig. 2. Threads creation

Each remote method invocation from different machines creates a Java thread. Thus a first concern is the thread creation performance. Fig. 2 shows the result of a simple experiment: a main thread creates a given number of threads, which are affected with Java MIN_PRIORITY before being actually launched. The thread creation rate is not sensitive to the number of running threads in the Sun JDK1.2.1 JVM running on Solaris. In the Linux configuration, the rate rapidly decreases and falls below one thread per second at high load.

The second experiment (fig. 3-A) was conducted so as to isolate the impact of network congestion from RMI calls. A client performs a light RMI call on a server which concurrently runs a fixed number of MIN_PRIORITY Java threads (in practice, the client iterates over RMI calls to measure an average; Java RMI is synchronous, so iterating over RMI does not create any network congestion and averaging makes sense). The remote method is light in the sense that is has no parameters and does not return a value, and only increments a counter. The behavior of the Solaris configuration is what can be expected: the average RMI latency is around 1ms and does not change with the number of adversary threads. The Linux system latency linearly increases with the number of adversary threads. The RMI latencies in presence of only one adversary thread are equivalent in both cases, showing that the RMI implementations are comparable.

Independent experiments have shown that rapid performance degradation with the number of active threads is shared by other JVM implementations on Linux, in particular the IBM one. The reason may be that Java threads are directly mapped to the native Linux threads (one-to-one scheme), which share the process scheduler, and thus are scanned each time the scheduler computes its goodness measures for electing the next process to run. However, the steep curve of fig. 3-A for a low number of adversary threads must reflect a problem specifically associated with thread creation: the actual thread work is so short that is very unlikely that it could invoke the kernel function *schedule ()* while running.

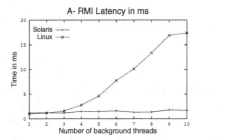 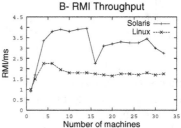

Fig. 3. RMI Latency (ms) in presence of adversary theads and RMI Troughput in RMI/sec

The last experiment (fig. 3-B) simulates at a small scale what could be the behavior of a complete XtremWeb system. Up to 32 heterogeneous machines connected through a LAN perform a light RMI call (averaged as before). The actual RMI throughput is measured. Before entering the RMI loop, the clients are synchronized, so as to ensure approximate simultaneity of the requests. Although Solaris neatly overperforms Linux, the difference is much less pronounced than in the two previous experiments. Two effects are at work here. First, the limited number of machines, possible network congestion and RMI overhead, all limit the number of outstanding requests for thread creation to a much lower level than in the first experiment, where only the thread creation rate was measured. The second effect is that the invoked method is very short. Thus, even if the thread associated with the RMI may wait before creation, not many threads will run concurrently, contrary to the second experiment.

The main conclusions of these early experiment are that server throughput depends on 1) the Java virtual machine implementation (which in turn depends on OS) and 2) the performance of all XtremWeb components : the servers, the workers and the network.

So, we must design a complete methodology (benchmark, experimental platform, result storage and interpretation) in order to measure and understand the respective contribution of each component to the global server throughput.

6   Application Example: The Auger Experiment

6.1   Background

The Pierre Auger Observatory [7] project is an international effort to study the highest energy cosmic rays, above 10^{19} eV. The origin of the very high energy cosmic rays is completely unknown. In fact, until the fortuitous detection of two events above 10^{20} eV, the theory did not allow for them to happen.

Such events are extremely rare: above the energy of 10^{18} eV, only When a cosmic ray particles (primaries) strike the earth's atmosphere, collisions with air molecules initiate cascades of secondary particles, called *air showers*. Two giant detector arrays, each covering 3000 km^2, will be constructed to measure the arrival direction, energy, and mass composition of cosmic ray air showers above 10^{19} eV over many years.

Air showers must also be numerically simulated, in particular by the Aires program.

The simulated results will be compared against the actual observations to infer the physical characteristics (speed, etc.) of the primaries, during the experiments. The inputs of the numerical simulation are the physical parameters of one primary particle plus parameters related to simulation control. The output is the simulated shower particles arriving at the earth level. The number of independent simulations to be run is very large: the simulation is based on a Monte-Carlo scheme, requiring many runs with the same input parameters to compute averages; primaries with various structural and kinetic properties must be simulated; finally, multiple physical models must be simulated. The requirement in computing power is equivalent to 10^6 years of a 300MHz PC per year. At this step of our work and of the Auger experiment, the XtremWeb project is a tentative resource complementary to the production of the classical high-performance computing facilities.

6.2   Implementation of AIRES on Top of XtremWeb

Aires provides an excellent testbed for experiments. The execution time can be predicted with reasonable accuracy from the input parameters. Moreover, with some modifications, the code can be considered as recursive: the shower particles can in turn be considered as primaries for smaller showers. Thus, the granularity can be arbitrarily down-sized [9].

For the Aires simulation, *WorkRequest* and *getWork* are merged, because there are only a few input parameters. Also the decoupling *WorkFinished* and *WorkResult* calls is mandatory. With a typical 10MB result file, the time scale and disk requirement of *WorkResult* is not consistent with the one of the other transactions.

Although the first version will include only a crude scheduler of complete showers based on the time of day, we plan to experiment in particular on the Rosenberg model [12]. This model considers a fixed startup cost accounting for network latency and a configurable workload, which is exactly the case of Aires.

XtremWeb and Aires are a good testbed for this model, and its extension to multiple workers.

7   Related Work

As in all grid-based or metacomputing projects and research, the goal of Xtrem-Web is to transparently exploit networked resources on a large geographic scale through the Internet. Contrary to most projects, it does not want to exploit these resources as a giant distributed computer.

The traditional execution model of MPP is message-passing. MetaCompu-ting or Grid-enabled infrastructures, such as Atlas [5] Globus [10] and Legion [8] extend this model to the world scale. They target tightly coupled computations, even if these cannot be as fined-grained as in a MPP context. In such compu-tations, the remote resources invoked by the application can, and probably will have to, communicate between each other. Thus these projects have developed their own communication environments. For instance, in the canonical model of Global Computation presented in [2], communication and queuing delays are considered only between the clients and the server, and not between clients. However, in these infrastructures, clients are allowed to unlimited access to the computing resources, which is a push model.

The XtremWeb architecture differs from the various previous projects in two points. The first one is that it plans to be a multi-application environment, allo-wing for multiple different multi-parameter applications to run simultaneously. The second difference is that it targets high performance applications, with re-latively coarse granularity.

8   Conclusion

In this paper, we have described the main design decisions about XtremWeb, a platform dedicated to study the capabilities of Global Computing.

Global computing system are much more challenging than existing cycle stea-ling systems which only run inside a LAN environment. We have presented the main issues. They are related to the typical number of machines involved in a Global computing system, the security and protection of the servers and the workers, the MTBF of the workers and the dynamicity of all these parameters.

Design decisions first concern the application domains considered for Xtrem-Web. XtremWeb is dedicated to *embarrassingly parallel* or *multi-parameter* ap-plications. The other design decisions which are 1) Pull and Steal model, 2) One-sided communication and 3) Native code execution correspond to a) the specificities of cycle stealing on WAN environment and b) high performance requirement. The first implementation of XtremWeb relies on Java based coordination and coupling.

Early experiments have shown the necessity of a performance analysis methodology reflecting the features and interactions of this new "parallel architecture" components, servers, networks and workers.

Finally, we have described the implementation of Aires on top of XtremWeb. Aires is a large-scale end-user application used in astrophysics.

Our immediate work is to complete the first XtremWeb version, which will be available soon. The next work is to define the relevant performance parameters, which implies to separate the impact of the network, the OS, and the Java infrastructure, and to define benchmarks that can measure these parameters across various configurations. With these two tools, we plan to build a performance model and to experiment on static scheduling. Finally, we will look for other applications.

The project development can be followed from the project web site: http://www.XtremWeb.net

References

1. Abramson, D., Buyya, R and Giddy, J. Nimrod/G: An Architecture of a Resource Management and Scheduling System in a Global Computational Grid, *International Conference on High Performance Computing in Asia-Pacific Region (HPC Asia'2000)*, Beijing, China. IEEE Computer Society Press, USA, 2000.

2. K. Aida, U. Nagashima, H. Nakada, S. Matsuoka and A. Takefusa. Performance Evaluation Model for Job Scheduling in a Global Computing System. In *7th IEEE Int. Symp on High Performance Distributed Computing*, pages 352 353, 98.

3. Anderson D., Bowyer S., Cobb J., Gedye D., Sullivan W. T. and Werthimer D. A New Major SETI Project Based on Project Serendip Data and 100,000 Personal Computers. in *Astronomical and Biochemical Origins and the Search for Life in the Universe*, Proc. of the Fifth Intl. Conf. on Bioastronomy, 1997

4. T. E. Anderson R. Wahbe, S. Lucco and S. L. Graham. E cient Software-Based Fault Isolation. In *Symp. on Operating System Principles*, 1993.

5. Baldeschwieler J. E., Blumofe R.D. and Brewer E.A.. Atlas: An Infrastructure for Global Computing. in *Proc. of HPCN'95, High Performance Computing and Networking Europe*, Lecture Notes in Computer Science 918, pp. 582-587, Milano, Italy, May 1995

6. J.Basney and M.Levy. *Deploying a High Throughput Computing Cluster*, volume 1, chapter 5. Prentice Hall, 99. R.Buyya Ed.

7. The Pierre Auger Observatory Cronin J. (University of Chicago) and Watson A. (University of Leed) http://www.auger.org.

8. A. S. Grimshaw and W. A. Wulf. The Legion Vision of a Worldwide Virtual Computer. *Communications of the ACM*, Volume 40, Number 1, Pages 39 45, January 1997.

9. G.Fedak. Execution delocalisee et Repartition de Charge : une Etude Experimentale. In *RenPar'2000*, 2000.

10. I.Foster and C.Kesselman. The Globus Project: a Status Report. in *Futur Generation Computer System*, 40:35 48, 99.

11. J. Maasen, R. van Nieuwpoort, R. Veldema, H. E. Bal and A. Plaat. An E cient Implementation of Java's Remote Method Invocation. In *Proc. ACM Symposium on Principles and Practice of Parallel Programming*. May 1999.

12. Rosenberg A.L.. Guidelines for Data-parallel Cycle-Stealing in Networks of Workstations. *Journal of Parallel and Distributed Computing*, 59:31 53, 99.

A Grid Computing Environment for Enabling Large Scale Quantum Mechanical Simulations

Jack J. Dongarra[1] and Padma Raghavan[1]

Department of Computer Science
The University of Tennessee
1122 Volunteer Blvd.
Knoxville, TN 37996-3450
{dongarra, padma}@cs.utk.edu

Abstract. This paper describes work-in-progress towards developing a simulation environment that utilizes recent advances in in the areas of grid middleware and computational kernels. Our goal is to develop an environment suitable for composing and deploying an overall high-performance, flexible and robust software solution for large-scale quantum mechanical simulations.

1 Introduction

Research in recent years has advanced the state of computational technology for enabling large scale science and engineering applications along two broad fronts. The first concerns the hardware and middleware infrastructure where the evolution is towards computational grids; disparate ensembles of high-performance computers, clusters, networks, and storage can now be integrated to form powerful unified systems [5,6,10,11]. The second concerns the large number of fundamental computational kernels that have been developed for parallel and distributed scientific computing. These have emerged from a variety of research on new parallel algorithms and software development and include advances in both dense and sparse matrix computations [1,4,15,20,22]. We plan to develop a simulation environment that utilizes recent advances in in the areas of grid middleware and computational kernels. Our environment is geared towards composing and deploying an overall high-performance, flexible and robust software solution for certain large-scale applications of interest.

We believe the main problem facing application developers is that of composing an overall high-performance solution by selecting judiciously from the array of available alternate methods for underlying subproblems. A typical large scale application requires the solution of several subproblems of differing granularity with differing amounts of parallelism, computation and communication requirements. Consequently, a simple parallel model of computation involving the same number of processors from start to end cannot result in an efficient solution. Furthermore, there are a variety of solution techniques for a given problem; the choice of the best alternative often depends on the problem characteristics as

R. Buyya and M. Baker (Eds.:) GRID 2000, LNCS 1971, pp. 102–110, 2000.

well as hardware and network speeds. Additionally, problem characteristics can change dramatically within the life of the same simulation. Finally, the overall characteristics of the application may allow various ways of decomposing it into subproblems further compounding the problems of composing an overall efficient solution.

We plan to develop a pipelined-parallel software architecture to harness the power of computational grids to enable large scale simulations. At the University of Tennessee, NSF has recently funded a five-year effort for building a "Scalable Intra campus Research Grid," henceforth called SInRG [8]. Our simulation environment will be developed on this grid. Our focus will be simulations involving large-scale eigenvalue computations associated with sparse matrices. These occur in a variety of molecular dynamics applications. Quantum nanotechnology simulations based on a "generalized tight binding molecular dynamics" [16,18, 21] are extremely compute-intensive; for example, each time-step in a simulation may require the solution of the standard eigenvalue problem to compute all the eigenvalues and eigenvectors of a symmetric, positive definite sparse matrix. Molecular dynamics for restricted closed-shell Hartree-Fock approximation through the Roothan equations [23] also require similar computations.

2   Computational Problem

The central problem in molecular dynamics applications of interest is that of computing $O(N)$ eigenvalues and eigenvectors of an $N \times N$ symmetric positive definite matrix. Such computations are intrinsically expensive; for $N \times N$ matrices, the storage requirements grow as N^2 while the number of operations grow as N^3 when the matrices are treated as *dense*. The constant in the N^3 cost term is larger for the generalized eigenvalue problem but the solution methods for the two problems are closely related. For molecular dynamics models of interest with several thousand atoms, the matrix dimension N is in the range 10,000 to 50,000. The eigenvalue problem has to be solved in each time-step of the simulation and a simulation typically involves a thousand time-steps. Consequently, for matrix dimensions of $\approx 10,000$, a simulation with one thousand time-steps requires computations in the order of 10^{15}. Making such simulations tractable is challenging and must necessarily involve utilizing performance gains from all possible enhancements including those from algorithmic improvements, efficient utilization of hardware resources, and selective composition of solution alternatives.

The standard eigenvalue problem can be generically stated as computing: $Hx = \lambda x$. Given that our application needs $O(N)$ eigenvalues and eigenvectors, *direct* methods are of primary interest. The direct solution process consists of the following three main steps:

1. Transform the matrix to a tridiagonal matrix T using orthogonal transformations.
2. Compute eigenvalues and eigenvectors of T.

3. The eigenvalues of T are the eigenvalues of the original matrix; the eigenvectors of the latter are computed by multiplying the eigenvectors of T by the orthogonal matrix composed of transforms used in the first step in the conversion to tridiagonal form.

For a detailed discussion and overview of fundamental eigensolution techniques, two excellent sources are the books Demmel and Parlett [7,19]. Good serial and parallel implementation exist in form of packages LAPACK [1] and ScaLAPACK [4].

For the three step solution process described above there are several algorithmic choices for each step. The simplest model might be to treat to the matrix as dense; now the choice of kernels for steps 1 and 3 are obvious. However, step 2 could be performed using at least three broad classes of methods: (a) based on bisection and inverse iteration, (b) using the QR method, and (c) using divide and conquer. The performance of each alternative depends to a large extent on the eigenspectrum of the problem as well as machine characteristics such as the computation to communication ratio.

The matrices arising from simulations of interest are sparse; i.e., and $N \times N$ matrix has typically some cN nonzeroes where c is a small constant. Sparsity of the matrix can be exploited for the first step; if the matrix can be put into a *band* form with a bandwidth of b, the intrinsic cost of the first step decreases from N^3 to $b^2 N$. The best algorithm for converting a banded matrix to tridiagonal form on parallel computers is still under research.

One interesting aspect of our application is that although $O(N)$ eigenvalues and eigenvectors are needed, they are not needed all at once. That is, it suffices to compute and use the eigenvectors one at a time. Hence at the very least , by reorganization of the underlying computation, the space requirement could be reduced from $O(N^2)$ to $O(bN)$ when band methods are used for step 1. A first alternative would be to compute only eigenvalues of the tridiagonal matrix T in the second step. The computations of eigenvectors could be postponed to the third step, where as earlier the eigenvectors of T could be calculated and then used to compute eigenvectors of the original matrix. Furthermore, a key issue in the parallel implementation of step (2) using divide-and-conquer (alternative c above) relates to the data-distribution of the eigenvectors as well as their re-orthogonalization. By moving eigenvector computation to the third step, one can easily explore models where the eigenvalues are divided into several groups (spectrum slicing) and the eigenvector computation for each group proceeds independently on a single processor. This could be done using explicit parallelization and LAPACK [1] kernels for eigenvector computation. Yet another interesting alternative would be to compute eigenvectors of the original matrix directly using inverse iterations. This could be especially advantageous when the sparsity of the matrix is utilized. This choice in turn leads to other alternatives, for example, a wide variety of choices for the sparse linear solution scheme for inverse iteration [2].

Our development effort is geared towards exploring such alternatives for the subproblems in order to compose an overall efficient solution. Another aspect of our approach relates to overcoming the traditional problem with decreasing speedups on increasing the numbers of processors using fixed-problem size. Consider for example, the simple solution process which involves treating the matrix as dense and using the routines from ScaLAPACK to solve the overall problem on a multiprocessor or a cluster. In our earlier work [17], we took exactly this approach and enabled a relaxation of a 1061 atom carbon cluster that forms part of a "knee" junction with interesting metal-semiconductor contact for connecting nanotubes of different diameters. The matrix dimension was 4244 and using 8-16 processors of a NOW with Intel Pentium-II processors and a Myrinet switch [9], computation time for a single time-step drops to under several minutes (speedups compared to one processor execution were nearly ideal). However, the overall simulation which required nearly 800 time-steps took several days of non-stop execution. Furthermore, this time cannot be reduced by simply increasing the number of processors; this lowers the per-processor utilization and we observed a slowdown with as few as 32 processors.

By developing a software pipeline, we can tackle as many different simulations as the number of pipeline stages. Now the actual time for a single time-step of any given simulation could be reduced by a factor equal to the number of pipeline stages. Each pipeline stage will be deployed on disjoint groups of processors. Parallelism within each stage will be exploited using the message passing model and MPI. The overall solution will be composed using NetSolve which will also be used to deploy the application on the SInRG computational grid.

3   Developing a Software Environment

The primary building block of the SInRG architecture is the Grid Service Cluster (GSC). A GSC is an ensemble of hardware and software constructed and administered by a single research group but also optimized to make its resources easily available for the overall user community. A GSC is a concentration of (possibly specialized) computing resources in an advanced local to wide-area network. Each GSC has three basic hardware components: a high-speed data switch capable of providing at least 1Gb/s per link, a data-storage unit connected to the switch, and computational resources customized for specific research. The latter could be an SMP, an MPP, a cluster of workstations, etc. Six GSCs are being established, with each one having typically in excess of the raw computing power of the state-of-the-art cluster of 32-node multiple-CPU computers. The total raw computing power over all GSCs will be in the range of Teraops/second. We next describe NetSolve, the software environment on SInRG and then outline our strategy for developing our simulation environment. We view this project as a precursor to the development of general-purpose software component technology based on object-oriented methods, an emerging field of research [12,13].

3.1   NetSolve

High-level access across all GSC's and to CPUs within each GSC is provided through NetSolve [5]. NetSolve is a software environment designed to transform disparate computers and software libraries into a unified, easy-to-access computational service. It aggregates the hardware and software resources of any number of computers that are loosely connected across a network and offers up their combined power through familiar client interfaces such as MATLAB, and C. It uses a *client-agent-server* paradigm to deliver this power to users without revealing the complexity of the underlying system. The user's data is sent to the server, where the programs or numerical libraries operate on it; the result then is sent back to the user's machine.

NetSolve provides the user with a pool of computational resources. These resources are in the form of servers that have access to ready-to-use numerical software. These computational servers can be running on single workstations, networks of workstations, or MPP (Massively Parallel Processor) systems. The user gains access by using any one of the NetSolve client interfaces such as MATLAB. The main function of the NetSolve agent is to process user requests and to choose the most suitable server for the underlying computation. An added advantage is that the agent performs load-balancing among the different resources.

When building NetSolve, one of the challenges was to design a suitable model for the computational servers. Features include uniform access to the software, configurability, and preinstallation. To make the implementation of such a computational server model possible, NetSolve has a general, machine-independent way of describing a specific numerical process, as well as a set of tools to generate new computational modules. The main component is a descriptive language which is used to specify the functionality of a computational server. The description files written in this language can be compiled by NetSolve into computational modules executable on any UNIX or NT platform. This approach allows machine independence as well as the ability to integrate arbitrary software components into NetSolve. Additionally, this framework also allows increased collaboration between research teams across institutions. Description files for a given numerical library need be written only once. These files can then be transferred to other locations and then compiled to create a new stand-alone NetSolve system or to contribute new servers to an existing system. Each time a new description file is created, the capabilities of the entire NetSolve system are increased. A number of description files have been generated for the following numerical libraries: ARPACK, FitPack, ItPack, MinPack, FFTPACK, LAPACK, BLAS, and ScaLAPACK. A Graphical User Interface (GUI) is provided to simplify generation of description files. This interface performs various error checking on user input in the form of choices from a menu. Using this interface is much easier than creating a description file manually, especially as the complexity of the problem increases.

3.2   A Pipelined Parallel Architecture

As mentioned in Section 2, the underlying eigenvalue computations can be divided into three main stages. We propose a pipelined parallel architecture in which each stage of the pipeline represents a major stage in the underlying computations. Now each one of the pipeline stages can be made to execute on the right number of processors such that per-processor efficiency is maintained while the pipeline stages are kept balanced. The pipeline stages are motivated by the three stage solution process described earlier. However, they are somewhat different both to reduce inter-stage communication and to easily allow the use of different kernels within the stages.

The first stage is responsible for conversion of the matrices to a tridiagonal matrix T. The second stage computes eigenvalues of the tridiagonal matrix; the eigenvectors of T are not computed in this stage. The third stage computes eigenvectors of the original matrix and this may involve using the traditional method of computing eigenvectors of T or new methods to be developed [2]. Our software will be designed is to select the optimal number of processors for each stage of the pipeline; each stage uses a disjoint set of processors. By careful selection of the number of processors per stage, the pipeline can be kept balanced, i.e., with each stage requiring approximately the same amount of time. By working on three different simulations at the same time, we can ensure that one time-step of a simulation will be completed in the time required for a single pipeline stage. If t units of time are required at most by any pipeline stage, then after the first $3t$ units of time, one time-step will be completed for a simulation every t time units. This pipeline architecture is shown in Figure 1.

We have selected the stages so that amount of information to be communicated between stages is typically $O(N)$. We expect the original sparse matrices to be transferred from each stage to the next. These matrices are very sparse and have only $O(N)$ nonzeroes. Additionally, from stage one and two, the tridiagonal matrix must be transferred and this obviously is $O(N)$ amount of data. From stage two to three $O(N)$ eigenvalues need be transmitted. In the last stage the eigenvalues are used to compute the corresponding eigenvectors, however if the simulation is to proceed for another time step all eigenvectors need not be computed and stored all at once. In the molecular dynamics model, each eigenvector and eigenvalue can be used as soon as it is computed to calculate its contribution to the force equations. Only the matrices for the next time-step need to passed from stage three back to one if the simulation is to proceed.

To implement the pipeline we will develop a NetSolve server which will contain suitably encapsulated kernels from ScaLAPACK, LAPACK and sparse solvers such as DSCPACK. The application interface will be through the MATLAB interface to NetSolve. We will begin with a static allocation of processors to pipeline stages as well as a static choice of kernels for each stage. We will migrate to dynamic, on-the-fly selection as the capabilities in NetSolve are enhanced. When resources permit, the three-stage pipelined parallel architecture can be replicated and farmed out to SInRG using NetSolve, thus enabling several independent groups of simulations. By utilizing the performance monitoring features of NetSolve, we will attempt to reduce simulation times through the use of scheduling strategies. Some recent work on application specific scheduling enhancements has yielded promising results [3] and these schemes will be integrated into NetSolve.

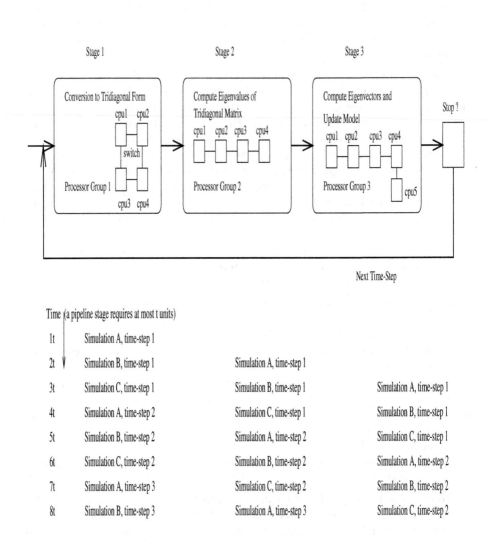

Fig. 1. A pipelined parallel software architecture to enable molecular dynamics simulations on a computational grid

There are also plans to incorporate fault-tolerance and visualization capabilities to NetSolve and these features will also be of potential use for our target applications.

4   Concluding Remarks

We plan to use our simulation environment to enable "generalized tight binding molecular dynamics" models of Carbon nanotubes developed by Menon. These nanotechnology simulations concern exploring the properties of complex and three-point, four-point and hetero-junctions of nanotubes to suggest experimentally feasible transistor-like devices [16,17,18,21]. These simulations are based on generalized tight-binding molecular dynamics scheme which has been shown to obtain equilibrium geometries for carbon clusters that are in very good agreement with *ab initio* and experimental results. Such simulations are essential for gaining a better understanding of the electronic and material properties of nanoscale clusters to allow design of nanoscale devices in the near future.

Acknowledgments. This work was supported in part through grants ACI-97-21361, CCR-98-18334, and CDA-99-72889 from the National Science Foundation.

References

1. E. Anderson, Z. Bai, S. Blackford, C. Bischof, J. Demmel, J. Dongarra, J. Du Croz, A. Greenbaum, S. Hammarling, A. McKenney, and D. Sorensen: LAPACK Users' Guide, Third Edition. SIAM, Philadelphia, PA (1999)
2. J. Barlow, P. Raghavan, K. Teranishi, C. Yang, and R.C. Ward: Computing Eigenvectors of Sparse Matrices Using Inverse Iterations. In preparation
3. F. Berman and R. Wolski: AppLeS: Application Level Scheduling. See http://apples.ucsc.edu
4. L. S. Blackford, J. Choi, A. Cleary, E. D'Azevedo, J. Demmel, I. Dhillon, J. Dongarra, S. Hammarling, G. Henry, A. Petitet, K. Stanley, D. Walker, and R. C. Whaley: ScaLAPACK Users' Guide. SIAM, Philadelphia, PA (1997)
5. H. Casanova and J. Dongarra: NetSolve: A Network Server for Solving Computational Science Problems. The International Journal of Supercomputing Applications, **11** (1997) 212 223
6. K. M. Chandy, A. Rifkin, P. A. G. Sivilotti, J. Mandelson, M. Richardson, W. Tanaka, and L. Weisman: A Word-Wide Distributed System Using Java and the Internet. Proc. of the Fifth IEEE International Symposium of High-Performance Distributed Computing (1996)
7. J. W. Demmel: Applied Numerical Linear Algebra. SIAM, Philadelphia, PA (1997)
8. J. J. Dongarra, M. W. Berry, M. Beck, J. Gregor, M. A. Langston, T. Moore, J. S. Plank, P. Raghavan, M. G. Thomason, R. C. Ward, and R. M. Wolski: A Scalable Intracampus Research Grid. Available at website: http://www.cs.utk.edu/ sinrg, Funded by NSF-CISE

9. J. J. Dongarra, J. S. Plank, and P. Raghavan: Enabling Technology for High-Performance Heterogeneous Clusters. National Science Foundation, $150,000 (1999)

10. I. Foster and C. Kesselman: Globus: A Metacomputing Infrastructure Toolkit. The International Journal of Supercomputing Applications (1997)

11. G. Fox and W. Furmanski: Web Technologies in High-Performance Distributed Computing. In Computational Grids (1998)

12. D. Gannon, R. Bramley, S. Diwan, B. Temko, N. Mukhi, K. Chiu, M. Govindaraju, M. Yechuri, and J. Villacis: Common Component Architecture. Available at website: http://www.cs.indiana.edu/ccat.

13. D. Gannon, R. Bramley, J. Villacis and A. Whitaker: Using the Grid to Support Software Component Systems. SIAM Conference on Parallel Processing (1999)

14. M. Snir, S. Otto, S. Huss-Lederman, D. Walker, and J. J. Dongarra: MPI: The Complete Reference. The MIT Press Cambridge, MA (1996)

15. G. Karypis and V. Kumar: METIS: Unstructured graph partitioning and sparse matrix ordering system. Technical Report, Department of Computer Science, University of Minnesota, Minneapolis, MN (1995)

16. M. Menon, E. Richter and K. R. Subbaswamy: Structural and Vibrational Properties of Fullerenes and Nanotubes in a Non-orthogonal Tight-Binding Scheme. J. Chem. Phys. **104** (1996).

17. M. Menon, R. Richter, P. Raghavan and K. Teranishi: Large Scale Quantum Mechanical Simulations of Carbon Wires. Superlattices and Microstructures **27** (2000) 577 581

18. M. Menon and K.R. Subbaswamy: Non-orthogonal Tight-Binding Scheme for Silicon with Improved Transferability. Phys. Rev., **55** (1997)

19. B. Parlett: The Symmetric Eigenvalue Problem. Prentice Hall, Engle-wood Cli s, NJ (1980)

20. P. Raghavan: DSCPACK: A Domain-Separator Cholesky Package for solving sparse linear systems on multiprocessors and NOWs using C and MPI. Available upon request

21. A. M. Rao, E. Richter, S. Bandow, B. Chase, P. C. Eklund, K. A. Williams, S. Fang, K. R. Subbaswamy, M. Menon, A. Thess, R. E. Smalley, G. Dresselhaus, and M. S. Dresselhouse: Diameter-Selective Raman Scattering from Vibrational Modes in Carbon Nanotubes. Science **275**(1997)

22. B. Smith, L. McInnes, and W. Gropp: PETSc 2.0 user's manual. Mathematics and Computer Science Division, Argonne National Laboratory, Report ANL-95-11- Revision 2.0.22, (1997)

23. R.C. Ward, Talk on applications of eigenvalue computations (1999)

A Web-Based Metacomputing Problem-Solving Environment for Complex Applications

Ranieri Baraglia[1], Domenico Laforenza[1], and Antonio Laganà[2]

[1] CNUCE-Institute of the Italian National Research Council
CNR Research Campus, Via V. Al eri 1, 56010 Ghezzano, Pisa, Italy
e-mail:(Ranieri.Baraglia,Domenico.Laforenza)@cnuce.cnr.it
[2] Dipartimento di Chimica, Universita di Perugia
Via Elce di Sotto, 8 - I06123 Perugia (Italy)
e-mail:lag@unipg.it

Abstract. In this paper a kernel of Problem Solving Environment aimed at managing complex chemical meta-applications based upon an *a priori* simulation of molecular structure and dynamics has been presented. By considering as a case study the simulation of a molecular beam experiment (SIMBEX), a metacomputing environment able to facilitate the SIMBEX execution through the Web has been designed. This choice is due to the rapid and impressive growth of Internet, Java and, Web technologies. The current work focus on the architectural aspects of the implemented environment.

1 Introduction

Modern Computational Sciences increasingly stimulate the development of advanced computing tools because of their need for realistic simulations of complex systems relevant to the modeling of several modern technologies and environmental phenomena. This type of simulations usually needs to include, though not necessarily in a completely rigorous manner, a detailed description of relevant molecular structures and processes. As a result, related computational procedures not only need to be run by coordinating several complementary expertises but also by integrating several extremely powerful computing platforms in a metacomputer system. From this derives the need to build smart and user-friendly Problem Solving Environments (PSE) enabling computational scientists to carry out their investigations without caring about the complexity of the computing platform being used. As defined in literature, a PSE is a computer system that provides all the computational facilities needed to solve a target class of problems. These features include advanced solution methods, automatic and semiautomatic selection of solving procedures, easy incorporation tools of novel approaches [1].

A European COST Initiative has been recently proposed [2] to promote the gathering of research laboratories having complementary expertises in clusters grafted on metacomputer systems (Metalaboratories). This action has been recently approved (D23) and a call for cooperative projects is being issued. These

R. Buyya and M. Baker (Eds.:) GRID 2000, LNCS 1971, pp. 111–122, 2000.

projects should tackle complex modeling problems without conveying in a single location all the required laboratories, programs and pieces of hardware. Our proposal focuses on building a Metalaboratory devoted to the *a priori* simulation of molecular processes, and in particular of crossed molecular beam experiments.

The metacomputing [3,4] approach harnesses different computational resources and uses their aggregate power as if it was contained in a single machine.

From a technological point of view, the rapid and impressive growth of the Internet has generated a rising interest in Web-based parallel computing. In fact, many worldwide projects are focused on the exploitation of the Web as an infrastructure for running coarse-grained distributed parallel applications. In this context, the Web has the capability to become a suitable and potentially infinite scalable metacomputer for parallel and collaborative work as well as a technological key to create a pervasive and ubiquitous grid infrastructure [5,7].

As a case study, we should consider here the simulation of crossed molecular beam experiments whose (on a small scale) prototype numerical procedure (SIMBEX) has already been discussed in literature [8].

Aim of the present paper is to briefly describe the main features of the simulation and the characteristics of the software tools developed to facilitate the SIMBEX execution on a metacomputer through the Web. These tools are designed to supply a completely transparent support to the user who does not have to care about the localization and the allocation of computing resources. All the needed functionalities were implemented on a properly extended Web server using, whenever possible, standard tools. In particular, use of the Java Servlet [9] and Directory Service facilities of LDAP [10,11] have been made. Moreover, a modular design has been adopted to guarantee an easy maintenance and extendibility of the product.

The paper is articulated as follows. In Section 2 is given a short description of SIMBEX. Section 3 focuses on the architectural aspects of the metacomputing environment. Related work on Web-based metacomputing environments is presented in Section 4. Finally, we summarize our work in Section 5.

2   A Short Description of SIMBEX

SIMBEX is a computational procedure based on *a priori* calculations of structures and processes of molecular systems. The procedure is articulated into several modules derived from the theoretical approach to the problem (see Figure 1).

Each module consists of alternative or coordinated computer codes which accomplish particular tasks. In particular, in module I the construction of the potential energy surface is performed (see Figure 2). This procedure may be bypassed when the potential energy surface is already available or used "on the fly" during dynamical calculations when a direct approach is chosen. If this step is not bypassed then the level of accuracy of *ab initio* calculations, the number and location of points to be considered, the fitting of calculated *ab initio* values to a given functional form have to be performed.

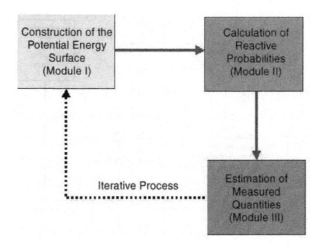

Fig. 1. SIMBEX: Computational Control Flow

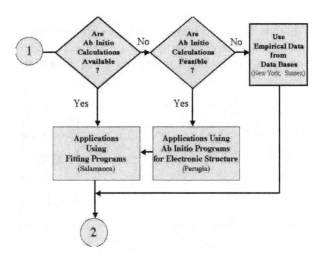

Fig. 2. SIMBEX: Module I Control Flow

In module II dynamics calculations are carried out (see Figure 3). These calculations too can be performed at different levels of accuracy. For small molecules it is possible to perform exact quantum dynamical calculations that can be either of the time dependent or of the time independent type. When considering larger molecules, approximations need to be introduced. This may consist of dynamics constraints leading to a dimensionality reduction in quantum calculations, or of a mixing of quantum and classical techniques, or of a use of pure classical methods.

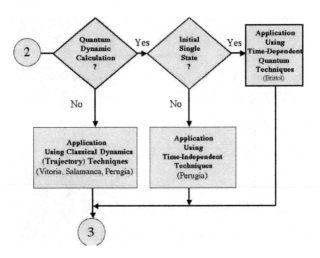

Fig. 3. SIMBEX: Module II Control Flow

Finally, in module III (see Figure 4), when scattering matrix elements or state to state probabilities have already been calculated, an averaging over unobserved variables needs to be made to reproduce experimental properties and distributions.

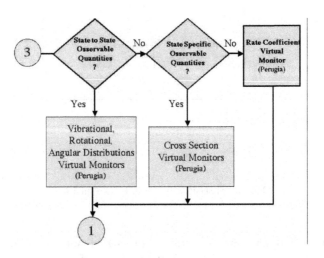

Fig. 4. SIMBEX: Module III Control Flow

More detailed information about SIMBEX can be found in [8,12].

3   The Metacomputing Environment: Architectural Aspects

To implement SIMBEX on a Web-based metacomputer platform we have designed a 3-tier architecture having the following components:

 – Client side: a Web browser;
 – Middleware: Web servers exploiting Java Servlets and Lightweight Directory Accesss Protocol (LDAP) functionalities;
 – Back-end: the ensemble of computing resources.

Figure 5 shows the architectural scheme singling out the key interactions among the mentioned components. The user, after being authorized when accessing the system, is offered a choice of applications available on the back-end. Next step deals with the handling of input data. In order to satisfy the requests of the users, the server makes use of the LDAP functionalities to localize available computing resources capable to provide requested services. LDAP provides information about the computing resources by accessing to a Directory Information Tree (DIT). The tree is made up of entries which represent the computing resources by a group of attributes. After collecting related information, the server activates a remote execution of the application on the selected machine. When the execution is completed, results are passed to the server that forwards them to the Client.

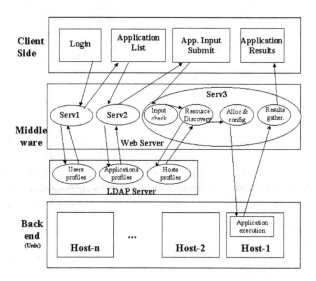

Fig. 5. The Architectural Scheme Singling out the key Interactions among the System Components.

3.1   The Client Side

The client is made of a Web browser representing the graphical interface driving the user in the selection of the required application, inputting the necessary data and collecting the results. HTML forms ensure the interaction of the user with the Web server: they activate the execution of the Java servlet that corresponds to the requested action (application selection, data input, etc.). Obviously, the address of the Web server providing the service has to be known in advance to the user. The initial page allows the specification of the *userid* and of his *password* which implies also the process of crediting a user (see Figure 6).

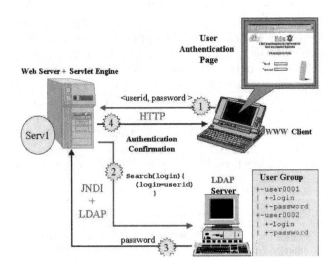

Fig. 6. User Authentication Process.

This implies the transfer on the network of private information that could be made using HTML forms. In order to check the integrity of the information transmitted we use a Java applet that implements a HMAC [15] mechanism which exploits the iterative cryptographic MD5 hash function.

In order to control the access to the system's resources, it is possible to define different user profiles according to predefined politics. This has been implemented using LDAP.

After authentication, the user is offered a list of applications that can be run on the machines belonging to the back-end system (see Figure 7). The application selection can be performed by clicking on the hyperlink related to the application.

Each application has an associated profile describing its computational characteristics (requirements): e.g., name, version, documentation available, type of input required, sources of data, etc. The application profile is stored in the LDAP server that is searched by the Web server in order to drive the input

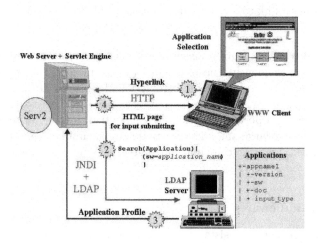

Fig. 7. Application Selection Process.

process. According to the characteristics of the application, by driving the input of data by the user, a HTML page is produced.

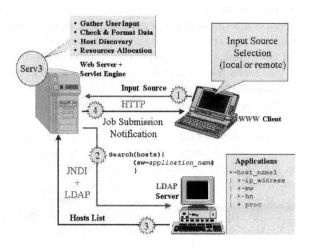

Fig. 8. Application Input Process.

The input data can be submitted (see Figure 8) to the application according to three different modalities:

- by a data entry phase;
- by selecting a file resident on the client local disk;

– by choosing a link to a remote data source (a file located on a metacomputer machine).

In general, the application execution is expected to take a significant amount of time. Consequently, the user can leave its metacomputing session after submitting the application. At job completion the user is notified by an e-mail message. The message allows the user to reconnect and access the page of the results built by a proper Java servlet. Serious difficulties may arise when dealing with the transfer of large amounts of data due to the limited bandwidth available on the network. Transfer time and data integrity cannot be guaranteed on the Internet.

3.2 The Middleware

The middleware layer consists of a Web and a LDAP servers. The Web server takes care of the interaction with the client and performs the Java servlets handling user's requests. The servlets residing on the Web server are:

serv1. Authentication of the user and his profile. According to the chosen policy, *serv1* handles the various phases of the authentication and the interaction with the client to establish his identity. To achieve this, the list of users allowed to make use of the services has to be accessed. This can be coded as an entry set of LDAP (see Figure 6). Among the attributes belonging to the user object there are those which identify the user profile (i.e. the applications he can submit for execution plus some auxiliary attributes useful for his identification). Auxiliary attributes can vary depending on the chosen policy. As an example, if an algorithm of the Challenge-Response type is implemented, the public key of the user should be stored (the assumption is that the decision on allowing access to the system should be hand made and left with the manager of the system).

These user profiles are necessary to state "who can do what" and "where should the results of a run be stored".

serv2. Application profiles management. According to the selected application, *serv2* needs to set the modality for transferring input data. To this end LDAP services are used too, in order to set input formats. In the DIT section of LDAP all entries related to a given application implemented in the back-end are defined. Its attributes define how data to be passed to executables have to be defined. As already singled out for the Client-end, there are three main ways of inputting data. According to the characteristics of the application *serv2* produces a HTML page that drives the user while inputting data (see Figure 8).

serv3. Validation of input data, resource localization, allocation and configuration, remote execution of the application, recollection and forwarding of results (see Figure 8 and 9). This is the most complex servlet which takes care of:

> **checking data format**. Data input by the client need to match requirements set by the application. In case they do not, a HTML page is generated to inform the user about the error;

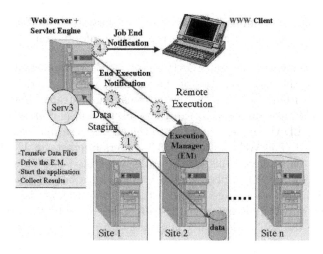

Fig. 9. Application Execution Process.

localizing resources. By interacting with the LDAP server it is figured out where the executable codes needed by the application are stored. It is worth noticing that LDAP is intrinsically static. Therefore, some mechanisms allowing a monitoring of the status of the resources of the back-end need to be introduced in order to allow also an update of the DIT entries guaranteeing the consistency of the information stored. This can be obtained by adding a further attribute to the object describing the characteristics of each machine. Aim of this attribute is to specify the date in which the last access to the resource has taken place. When the difference between the actual time and the time indicated by the attribute is larger than a predetermined amount, one can reasonably assume that the machine is available. Otherwise, the check is pushed to a lower level by using commands like *ping, top, procinfo* to update the entry related to the considered machine;

allocating and configuring resources previously localized. To this end a session is activated on the account of the user made available by the the back-end machine using remote shell mechanisms. Input files are transferred into a given directory of the machine and a script to activate the executable codes of the application is configured;

remote executing of the application. A script is launched to start the execution of the application. System mechanisms like *pvm daemon, mpirun, Condor*, etc, local to the chosen machine, take care of configuring the virtual machine, of executing the parallel application and of storing the results on a file;

collecting and forwarding results. *serv3* waits until the application is ended before starting the collections of all its results. Then it opens a

HTML page containing them or a link and forwards a mail to the user so that he can connect and access the desired information.

As already mentioned, the LDAP server, keeps the information about registered users, the characteristics of the available software and hardware. This information, initially provided by the systems administrator, due to the static nature of LDAP, is maintained by the *serv3* servlet that periodically updates the content of the LDAP entries according to the checks performed on the resources of the back-end. The Web and the LDAP servers interact via JNDI [16,17], an interface written in Java. This can be easily integrated into Java applications. The reason why JNDI has been chosen is that it has been developed with the aim of prividing access to a generic directory service and, at the present, it can interface not only LDAP but also NIS [16], DNS [18], and CORBA [19]. This guarantees to the applications that make use of it an easy extensibility.

3.3 The Back-End

The back-end is made by high performing computing resources, multiprocessor systems, workstation networks which provide computing power to the applications of the metacomputer. On these machines the Web server has user accounts that allow the execution of the applications.

4   Web-Based Metacomputing Environments: Related Work

There is a growing number of worldwide projects related to metacomputing and grid computing [6,7]. Some of those focus on the exploitation of Java technology for Web-based metacomputing.

This section presents some of the most significative projects that are representative of the Web-based approach.

Charlotte [20], developed at New York University, was the first environment that has allowed any machine on the Web to participate in any ongoing computation. Charlotte is built on top of Java without relying on any native code.

Javelin [21] is a Java-based infrastructure for global computing. The system, developed at the Department of the University of California, Santa Barbara, is based on Internet and Web technology.

WebFlow [22], developed at the Northeast Parallel Architecture Center, is a computational extension of the Web model that can act as a framework for the wide-area distributed computing and metacomputing. The main goal of the WebFlow design was to build a seamless framework to publish and reuse computational modules on the Web so that end users, via a Web browser, can engage in composing distributed applications using WebFlow modules as visual components and editors as visual authoring tools.

NetSolve [23], developed at University of Tennessee and Oak Ridge National Laboratory, is a client/server application designed to solve computational science problems in a distributed environment. Netsolve clients can be written in C and Fortran, use Matlab or the Web to interact with the server. A Netsolve server can use any scientific package to provide its computational software.

Although our approach inherits some interesting solutions exploited in the previous mentioned projects, it is less general. In fact, our project focuses mainly on the creation of a Web-based metacomputing PSE to supply a completely transparent support to the user who does not have to care about the localization and the allocation of computing resources.

5 Conclusions

In this paper we have presented the main features of a PSE designed to facilitate the execution of a complex chemical application (SIMBEX) on a metacomputer through the Web. This project is developed in the framework of a European Communities COST Initiative-Action D23.

Our prototype is based on Web technologies and it is written in Java. The Java programming language successfully addresses several key issues related to grid environments. It also removes the need to install programs remotely; the minimum execution environment is a Java-enabled Web browser.

Many researchers agree with the fact that frameworks incorporating CORBA services will be very influential on the design of grid environments in the future. For this, we would like to investigate on the usage of CORBA technology to enhance some features of our PSE prototype.

Acknowledgments. We would like to thank the Master Thesis students, Fiorenzo D'Alberto and Andrea Vasapollo, who worked with us during the design and the development of this software environment.

References

1. S. Gallopoulos, E. Houstis, and J. Rice, *Computer as Thinker/Doer: Problem-Solving Environments for Computational Science*, IEEE Computational Science and Engineering, Summer (1994).
2. Metachem Workshop, European Community, Brussels, 26-27 November 1999.
3. C. Catlett, L. Smarr, *Metacomputing*, Communications of the ACM, 35(6), 44 (1992).
4. Baker M., Fox G., *Metacomputing: Harnessing Informal Supercomputers*, In High Performance Cluster Computing: Architectures and Systems, R. Buyya Ed., Volume 1, Prentice Hall PTR, NJ, USA (1999).
5. *The Grid: Blueprint for a Future Computing Infrastructure*, I. Foster and C. Kesselman Eds., Morgan Kaufmann Publishers, USA (1999).
6. W. Gentzsch (editor), *Special Issue on Metacomputing: From Workstation Clusters to Internet computing*, Future Generation Computer Systems, No. 15, North Holland, 1999.

7. M. Baker, R. Buyya, and D. Laforenza, *The Grid: International Efforts in Global Computing*, International Conference on Advances in Infrastructure for Electronic Business Science,and Education on the Internet (SSGRR'2000), L'Aquila, Italy, July 31 - August 6. 2000.
8. O. Gervasi, D. Cicoria, A. Lagana, and R. Baraglia Pixel 10, 19 (1994)
9. A. Patzer, *Introduction to Servlets, in Professional Java Programming*, Wrox Press Ltd (1999).
10. M. Wahl,T. Howes, and S. Kille, *Lightweight Directory Accesss Protocol*, RFC 2251, December (1997).
11. T.A. Howes, *The Lightwweight Directory Accesss Protocol:X.500 Lite*, Center for Information Technology Integration, July (1995).
12. A. Lagana and O. Gervasi,*A structured computational approach to chemical reactivity*, Chem. Phys., in press.
13. A. Lagana, G. O. de Aspuru, and E. Garcia, J. Chem. Phys. 108, 3886 (1998).
14. A.J.C. Varandas, *Multivalued Potential Energy Surfaces for Dynamics Studies*, A. Lagana and A. Riganelli Eds., in Lecture Notes in Chemistry, Springer-Verlag, in the press.
15. H. Krawczyk, M. Bellare,and R. Canetti, *HMAC: Keyed-Hashing for Message Authentication*, RFC 2104, February (1997).
16. M. Wilcox, *Server Programming with JNDI, in Professional Java Programming*, Wrox Press Ltd, December (1999).
17. JNDI - www.javasoft.com/products/jndi/index.html.
18. P. Mockapetris, *Domain Names - Concepts and Facilities*, RFC 1034, November (1987).
19. Object Management Group, Common Object Request Broker: Architecture and Speci cation, OMG Doc. No. 91.12.1 (1991).
20. A. Baratloo, M. Karaul, , Z.M. Kedem, and P. Wycko , *Charlotte: Metacomputing on the Web*, Special Issue on Metacomputing, Future Generation Computer Systems, pages 559-570, North Holland 1999. http://www.cs.nyu.edu/milan/charlotte/index.html
21. M.O. Neary, B.O.Christiansen, P.Cappello, K.E.Schauser *Javelin: Parallel computing on the Internet*, Special Issue on Metacomputing, Future Generation Computer Systems, pages 659-673, North Holland 1999. http://www.cs.ucsb.edu/
22. Haupt T., Akarsu E., and Fox G., Furmanski W, *Web Based Metacomputing*, Special Issue on Metacomputing, Future Generation Computer Systems, North Holland (1999) http://osprey7.npac.syr.edu:1998/iwt98/products/webflow/
23. H. Casanova and J. Dongarra, *NetSolve: A Network Server for Solving Computational Science Problems*, Intl. Journal of Supercomputing Applications and High Performance Computing, 11, 3, (1997). http://www.cs.utk.edu/ casanova/NetSolve/

FOCALE: Towards a Grid View of Large-Scale Computation Components

Gaëtan Scotto di Apollonia, Christophe Gransart, and Jean-Marc Geib

LIFL (Laboratoire d'Informatique Fondamentale de Lille),
USTL (University of Science and Technology of Lille),
F-59655 VILLENEUVE D'ASCQ CEDEX, FRANCE
{scottoda, gransart, geib}@lifl.fr

Abstract. In the model of grid computing, we have several views of the components of the grid. One would prefer a large grid of small data-driven computations, while another one would rather use coarse grain components with great computing power. This paper presents our project, FO-CALE, which provides genericity for large components interconnection through Java and CORBA.

Keywords: CORBA and JAVA, distributed computing, objects and components

1 Motivations

Grid computing is today one of the greatest issue in the world of large-scale distributed applications. This concept not only promotes the distributed platform research projects, but it also involve major technical improvements, such as computing centers power, and network throughput and latency. In the United States, large universities and laboratories are already connected by such high-speed backbones, and serve as a testbed for the future of large applications and platforms supporting them. In other countries, whereas it is not as developped, great steps have been taken to attain that goal. In France, the education administration has put up a national network joining the major universities and public laboratories, and this network recently improved its speed with ATM technology. Some researchers also work on an ambitious program making this network attain the Gigabit/s bandwith.

However, in the general case, the main projects around a new item involve creating a new standard, changing everyone's programming method, and developping the applications from scratch. We intend to develop a platform over these networks permitting to any program, already existing or not, to be connected to any other, in a tree of connections that will form our distributed application. Such an application can be whatever the application provider will want, as he can either use already known components, or provide newly-created ones. Applications worth being distributed upon such a large-scale platform include, but are not limited to, all mathematical and applied mathematics computations, database management and datamining, virtual reality and visualization.

R. Buyya and M. Baker (Eds.:) GRID 2000, LNCS 1971, pp. 123–134, 2000.

Our project is named FOCALE, which stands for Federation of Objects for Computing on a large scALE[1]. As a starting step, FOCALE is being developed in Java, with use of the CORBA standard to permit its future implementation in any[2] language (like C++, for better preformance), and its communication with clients also written in any language. CORBA use is not required from the computing components, because that would mean rewriting some of the world's most used computing libraries, and these libraries are not always written in a CORBA-compliant language, like Fortran.

Let we present some interesting projects, related to ours by the fact that they manage and use either Java components, computing platforms, CORBA technology or world-wide interconnections.

1.1 Java-Based Execution Platforms

Ajents [6] is an environment for mobile java applications. With its purposes, it addresses mainly the world of java-written mobile agents. Ajents makes use of JAVA possibilities, and RMI for mobility.

ProActive (formerly known as Java//) [1] is a project which provides "seamless metacomputing" in JAVA. It does not use CORBA, though, but is based on a MOP (Meta-Object Protocol) and issues polymorphism between remote and local objects in a portable JAVA library.

1.2 Components-Based Environments

NetPebbles [12] is an environment dealing with network components, with the interesting aspect of a script language with which users can create components and interact with the system.

Comet [18] is an architecture based on components, for the construction of distributed applications. It provides means for components to adapt to their environment, as well as acting on it. The model used here is the separation of control from functionalities.

Regis [10] is a system which supports configuration programming, that is, separating the configuration phase from the code. The authors of Regis also made a graphical user interface, the Software Architect's Assistant [13] where users can plug their components one to another, to help the design of the application. They also have written a specifying language, called Darwin [9], that deals with the the high-level organisation of components and the interaction between them.

1.3 High-Performance Interconnection

At the hardware level, networks are always increasing their throughput. High-speed national-wide backbones projects already exist in several countries. It is one of the aspect of raising technology to higher levels: it is either for technology itself, or for its users.

---

[1] this has a better meaning in French, but this is close

[2] almost any

The Cobra project [19] proposes a runtime based on CORBA and working on top of a network of multiprocessor workstations, interconnected with SCI [2]. The special involvment here is the use of a high-speed local area network.

1.4 World-Wide Projects

Legion [8] and Globus [5] are wide-spread projects, that also aim to provide ease of use and fast access to metacomputing to end-users. Legion architecture was designed with computing speed in mind, and multi-language support is, however present, somewhat limited to C/C++ and Fortran/HPF.

Globus and Legion were born before the recent versions of CORBA and their teams are currently working on the integration of CORBA support in them.

Globe [4] is also an object-based framework for developing wide-area distributed applications. Its authors make use of CORBA possibilities to implement worldwide scalable Web documents.

1.5 Incoming Corba Technologies

In the near future, CORBA will be enhanced by some aspects that directly interest us. Some requests for information and proposals have been posted, like *Parallel* CORBA [15] and *Aggregated Computing in* CORBA [14].

The Advanced Computing Laboratory[3] has grouped some of its projects into a response to these RPFs. Ligature [7], one of them, is a database of software components designed to interact with each other through programmer-defined interface.

1.6 Comparing with Us...

All of these projects have very interesting functionalities, but were not designed with the same ideas as FOCALE, and as such do not provide the same tools. The following ideas are present in one or more of the described environments, and particularly interest us:

– **Component description language**
  Such a language[4] is important to help end users manipulate FOCALE objects, without entering into the technical part of establishing and maintaining links between their objects.
– **Corba support**
  "Native" CORBA support is usable for the platform itself, and we will see that our platform makes extensive use of it. The console we developed also uses CORBA to communicate with FOCALE servers.
– **Separation of control and functionalities**
  To permit a good developpement of the platform, we separated these aspects, so that developping a control aspect does not hinder the writing of each level's code (see next section for a description of FOCALE architecture's levels).

---

[3] Los Alamos National Laboratory
[4] whether it is IDL3 or any personally-de ned language

- **Genericity of operations**

  The FOCALE project aims to build applications by interconnecting user-defined computing components. Such components can use CORBA to communicate, but some of the best-known implemented computing algorithms don't. As it is, we prefer a platform that can connect and run generic components than focus on one language and/or API and then be stuck with it, forcing willing users to rewrite their code once more. This aspect is the main difficulty of our platform development, but this is also what separates us from most of the previous examples of related work.

  By developping these aspects (and others), we do not fit exactly in one of the previous examples, but it is obvious that some areas overlap.

2   Focale Architecture

The construction of our project was made upon a top-down analysis of Grid-computing platform needs. This analysis permitted to separate aspects of the differents execution levels involved. However, in separating levels, we often forget non-functional capabilities, like the persistence of data, or the event management in the different levels. As we are building FOCALE with CORBA, we have the CORBA Common Services list in mind not to forget about those capabilities.

Here is a description of the levels, with an brief explanation of how they work, and of the non-functional capabilities associated to them, when applicable.

2.1   The Federation Level

Under this term, we put a group of machines, each with a FOCALE server running, and interconnected (see figure 1). The functionalities of one server are described in the next paragraph. Users can access this group by any server, although they would prefer to select the nearest one - in terms of either physical distance or network latency. The federation management is not centralized, as it would reduce its global fault-tolerance. Therefore, each server acts as a grid node, with equal power over its local array of components.

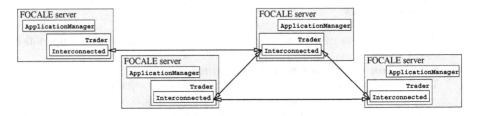

Fig. 1. A Federation consists of interconnected FOCALE servers

2.2   The Server Level

A FOCALE server must be run on a machine for it to be usable with our federation. Although it is not encouraged to do so, some users can propose more than one FOCALE server on one host.

Client Interaction

Our server provides an interaction with the users, through OMG-IDL-defined contracts. Among these, we defined the following interfaces, which will be explained in this section:

Interconnected, HasProperties, FactorySet, FactoryTrader and ApplicationManager.

Server Interconnection

A requested capability of our server is to be interconnected with its peers (see figure 1). This can be done by two ways: first, a user can launch a server on a machine, then notify one of the registered servers of its availability; the second way is more automatic, as a starting FOCALE server can browse the CORBA Naming Service, and find there its peers.

The technical part of the connection involves the new server asking another to register, through an OMG-IDL-defined operation register. The requested server then invokes a notifyRegister on itself and on the asking server, to permit a bi-directional communication.

Server Properties

An object implementing our OMG-IDL interface HasProperties has a set of properties, that the user can browse and manipulate. Each of these properties is defined by a name and a value. Some properties have a meaning, and a FOCALE server, by checking its environment, sets values for OS, architecture, ORB and user, at least.

These default properties are set to permit the management of code execution: if a server runs on a Sun/Solaris, and a code written for a PC/Windows has to be run, it will not be done there. These properties can also be checked to tell if the server's underlying machine works with little-endian or big-endian integer, and so on... Speaking of code leads naturally to the following aspect of a FOCALE server: the FactorySet.

Factories Set

What is a Factory ? In our project, we used the definition of E. Gamma *et al.* [3] for the *Factory design pattern*. We enter in more details about factories in the section 2.4. For this paragraph, we talk about a Factory set: each FOCALE server implements a way to store many factories, and retrieve them, locally (we will present the "remotely" aspect in the following section). *Persistence* of the FactorySet is achieved through individual Factory's persistence, but using a Cache mechanism delegated to the server level.

To create a factory in this set, a user has to submit all the **Factory** fields (see section 2.4). Once this is done, the newly-created factory is available for instanciation or local copy by all servers of the federation.

Trading Service

For a server to be able to retrieve a Factory that is stored somewhere in the federation, but not locally, we designed a (very) simple trading service. This trader is inspired by the CORBA Trading Service, but not fully compliant, because it is to be used only internally.

How does it work ? First of all, each Factory has a set of properties, for the code name, job description, version, provider, number of uses, etc. and retrieving a Factory is made by using these properties as criteria for a Trader search. For example, you could ask for the most-used matrix inversion component Factory, or the last version of the Factory named "Transpose".

If a corresponding Factory is not present locally, the servers **Interconnected** to this one will be asked for it, in a depth-first tree browsing. Although the servers are interconnected as a graph, cutting the cycles of this graph will form a tree. The cycles are cut when the search process encounters a server it has already browsed.

Applications Manager

In the same way as the **FactorySet**, the **ApplicationManager** OMG-IDL interface provides ways to create, obtain and remove Applications to a FOCALE server. The description of one individual Application follows, in the section 2.3.

2.3   The Application Level

In FOCALE, an Application follows the *Factory design pattern*, but at a higher level: an Application is described as a set of interconnected factories, and is instanciated by instanciating the described factories, then connect them (one's output is linked to the other's input, see section 2.6 for description of the *Connectors*) then launch them (see figure 2).

We remark here that instanciating and running a Factory are two different steps. These had to be separated to permit the interconnection between them, so that the producer does not start its job before having properly been connected to its consumer. Therefore, we will introduce a lower level after the Factory level description: the Instance.

2.4   The Factory Level

Conceptually, a Factory is an object that can create a (possibly) unlimited number of instances of one class. It can destroy them too, although in FOCALE, this could generate some problems: in Java, we are not able to take a snapshot of the stack trace, to restore it afterwards. So, users wanting a factory to destroy its instances must be sure of what they are doing.

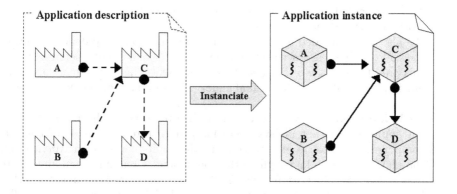

Fig. 2. Instanciating an Application instanciates all its Factories

In FOCALE, a Factory consists of a `Code` structure and methods to manage it (initializers, instanciate, run...), as well as a `HasProperties` interface implementation (see section 2.2 on Properties). The `Code` structure contains the following items (see figure 3), which can be accessed independantly — as defined in the `Factory` interface — to reduce the amount of unnecessary network traffic.

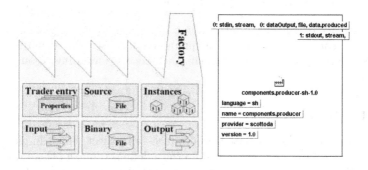

Fig. 3. The factory's content, and its console representation

− `FactoryTrader entry`

This field is a set of properties (see section 2.2, again). Such properties include the component name, its implementation language, version, provider, etc. There is no restriction on the properties, so that each user can add the property he wants, like comments on the code, or its quality of service.

− **information about the code execution**

In order to be able to launch the given code, the platform must know its execution command in the case of a process-level component, or the name of the main method for a class (see the next section, 2.5, for further details).

This field includes also the original code path which is mapped locally in the FOCALE server's cache.

We also have included a set of trader entries to define the dependencies of the code, that is, a description of the codes to load locally before running this one. In the case of a JAVA class component, this is not mandatory, as our implementation of the ClassLoader will do a part of this job.

– **basic knowledge of the component input/output channels**
  An application is not always — in fact, quite rarely — made of a single component, and to be able to connect the components of an Application, the platform has to know where the component is reading from, and where it is writing to. This item contains 2 arrays (one for the input, the other for the output) of the Resource structure. This structure contains the following fields: name, type and location. See section 2.6 for details on how the connection is achieved.

– **the code itself**
  When uploading the component into the federation for the first time, its provider has to give its binary form[5], so this is a part of the Code structure. However, as we wanted to be able to transmit all the informations about a Factory without requiring this field (which is rather big), we grouped all the Factory fields except this one into a Descriptor, which can be accessed directly thanks to the Factory interface.

Persistence of a Factory data is done by storing its Code in a file. Of course this could lead to problems (with quota-enabled users for example), but we will assume that users proposing their machines as computing resources are not "just" these machines' users.

2.5 The Instance Level

When a Factory is instanciated, it produces an object which implements the Instance OMG-IDL interface. This interface defines (among others) methods to connect this instance to others, run the created instance and test if its job is finished. As we wanted the platform to be the most generic possible, we have factories handling code that can be either Java classes, or processes (including all other programming languages: C/C++, Fortran, shell scripts, IDLscript programs, etc.). In the case of a Java class, the initialization of the Instance finds the given class and its main method, whereas the launch function invokes that method. In the case of a process, the initialization just keeps the external command, and the launch function executes it.

To connect an instance to another, users have to call the connectOutput function on the instance producing data, and connectInput on the instance consuming it. Each of these functions return a Connector (see next section), that we have to connect to each other, by calling the connect method on one, giving the second as argument. As the Interconnected aspect of the FOCALE server

---

[5] We can also work from a source code, but this will not be presented here.

(see section 2.2 on Interconnection), this will call a notifying method on both connectors. Once an producer instance output if connected to its consumer, all of the data going through the output connector's given resource will be redirected to the consumer's input connector's resource.

If the output connector of an instance is not connected, we will assume that its data will form the result of this component's job. If the user is logged to the federation, he is notified of the termination, and the result is shown. If he logged out after having submitted his job, he will be notified the result when he will log back.

2.6   The Connectors

Conceptually, a `Connector` is like a system pipe, extended to CORBA.

A `Connector` contains a `Resource` structure (see section 2.4), which is used to specify which resource is being used to transmit data. These resource can be the input/output standard streams of the `Instance`, a file or a socket. It is not mandatory for an input connector to map the same resource type as the output connector, as the resource is given for only one of the connectors. Actually, it is possible for a standard output stream to be linked to a file or a socket, for example.

We have plans to provide also URL resource (publishing and fetching data through URLs), and also a Method resource which will be run to fetch data or send it (mostly for specially designed new components, and more in the style of the CORBA Component Model [16]). An output `Connector` consists of a thread watching the given resource, and upon data arrival, sending it to the input connector. When data arrives, the input connector moves it to its given resource, so that it is available to the consumer. These steps are illustrated on figure 4.

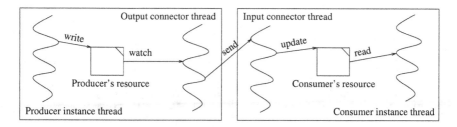

Fig. 4. The steps of the communication between two connected Instances, one producing data and the other consuming it

It is possible that two components cannot communicate directly, because of the differences of information representation between the produced data and the consumer input format. In this case, the Application provider can put a "translation" component between the consumer and the producer, so that the producer data can be translated into the consumer input format.

3   The Console

Using the FOCALE federation can seem complicated, with all these levels and
interfaces. Even with CORBASCRIPT [17] [11], it is not easy to feed the servers
with new factories, although the manipulating methods are easy to find and
invoke. This fact, along with the end-user availability of our platform, made us
create a console above FOCALE federation. This console has a graphical user
interface, made with Java/Swing, using different frames to display different levels of the federation. With it, you can create/connect/remove servers from
the federation, add/move/delete factories from the servers (figures 3 and 5),
create/modify/run/destroy applications from the servers (figure 6), and many
other functionalities, like catch events from any item[6], or display information on
any level of the federation.

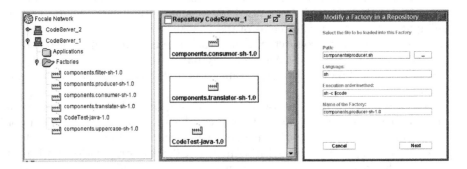

Fig. 5. Console display of a server factories, as a tree and as a window, and the factory
installation wizard window

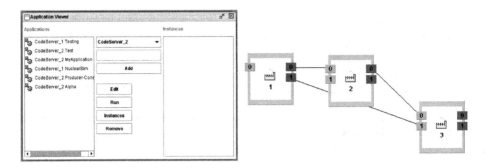

Fig. 6. Console display of the applications list, and one application factories interconnection

---

[6] our implementation of the Observer/Observed design pattern used will not be explained in this document

Of course, users can develop their own clients, that can access FOCALE federation through CORBA, by using the OMG-IDL contracts of FOCALE. In this case, the console is not needed, but it can always serve to monitor the client progress.

4   Conclusion

The platform described in this article, as well as its console is now working, and it is available from `http://corbaweb.lifl.fr`. Generic components can be installed, deployed, and run in applications. It is interesting to note that, although formerly developped only for scientific applications, FOCALE uses enough genericity to permit any form of application to be launched upon it.

The performance of our platform was not discussed here, as it is not the main issue in FOCALE: we provide a simple mean to deploy and interconnect computation components, and when this is done, they run at their own speed. Actually, the performance of the platform itself does not reside in the running speed of these components, but in its capacity to deploy, find and connect them.

5   Future Works

Globally, the platform is not very fault-tolerant (although if one server is missing, others can fetch factories from elsewhere), due to the evident fact that computing nodes spread over the Internet are not very reliable. One of the main next step of FOCALE improvement will then be improving its fault-tolerance and quality of service.

It has also been noted that the performance of the platform was somewhat limited to loading and connecting components, but if a server becomes too loaded, there is no way, yet, to reduce it. To deploy components, we will use theoretical issues such as optimisation and graph theory, that can provide means to speed up the positioning of components on the federation and the search of those components afterwards. For the components' execution, we intend to include a load balancing policy to increase the performance of this phase.

To the end-user point of view, it would be interesting to have a "preview" of the deployment and execution of its application. Therefore, we intend to include a cost prevision module, which will present a rough measure of time for the deployment and execution phases. Such a module will obviously display its information for special use of the platform and the components, as it is not known beforehand if other users will use it, and if servers will crash during the process.

References

1. Denis Caromel, Wilfried Klauser, and Julien Vayssi re. Towards seamless computing and metacomputing in Java. In Geo rey C. Fox, editor, *Concurrency Practice and Experience*, volume 10 (11-13), pages 1043 1061. Wiley and Sons, Ltd, Sep/Nov 1998.

2. Paul Sweazey *et al.* SCI - Scalable Coherent Interface, P1596/D2.00. Technical report, 1992.
3. E. Gamma, R. Helm, R. Johnson, J. Vlissides, and G. Booch. *Design Patterns: Elements of Reusable Object-Oriented Software.* Addison-Westley Professional Computing, USA, 1995.
4. Globe web site.
   http://www.cs.vu.nl/globe.
5. Globus web site (papers available).
   http://www.globus.org.
6. Matthew Izatt, Patrick Chan, and Tim Brecht. Ajents: Towards an Environment for Parallel, Distributed and Mobile Java Applications. In ACM 1999, editor, *Java Grande Conference*, pages 15 25, June 1999.
7. Katarzyna Keahey, Peter Beckman, and James Ahrens. Ligature: Component Architecture for High-Performance Applications.
8. Legion web site (papers available).
   http://legion.virginia.edu.
9. J. Magee, N. Dulay, S. Eisenbach, and J. Kramer. Specifying distributed software architectures. In *Fifth European Software Engineering Conference*, September 1995.
10. J. Magee, N.Dulay, and J. Kramer. Regis: A constructive development environment for distributed programs. *Distributed Systems Engineering Journal*, 1(5):304 312, September 1994.
11. P. Merle, C. Gransart, and J.-M. Geib. Using and Implementing CORBA Objects with CorbaScript. *Object-Oriented Parallel and Distributed Programming*, 2000. Ed. Hermes.
12. Ajay Mohindra, Apratim Purakayastha, Deborra Zukowski, and Murthy Devarakonda. Programming Network Components Using NetPebbles: An Early Report. In *USENIX Conference on Object Oriented Technologies*, April 1998.
13. K. Ng, J. Kramer, and J. Magee. A case tool for software architecture design.
14. Object Management Group. Supporting Aggregated Computing in CORBA. OMG TC Document 1999-01-04, Object Management Group, First Needham Place, 250 First Avenue, Suite 201, Needham, MA 02194, U.S.A., 1999.
15. Object Management Group. Parallel Application Support for CORBA. OMG TC Document 2000-02-06, Object Management Group, First Needham Place, 250 First Avenue, Suite 201, Needham, MA 02194, U.S.A., 2000.
16. OMG. *CORBA Components: Joint Revised Submission.* Object Management Group, August 1999. OMG TC Document orbos/99-07-{01..03,05} orbos/99-08{05..07,12,13}.
17. OOC and LIFL. *CORBA Scripting - Joint Revised Submission.* Object Management Group, August 1999.
18. Fr d ric Peschanski. COMET, reflective architecture based on components, for the construction of parallel and distributed applications.
19. Thierry Priol and Christophe Ren . Cobra: a CORBA-compliant Programming Environment for High-Performance Computing. In *Europar'98, Southampton, UK*, pages 1114 1133, September 1998.

Web Enabled Client-Server Model for Development Environment of Distributed Image Processing

Haresh S. Bhatt[1], V. H. Patel[1], and A. K. Aggarwal[2]

[1]Space Applications Centre
Jodhpur Tekara,
Satellite Road,
Ahmedabad – 380 053
INDIA
{haresh,vhpatel} @ipdpg.gov.in

[2]Department of Computer Science
Rollwala Computer Centre
Gujarat University
Ahmedabad – 380 009
INDIA
aka19@hotmail.com

Abstract. Image processing applications (IPA) requirements can be best met by using the distributed environment. The authors had developed an environment over a network of VAX/VMS and Unix for distributed image processing. The efficiency was as high as 90-95%. This paper presents an augmentation and generalization of the environment using Java and web technology to make it truly system independent. Although the environment has been tested using image processing applications, the design and architecture is truly general so that it can be used for other applications, which require distributed processing.

Keywords: DEDIP, Parallel Image Processing, Distributed image processing

1. Introduction

Image processing applications (IPA) require processing on large volumes of data. These also require various types of resources like high-resolution graphic displays, drives for magnetic tape/cartridge/floppies, optical disk, database, etc. The resource requirement changes with time due to the availability of new and better resources. Hence, it is not possible to assume the availability of all resources on a single system. The distributed processing environment not only helps in optimum utilization of such resources but also helps in achieving better throughput using multiple processors in parallel. However, if one has to use multiple heterogeneous machines in a network to execute a set of tasks, one may have to execute a tedious set of commands. It is not possible to expect an operator to carry out such operations on a regular basis. Moreover in such a system, any error, occurring either during data transfer or during processing, creates difficulties for the operator.

Development of an application having built-in automated data transfer, capability of using multiple machines in parallel, and robust error handling is a challenging job. This paper presents the authors' contribution in providing a tool that makes such a development very easy.

R. Buyya and M. Baker (Eds.): GRID 2000, LNCS 1971, pp. 135-145, 2000.
© Springer-Verlag Berlin Heidelberg 2000

The research work carried out by eminent computer professionals [1-10] focused on the parallel-processing experts' needs. The image processing applications are developed by scientists (mathematicians, physicists, remote sensing experts, etc) not by parallel processing experts. *Smooth operational environment, Operational setup,* and *ease of use* are the critical issues for scientists compared to parallel processing experts.

We focused on the requirement of this vast community. We presented a full fledged Development Environment for Distributed Image Processing (DEDIP) that makes the development & operationalization of distributed applications very easy [11]. This paper presents a WebDedip, which is redesign and generalization of DEDIP to make it more user friendly and truly heterogeneous.

2. Generalization and Extension

The WebDedip has a novel design, which explores object oriented modeling technique in the web domain. The new model uses three-tier architecture instead of master-slave one. The DEDIP had provided GUI only on the host system. The WebDedip provides browser based GUI on all nodes connected to the system. It enables the user to use the WebDedip from any system on Internet. Thus, it provides the roaming profile to application designers, operation managers and operators. Users have to edit a few text files to configure their application in DEDIP. WebDedip has made this task easier by adding new user friendly GUIs. The augmented design addresses all the important redundancy issues making the WebDedip fault tolerant.

3. WebDedip Overview

The WebDedip has a three tier architecture; GUI, DedipServer and Agents, as shown in figure-1.

The GUI is the web enabled graphical user interface to make the entire user-interaction truly system independent. It supports various Java Applets for application configuration, application building, application operation initiation, application progress monitoring, and session controlling. The user initiates the interaction by visiting a predefined site using a standard browser. The standard web server loads the required GUI on the web browser.

It has a back-end DedipServer running on the web site. When the GUI submits the request to the DedipServer, it reads the application configuration information from the configuration file. The DedipServer initiates the execution of the first process in the interdependency chart. Normally, most of the applications have a single starting process. If any application has multiple starting processes, it initiates execution of all such independent processes. It informs the agent(s) on the target node to start the execution of the process. The agent sends the status information back to the DedipServer when the process is completed. The DedipServer finds out the dependent processes on the successful completion of a process and initiates the execution of each such process. The required files are transferred from one node to another. WebDedip has a callable library in Java to interface with the FTP server [12] that helps in transferring files. The required process is automatically inserted in the configuration when IP designer inserts the IO dependency information (figure-5) between two processes.

The DedipServer stores complete information about all the applications configured on the web site. The DedipServer exchanges information with the DedipBackupServer making the model fault tolerant.

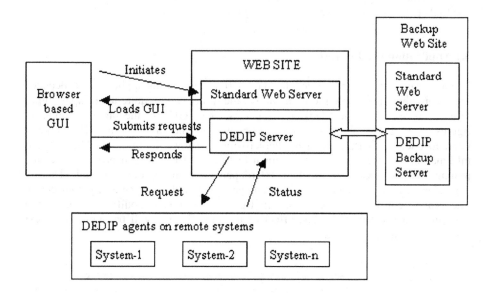

Fig. 1. WebDedip Model

The task of the agent is very simple. It accepts requests from the DedipServer, executes them and provides the status information when completed. It has process building (compilation), execution, and monitoring capabilities. It can schedule multiple processes in parallel. It does not control the synchronization among the parallel processes, instead it depends on the DedipServer for this job. It treats each process as a single independent entity.

The WebDedip not only caters to the requirements of the application designer, but also addresses all the requirements of the operation manager as well as operators. The application configuration and building is a privileged task, carried out either by the application designer or operation manager. During the regular operations, the operator can initiate any required application, monitor progress, do error handling, and terminate the application, if necessary. The web server capability is used to provide the required access control rights.

Object-oriented modeling (implemented in Java) is used for the design of the WebDedip [13]. The application is modeled as an object while the process is modeled as an embedded object. The object inter linking capability is used to maintain interdependency information for an application. Java distributed object architecture is used along with the object serialization for network communication among GUI, DedipServer and agents. Hence, WebDedip can be used on a LAN, WAN or on Internet. Agents may run on any system over Internet. On start, an agent makes connection with DedipServer on a predefined port and volunteers for computation workload. Java object persistence is used in storing the information, including dynamic information. The same is explored in communication among the GUI, DedipServer and agents.

The Windows-explorer is used as a metaphor in developing the navigation GUI due to its popularity and ease of use (see figure-2).

3.1 Application Configuration

The application designer first decides the configuration of his application. It depends on the distributed resource requirement, parallel processing requirement, input/output of each process, etc. The WebDedip supports a nice GUI for the same as shown in figures 2-5. Figure-2 shows the overview of the application. The typical interdependency chart, generated interactively, is shown in figure-3. The detailed information about each process is shown in figure-4 for a typical process. The line joining two processes shows their interdependency in top-down model. The IO dependency, if any, is a part of this interdependency and it can be easily configured. The typical configuration is shown in figure-5. User can modify his application configuration file any time. The effect of the modification will be applied on next execution of the application.

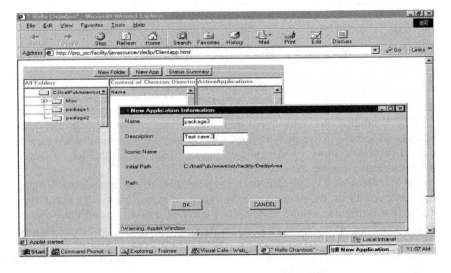

Fig. 2 Basic Information of the Application

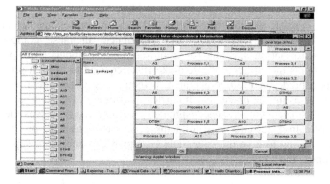

Fig. 3 Process interdependency Information

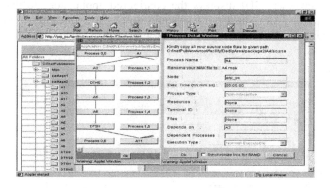

Fig. 4 Process Information

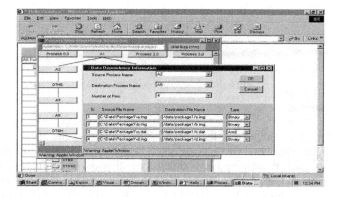

Fig. 5 Data dependency information

3.2 Application Building

An application consists of many processes. All these processes need to be compiled on the target node. The WebDedip has automated all these compilation. The configuration information has all the required details about each process. The DedipServer copies the source code & make-file, required to build a process, on the target node in a predefined temporary area. It then requests the agent on the node to build the process using the make-file. It carries out this task for each process given in the configuration. The agent creates designated directory and preserves the executable in it. The application designer can build the processes externally on all systems in case he is not willing to give the code. The GUI provides necessary support for such external readiness indicator.

3.3 Application Execution and Monitoring

The operator can start execution of any application from any machine on the net using the standard browser. GUI displays the configured applications to the operator for selection. Operator can start/abort/suspend/resume an application.   Figures 6 & 7 show the GUI for session and application progress information.

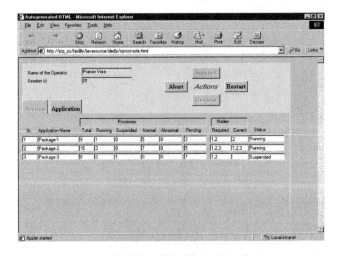

Fig 6 Session progress information

3.4 Error Handling

In case of abnormal completion, the DEDIP Server displays the error message with error code to the operator. These error codes and error messages are provided by application designer. WebDedip keeps this information in the configuration file. The operator can restart the process after taking the necessary actions. In addition, the operator has the options of either restarting the entire application or aborting it.

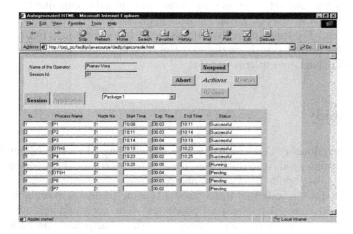

Fig 7 Application progress information

3.5 Session Management

Each time an operator logs in, DEDIP scheduler starts/restarts a session for him. Each session has a unique session identification number. It keeps all the information about the session on the server. The operator has multiple options to log out. He can close the session, terminate the session, suspend/resume the session, or submit the session for progress in background before logging out. He can close the session only after normal completion of all the requests he has submitted. He can terminate the session immediately in case of emergency. In case of termination, the WebDedip kills all the processes of all the requests submitted by the operator irrespective of the status. The background processing is very effective in the case of non-interactive processes. The WebDedip gives the detailed status to the operator at the next logon.

3.6 WebDedip System Management

The WebDedip system consists of a DedipServer and agents. The DedipServer can detect the agent termination. It displays the message on operators' console as well as operation manager console.

The DedipServer is the most important process in the entire system. Its failure, for example, due to system crashing, can cause a severe problem. DedipBackServer is designed to handle the failure of the DedipServer. The software package DedipbackupServer runs on the machine of the backup server and duplicates the required information from the DedipServer. An agent sends a trigger to DedipBackupServer when it fails to communicate with the DedipServer. The DedipBackupServer validates the DedipServer failure. It takes over the complete responsibility from that moment onwards and informs the operation manager. The servers are exchanging information only in case of external events like termination of process, start of new process, initiation of an application by the operator, the start of new session, etc. The frequency of such possible events is very low. Furthermore, the volume of the information is negligible. Hence, the communication overhead for maintaining the back-up server is very low.

4. Case Study

WebDedip functionality and efficiency was tested using Microsoft NT as host and IRIS workstations as slaves. IIS 4 was used as web server. The front-end GUI is tested on two most popular browsers IE and Netscape

The WebDedip was tested for three cases [11] using simulated executables by three operators in ten runs. The simulated processes were generated resembling actual processes for image processing interaction/processing. The process dependency chart is given in figures 8-10. The processing node is shown in the bracket if it is different than host. DTHS stands for Data Transfer from Host to Slave while DTSH stands for the reverse process. 'T' indicates the tape unit requirement by the process. 'W' & 'W2' indicates that the process is scheduled on workstation1 and workstation2 respectively. The time (in minutes) required by each process is shown in bracket.

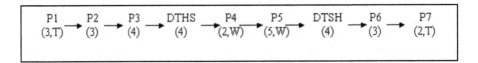

Fig. 8. Simulated case-1 for testing

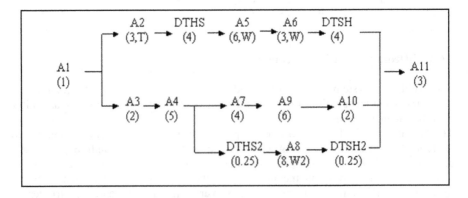

Fig. 9. Simulated case-2 for testing

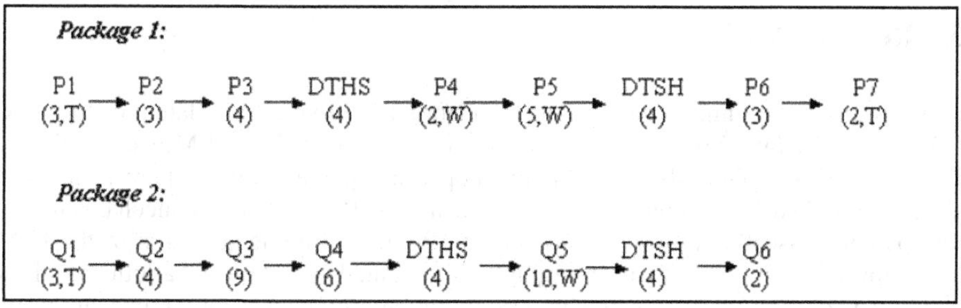

Package 1:

P1 $\to$ P2 $\to$ P3 $\to$ DTHS $\to$ P4 $\to$ P5 $\to$ DTSH $\to$ P6 $\to$ P7
(3,T) (3)   (4)   (4)   (2,W) (5,W) (4)   (3)   (2,T)

Package 2:

Q1 $\to$ Q2 $\to$ Q3 $\to$ Q4 $\to$ DTHS $\to$ Q5 $\to$ DTSH $\to$ Q6
(3,T) (4)   (9)   (6)   (4)   (10,W) (4)   (2)

Fig. 10. Simulated case-3 for testing

Case 1: Single package requiring sequential scheduling is shown in figure 8 depicting the simplest case.

Case 2: Single package requiring parallel scheduling is shown in figure 9.

Case 3: Parallel execution of two packages, each package requiring sequential scheduling, is shown in figure 10.

Table 1 : Results for the case studies (time in minutes)			
Case	**Theoretical**	**Without Dedip**	**WebDedip**
1	30.0	32	32.0
2	23.5	52	25.0
3	42.0	74	46.0

The efficiency results are almost the same as those achieved in the earlier version, ie 90-95%. The page & applet loading time over the network is excluded. The access time in case of WebDedip is mainly due to two reasons: (1) action communication delay and (2) DedipServer overheads. This action communication delay was measured for various actions by repeated exercises. It was found out to be approximately 10 to 40 seconds on this type of action. The remaining are the DedipServer overheads.

Recently, a few scientists were engaged in developing web-based project management & work flow applications [14] like hierarchical progress reporting & compilation, meeting management, project task management, personal task management, document authentication, resource booking, complaint management, job work flow and remote system configuration detection. These applications were having distributed processing requirement amongst the browser based remote machines, web server, database server and mail server. They used WebDedip instead of Java servlets. The used their own GUI could communicate to DedipServer and agents using RequestObject, a message passing object from WebDedip library [13].

5. Related Work

In this section, we summarize the research efforts that are closely related to our work. JPVM [1], and Java MPI [2] are the Java extensions of PVM and MPI respectively. JavaParty [3], ParaWeb [4], Charlotte [5], Popcorn [6], and Javelin [7] are Java based systems for distributed computing using Java. JavaParty provides mechanisms for transparently distributing remote objects. ParaWeb is an implementation of the JVM that allows Java threads to be transparently executed remotely. Charlotte provides high level solution that decouples programming environment from the execution. Its disadvantage is that the programmer does not have explicit control over resource utilization. However, its eager scheduling enables the runtime systems to efficiently provide load balancing. Popcorn provides a Java API for writing parallel programs for Internet distribution. Applications are decomposed, by the programmer, into small, self-contained subcomputations, called computelets. The Popcorn is based on buyer-seller concept. It has a centralized entity called market that determines which CPU seller executes the computelet. Javelin is an infrastructure for Internet based parallel computing. Any free computer system can volunteer to execute a task using the applets supported by the Javelin. It follows a client-broker-server architecture. Bayanihan [8] and Ninflet [9] are also very similar to the Javelin.

The methods, reported in most of the above, concentrate in providing computation power to a large and complex application efficiently. All of them expect efficient parallel and distributed programming skills. Their definition of ease of use is around application compilation, scalability, load balancing, fault tolerance, etc. The WebFlow [10] is closest to our work. It provides Java-Swing based visual programming environment for metacomputing using Java. It supports Globus [15] metacomputing toolkit at the backend.

The programmer needs to use Java for metacomputing language in the above models. Furthermore, the GUIs of the above models support the monitoring and controlling an application (large & complex) in stand-alone mode. Therefore, they do not require elegant & easy GUI for simultaneous execution, monitoring and controlling of multiple applications.

WebDedip (& DEDIP) concentrated on the vast community of scientists rather than efficient programmers. It made the distributed application development very easy. It supports all languages like Fortran, C, C++ and Java. Its GUI supports all the needs of operational environment executing multiple heterogeneous applications simultaneously. It has its own backend support for process scheduling and monitoring.

6. Conclusion

The WebDedip provides a useful facility to the designer to develop the distributed image processing application in a user-friendly environment. The browser based GUI enables him to use the system functionality from anywhere over the Internet. The graphical user interface makes it easy to visualize and configure the application. Furthermore, WebDedip addresses all the critical elements for smooth operations. The option of back-up server support makes the entire system robust.

The results obtained from the simulated test cases for the WebDedip match with those of the earlier version. The communication delay over the network is the only additional delay. The earlier version of the model was used by 15 scientists for development and operationalization of 10 distributed image processing applications for Indian Remote sensing Satellite (IRS). The same is likely to be replaced by the new WebDedip.

Although the WebDedip has been tailored for the requirement of image processing applications, its design and architecture is truly general so that it may be used for other applications also. Collaboration is being worked out with Nirma Institute of Technology to use WebDedip in field of advanced computing for civil engineering.

A study is being carried out for interfacing WebDedip and PVM.

References

1. A.J. Ferrari, JPVM - *The Java Virtual Machine*, http://www.cs.virginia.edu/ajf2j/jpvm.html.
2. S. Taylor, *Prototype of Java-MPI package*, Available at http://cisr.anu.edu.au/sam/java/jav.mpi.prototype.html.
3. M. Philippsen, M. Zenger, *JavaParty – trasnperent remote objects in Java*, Proc. of ACM 1997 PPoPP Workshop on Java for Science and Engineering Computation, (1997).
4. T. Brecht, H. Sandhu, M. Shan, J. Talbot, *ParaWeb: towards world-wide supercomputing*, Proc. of 7th ACM SIGOPS European Workshop, (1996).
5. Baratloo, M. Karaul, Z. Kedem, P. Wijckoff, Charlotte: *Metacomputing on the Web*, Future Generation Computer Systems, Vol. 15, (1999), 559-570.
6. N. Camiel, S. London, N. Nisan, O. Regev, *The POPCORN project: Dsitributed Computation over the Internet in Java*, 6th International World Wide Web Conference, (1997).
7. M. Neary, B. Christiansen, P. Cappello, K. Schauser, *Javelin: Parallel computing on the internet*, Future Generation Computer Systems, Vol. 15, (1999), 659-674.
8. L. Sarmenta, *Bayanihan: Web-Based Volunteer Computing Using Java*, 2nd International Conference on World Wide Computing and its Applications, (1998).
9. H.Takagi, S. Matsuoka, H. Nakada, S. Sekiguchi, M. Satoh, U. Nagashima, *Ninflet: a Migratable Parallel Objects Framework using Java*, Proc. of the ACM 1998 Workshop on Java for High_performance Network Computing, Palo Alto, CA, (1998).
10. T. Haupt, E. Akarsu, G. Fox, W. Furumanski, *Web based metacomputing*, Furture Generation Computer Systems, Vol. 15, (1999), 735-743.
11. Haresh Bhatt, CVS Prakash, A K Aggarwal, *DEDIP: Development Environment for Distribute Image Processing*, Submitted to DS Online, http://computer.org/channels/ds/
12. *Java based client object library for interfacing with FTP servers*, Technical report, DWPIP project, (1999).
13. *Design of Web based DEDIP using UML*, Technical report, DWPIP project, (2000).
14. *Design overview of project & work-flow management automation*, Technical report, CNF/SIIPA, Space Applications Centre, Ahmedabad, India.
15. *Globus project-* http://www.globus.org/

An Advanced User Interface Approach for Complex Parameter Study Process Specification on the Information Power Grid

Maurice Yarrow, Karen M. McCann, Rupak Biswas, and Rob F. Van der Wijngaart

Computer Sciences Corporation, Mail Stop T27A-1, NASA Ames Research Center, Moffett Field, CA 94035, USA
{yarrow,mccann,rbiswas,wijngaar}@nas.nasa.gov

Abstract. The creation of parameter study suites has recently become a more challenging problem as the parameter studies have become multi-tiered and the computational environment has become a supercomputer grid. The parameter spaces are vast, the individual problem sizes are getting larger, and researchers are seeking to combine several successive stages of parameterization and computation. Simultaneously, grid-based computing offers immense resource opportunities but at the expense of great difficulty of use. We present ILab, an advanced graphical user interface approach to this problem. Our novel strategy stresses intuitive visual design tools for parameter study creation and complex process specification, and also offers programming-free access to grid-based supercomputer resources and process automation.

1 Motivation and Background

Only a decade ago, the solution of the partial differential equations required for the evaluation of aerospace vehicle flow-fields typically involved a single discretization zone and was performed on a single processor of a high-speed compute engine that was usually situated locally. These compute tasks were so costly in CPU cycles that the notion of performing parameter studies was usually ignored. Now, however, the flow-solvers are typically parallel codes. The compute engines are frequently large parallel machines with multi-gigabyte memories and terabyte disk farms. Researchers have available the resources not only of their own laboratories but also those at other computer centers accessible via fast networks. Parameter studies are now quite feasible and are being performed on a regular basis by researchers who require solution information throughout a given aerospace vehicle flight regime. The difficulties, however, have shifted to the manual creation of these parameter studies and to tasks associated with launching and managing the large number of jobs required by these studies. Modern aerospace flow-solvers frequently require large sets of discretization grids which describe the geometry of the aerospace vehicle. They produce as output large collections of data files. Currently, most parameter studies are performed with two-dimensional flow solvers, but three-dimensional solvers are also beginning to be used.

Recent developments in grid-based "metacomputing" such as Globus [1]. and Legion [2] have created opportunities for running parameter studies on remote networked

R. Buyya and M. Baker (Eds.:) GRID 2000, LNCS 1971, pp. 146–157, 2000.

high-performance compute servers which constitute a shared resource for participants. But these opportunities come at a price: the proliferation of *job control language* (JCL) to support these capabilities. This has placed an onus on users of these metacomputing grids, who are typically engineers and researchers not well prepared or enthusiastic about learning or creating the requisite control language scripts for managing distributed parameter studies. NASA is currently building a national metacomputing infrastructure, called the "Information Power Grid" (IPG) [3], intended to provide ubiquitous and uniform access to a wide range of computational, communication, data analysis, and storage resources, many of which are specialized and cannot be replicated at all user sites. However, the interface to the IPG is still under development.

We briefly describe the notion of a "parameter study" by giving two general examples. Simulation codes produce solutions to scientific or engineering problems for some set of input values ("parameters"). Varying these parameters through some prescribed range (the "parameter space") yields a set of related results, called a "parameter study" (sometimes written as "parametric study"). As a second example we point to Monte Carlo simulations. Monte Carlo codes are typically run many times in order to to produce statistically meaningful ensemble averages. This too can be considered a parameter study, where the parameter to be varied is merely the seed for random number generation, and does not actually have any physical significance.

The end product of creating and launching parameter studies is typically a large suite of result files which must be postprocessed and/or moved to some form of long-term storage. Furthermore, parameter study users must be able to keep track of these results and log into a scientific diary such particulars as nature of the solved problem, location of the result files, history for the individual runs, and any other associated information. Being able to easily recreate and then modify the parameter study is also an important need for many users.

We conducted a literature survey to identify existing parameter study capabilities that fulfilled the need of users at NASA Ames Research Center. The only tools deemed applicable for these tasks were the historically related Clustor and Nimrod codes [5]. Both are able to generate and launch simple parameter studies. They also implement an internal "meta-language" for describing parameter study creation. Additionally, they make it easy to parameterize command line arguments.

However, they did not fully meet the requirements of our users. Some of these are as follows. Users must have access to multiple job submission environments. These must include any combination of PBS [6], LSF [7], MPI, Globus, Condor [8], and Legion. Also, users require the ability to create what we call "multi-stage" parameter studies (a detailed example appears in section 7). Users also need a "fire-and-forget" capability, i.e., once the parameter study suite is created, it should be possible to initiate job launching and then shut down the parameter study tool entirely. Job submission should continue autonomously, and without the continued presence of the parameter study tool. Users also require a fairly comprehensive level of job auditing and scientific diary capability, the secretarial side of a problem solving environment (PSE). On the development side, we needed to design a parameter study tool that could be easily extended using a high-level rapid-prototyping language (such as Perl). This is because we envision using the tool as a testbed for experiments in parameter study creation models, job submission models, and complex process specification models. We also need to be able to use the tool to generate shell scripts designed for parameter study job submission and for complex process job submission (visual scripting). It is essential that the script generation process be very flexible.

2   Problem Definition

Creating and launching parameter studies without the assistance of automating tools is laborious, tedious, and error-prone. Examining the stages of this task allows us to discern the nature of the inherent problems. The first stage is to create the parameterized input files which incorporate the sets of values representing the parameter study. These sets are the Cartesian product of the individual sets of values over which each of the parameters of interest varies. The total number of combinations (the *parameter space*) can quickly get to be very large, and creating these sets of input files manually is time-consuming and error-prone. Each of the resultant input files represents a run of the user program (a job). Launching jobs involves setting up partitioned file spaces in which they can run, supplying each with all required input files, submitting them, and then monitoring progress and managing output. Our first design requirement was that all of these functions be automated and integrated into a single Graphical User Interface (GUI). The second requirement was that of simplicity of use. We believe that users are very sensitive to ease-of-use issues, and that they will avoid process automation tools that are deemed difficult or non-intuitive. The third requirement is that a parameter study tool be able to self-document its actions. If it cannot, users will quickly be mired in a morass of hundreds, even thousands, of old runs whose origin and purpose are no longer obvious; a complete parameter study tool must be part PSE and part scientific diary. The fourth requirement is that of job submission flexibility in a scientific computation environment currently in flux. This is because "Grid-based" computing has added new complexities and layers of JCL to the task of submitting jobs. ILab meets all of these four user requirements.

3   Basic Assumptions and Requirements for Distributed Processing

We have started with two basic assumptions about NASA's distributed computing environment into which jobs will be launched. The first is the need to maintain production level capability. This has significant implications, because all compute-intensive application processing must occur under the aegis of a job scheduler and queuing system. Any other manner of submitting to shared computational resources would violate "good neighbor" policy. The second assumption about our distributed computing environment is that it should be able to leverage the Globus metacomputing middleware currently being developed at Argonne National Laboratory. It must also be possible for parameter study users to bypass the Globus layer and still submit jobs into a distributed environment. This has resulted in a design incorporating several job models for spawning parameter studies in a distributed fashion.

4   ILab: The IPG Virtual Lab

We describe important features of the ILab parameter study tool, in particular parameterization operations and aspects of the internal coding design.

4.1   Parameterization of Program Input Files

In order to minimize the difficulty of building a set of parameterized input files, ILab includes an integrated, special-purpose text editor. This editor has unusual capabilities: it allows the user to mark *graphically* the appropriate parameter data fields and to designate the set of values for each selected field. This parameterizer is depicted in Fig. 1. Value sets

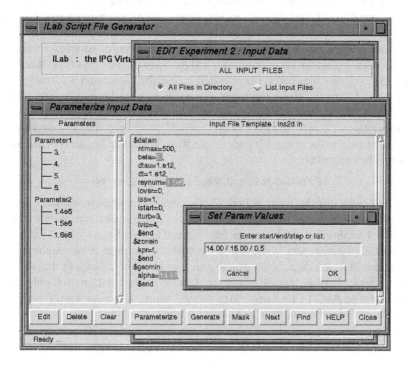

Fig. 1. ILab parameterization screen

can be specified either as a list or by min/max/increment. The user first selects (highlights) with the mouse those ASCII text fields within the input file which will be parameterized. In Fig. 1, "beta" and "reynum" (known to ILab as Parameter1 and Parameter2) have already been parameterized; their value sets are displayed in the left window. Currently the user is specifying the third parameter in the "Set Param Values" dialog. If several fields must be parameterized in tandem (example: multiple occurrences of "timestep" for each of several related discretization zone input files), that can be indicated at this stage. After text selection of the appropriate fields, the user enters a list or range of values for the selected fields. Lastly, the set of parameterized input files is generated. These files constitute the Cartesian product of the individual parameter sets. As an example, if three input values are to be parameterized (a 3-dimensional parameter space), the first with the set of values $\{1, 2, 3, 4\}$, the second with $\{hello, goodbye\}$, and the third with $\{3.14, 2.718, 1.618\}$, then a total of $4 \times 2 \times 3 = 24$ parameterized files will be produced.

Because the file parameterizer is integrated within the ILab GUI and because its use is intuitive, the process of parameterization of the input files has been made trivial. Additionally, a "most-recently-used" (MRU) capability saves the current parameterization state for future reference and for reuse or modification.

4.2   Job Masking Capability

One of the necessities of a parameter study program is to provide "masking" capability for a set of parameterized input files. Users require this ability when they know that certain parameter combinations will produce an unsuccessful run of the scientific program under consideration. Typically, they want to specify combinations of parameter values that will be excluded from the set of input files and their associated script files. ILab's "Edit Parameters" screen - the special purpose editor described in section 4.1 - has a pop-up dialog for this purpose. Users can enter any number of masking rules, and each rule must specify two or more parameter comparisons. For example, if the user is varying Parameter1 from 1 to 10, and Parameter2 from 55 to 75, and wants to exclude those combinations where Parameter1 is greater than 9 and Parameter2 equals 60, the masking rule would be entered as:

```
Parameter1 > 9 && Parameter2 == 60
```

This syntax, which is the same in Perl, C, C++, and Java, was chosen since users are likely to be familiar with it. The names Parameter1 and Parameter2 are assigned in order by ILab to the values being parameterized. (ILab, of course, has no way of knowing the actual names of parameters in the user's input files since there is no requirement that the input have labeled data. In the example in Fig. 1, it just so happens that the user is parameterizing a Fortran "namelist" file with labeled fields, but ILab itself only requires that the input be ASCII.) By using Perl's "eval" function, we can easily interpret the above rule with minimal parsing, and use it to delete job objects from the user's list of experiments.

4.3   Coding Model and Language Choice

We have chosen to build our ILab GUI using Perl5 and the Tk user interface construction tool kit. In addition, we have used the Perl generation capabilities of the "SpecTcl" Tk GUI generation IDE [9], a free software tool available from Sun Microsystems. Our choice of Perl5 was based on its strong character string manipulation and built-in regular expression capabilities, strong list and sortable associative-hashtable datatypes, and its simple-to-use object-oriented features. Also, Perl is relatively ubiquitous and is amongst the fastest interpreters commonly available today. Altogether, these features make Perl an excellent choice for true rapid-prototyping. Though we cannot exactly quantify the savings in the coding effort, we believe, based on prior experiences, that the equivalent functionality would require two to three times as much C++ or Java.

4.4   Object-Oriented Data Structures and Strategies

We used Perl "packages" (the equivalent of classes in C++ and Java) to hold all ILab data, both persistent and transient. Fig. 2 depicts the data structures hierarchy.

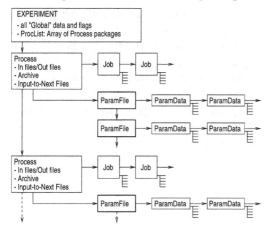

Fig. 2. ILab data structures

An Experiment package holds all persistent data: the data is serialized (written *en masse*, retaining data structure hierarchies) to and from disk with the use of Perl's Data::Dumper module. To reduce the size of the Experiment package, several other arrays of packages apportion data that has to be held in lists or arrays: a ParamFile package for each input file to be parameterized, a ParamData package for each variable being parameterized in each input file, and a Job package to hold run-specific data. ParamFile and ParamData hold file- and variable-specific data while the Experiment is being created and edited. To run a user's parameter study Experiment, a list of Job packages is created: some ParamFile and ParamData data is transferred to Job packages, and additional data is attached. The organization of data in ParamFile and ParamData is "orthogonal" to the way the same data is organized in the array of Job packages: this simplifies script creation, submission, and monitoring. Essentially, data is in arrays of arrays during editing/creation, while during submission/monitoring the same data is flattened out into a one-dimensional array of Job packages. Both sets of data are serialized when an Experiment package is serialized.

Each window or dialog box is also a package, which holds transient data: user interface references and data as necessary, and also "mirror" portions of the current Experiment data. This duplication of data makes it easier and more robust to edit previously entered data, since a user can make changes and then cancel the changes without having to restore the original data. Another important advantage is gained from the "mirror" and "orthogonal" approaches: the trade-off is more data, less code. Problems in the data are easier to find and fix than problems in the code. Debugging is also facilitated by the following strategies: (1) each package has a "dump" function to print out all variables and (2) each package error-traps the setting of any variable inside the set portion of a get/set function. Caveat: data duplication is not a good or dependable strategy, unless it is closely integrated with code design. This integration means constantly reviewing the data members of packages, and moving data members as appropriate to avoid inconsistencies and incoherencies in the package design.

To keep the code structure simple and intelligible we avoided as much as possible the use of inheritance. Some of ILab's dialog packages are derived from existing Tk packages, but this derivation is only one level deep, and fairly transparent. The only data structure that requiring inheritance is our JobModel package, because (1) we have several "job models" already, and they have enough similarities and differences to justify the existence of a base class and (2) more derived job models will need to be added in the future, as ILab is expanded to accommodate more meta-computing environments. The various job models are described in section 5.

Perl is a highly flexible language. We were able to further simplify our packages by giving the package members and the get/set functions the same names, since the Perl interpreter distinguishes the variable from the function syntactically; the variable is $reference->{name}, and the function $reference->name. Note that Perl already makes it easy to collapse get and set functions into one function, so that only one function accompanies each data member.

Here is an example of this approach in our Job package, showing the new (constructor) function, two data members, (JobID and Status) and the Status (get/set) function associated with the Status data member:

```perl
package Job;

sub new {
    my $class = shift;
    my $self  = {};
    $self->{JobID} = undef;
    $self->{Status} = 'NotStarted';
    bless $self, $class;
    return $self;
}

sub Status {  # Only allow one of six strings for this field
    my $self = shift;
    my $temp = $_[0] if @_;
    if ( defined( $temp ) ) # set variable if argument passed in
        {
        if ( $temp eq 'NotStarted' || $temp eq 'Queued'  ||
             $temp eq 'Running'    || $temp eq 'Stopped' ||
             $temp eq 'Failed'     || $temp eq 'Done' )
            { $self->{Status} = $temp; }
        else  { print "illegal job status = $temp\n"; }
        }
    return $self->{Status}; # get func. always returns variable
}
```

In a large program this "same-name" model reduces the number of occurrences where the programmer has to reference another part of the code to ensure that names are correct. For those packages that need to be made into base packages (for derivation of mostly similar but slightly different packages), we extend the object-oriented approach by putting the package variables into a "closure", thereby making these data members less accessible to programming users of the base class.

5   Job Models

We describe the various job models that ILab currently supports in order of increasing complexity. The simplest represents an entirely local capability, i.e., all jobs making up the parameter study are submitted for execution on the local machine. The runs occur without the assistance of a scheduler, but may include a parallel job launcher such as "mpirun". ILab generates for each run in the parameter study a single shell script, which constructs a main directory for the whole study (if one doesn't already exist), and then builds its own subdirectory, uniquely named with an automatically generated parameterization identifier. Files required for input by the user's executable are copied into the respective subdirectories. The executable is then started. Because no scheduler is assumed, jobs are run sequentially to avoid oversubscribing the local system. This is accomplished by chaining the shell scripts: the first script does its work and then submits the next script in the chain, etc. This chaining proceeds even if some command within a script fails (e.g., the user's primary compute executable).

The second job model launches jobs onto a cluster of machines (which may include the originating machine), on which the user has accounts and an appropriate ".rhosts" file. Each job is implemented with a pair of shell scripts. The first remote-copies (Unix "rcp") the second script to the remote machine and then executes (Unix "rsh") it there. It is the second shell script that creates and organizes directory layout on the remote host, and which starts the chain of computation. This job model currently makes no use of schedulers. We have not built in any mechanism for limiting the number of concurrently running jobs on any individual resource. This implies that the individual compute resources may become oversubscribed. We are planning to add a non-scheduler-based job "limiter" into this job model.

The third job model is similar to the second, except that the presence of a scheduler is assumed. When the scheduler is PBS, the first shell script submits to the scheduler a script containing PBS directives followed by shell commands.

The fourth job model assumes that the Globus metacomputing middleware is used for remote job submission and file manipulation and that a scheduler (PBS) is used for queuing and starting jobs. The remote script is similar to that of the third job model.

None of the above shell scripts need to be provided by the user; they are automatically generated by ILab. In each of the above cases, a parallel job loader (currently MPI is supported) may be specified.

Currently files are not cached on the remote systems at the time of job submission. We assume a production level environment requiring routing through a job scheduler. This implies that the third and fourth job models will be the most heavily used. The typical usage scenario is that a suite of jobs is submitted through a scheduler, and that the compute resource is shared with other users. The time for the parameter study to complete will often be numbered in days, not hours or minutes. This is based on experience at NASA research centers and on knowledge of the types of parameter studies users are contemplating. Such computations frequently utilize volatile scratch file systems when user allocations of permanent file-system space are insufficient to accommodate the input and output files of substantial parameter studies. Advance copying of files is therefore risky, since cached input may have been purged by a file scrubber by the time an individual job is started by the scheduler. However, we have devised a method for just-in-time caching. It guarantees that (1) only one process copies an input file to a cache, which avoids clobbering (involves lock file), and (2) that files previously cached, but subsequently deleted by a scrubber, are re-cached on demand by the client job. We will add these capabilities to the third and fourth job models.

Utilizing shell scripts has several advantages. Unix shell languages are the "lingua-franca" of Unix JCL. Our choice is the Korn shell [10], a highly expressive language for constructing sequences of commands, and for error-trapping them. In the Korn shell, background processes and "co-processes" (background processes that can communicate with the parent process) are easily created. Processes may also be easily monitored, and killed if necessary. Another advantage of using shell scripts is that they may be invoked independently of the GUI. There is no requirement that only the ILab GUI start user processes. Users may modify the shell scripts for their own purposes; they are"recyclable." The commands in the scripts are interleaved with output statements, which leave a record of their workings which acts as a log.

ILab may, in part, be described as a GUI that collects information on the locations of the user's executable and input files, and assembles shell scripts for running this executable. It is fairly easy to change existing job models or add new ones, which is accomplished simply by modifying the script generating code within ILab. In order to simplify the addition of future job models to ILab, we used the object inheritance capabilities of Perl to create a base `JobModel` package and several derived packages (`LocalJobModel`, `GlobusJobModel`, etc.). New derived job models, e.g. for the meta-computing environments Condor and Legion, can be easily inserted into the existing framework.

It is possible, and easy, to use ILab to launch single jobs (i.e. a singleton parameter study) into a local or remote compute environment that may require any of Globus, PBS, and/or MPI. Thus, ILab may be used simply as a convenient Unix JCL script generator for launching single jobs. This is especially beneficial when a job will be run on a remote system and requires the migration of input files and executable.

6   Parameter Study Example - A Case Study

Until recently, parameter studies of aerospace vehicle flow characteristics utilized mostly two-dimensional computational fluid dynamics (CFD) solvers. This was partly dictated by limitations in the available compute resources (CPU time and memory size). Recently, however, because of the increased availability of multi-processor machines with large memories, parameter studies based on three-dimensional CFD codes have become feasible. Nevertheless, the overhead for such large studies remains high. As an example, we chose the Overflow three-dimensional Navier-Stokes flow solver [11], which employs the overset grid method (overlapping curvilinear grids exchange interpolated boundary information at each time-step). The MPI parallel version of Overflow groups neighboring grids for solution onto individual processors. We used Overflow to compute the flow field of the X38 Crew Return Vehicle (CRV), a NASA space vehicle. Fig. 3 depicts the X38 CRV and several of the body-fitted curvilinear grids defining its surface. The complete configuration consists of 13 curvilinear body-fitted grids and 115 rec-tilinear off-body grids, totaling approximately 2.5 million points. Overflow uses some

40 double-precision words of memory per grid point, which results in a total memory requirement of approximately 800 MB per run.

We chose to create a 16 × 12 parameter study for two significant flow variables in a portion of the glide regime of the X38: Mach number (normalized vehicle velocity) and Alpha ("angle-of-attack"). This results in a two-dimensional parametric study consisting of 192 runs. Each run for the X38 vehicle requires four processors.

Using ILab involves the following steps. First, the user supplies a name and directory for the "experiment", which is where the records for this study will be kept. Then, the local and remote machines on which the runs will occur are selected. Next, an input file directory, and the input file(s) to be parameterized, are specified. Input files are displayed in the special-purpose graphical editor, and parameterized as described in section 4.1, producing 192 parameterized input files. Next, the user identifies the executable name and location and also a directory where the run subdirectories will be rooted on each of the executing hosts. Options for specifying MPI, Globus, and PBS, and number of processors (four per run, in this case) are set. At this point, the appropriate shell scripts are generated and then initiated. This entire entry process takes under five minutes. If starting from a previous experiment, an MRU file may be selected, permitting the user to make appropriate modifications through the same widgets used to create a new experiment. For cases like that described above, it usually takes under a minute to create and start an entire parameter study.

Two machines were selected for running the jobs, each supporting MPI, Globus, and PBS. The scripts generated by ILab conformed to our fourth job model. ILab submitted all jobs to PBS queues on the selected machines, and within approximately 24 hours all jobs completed. From the resulting solutions we constructed a plot of the coefficient of lift over drag (Cl/Cd) for the X38 CRV. See Fig. 4. Every point in the lattice represents a complete flow solution.

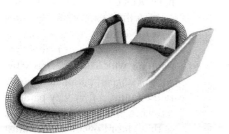

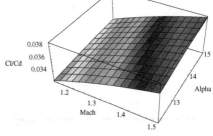

Fig. 3. X38 Crew Return Vehicle with several of its computational body grids

Fig. 4. Coefficient of lift over drag for the X38 CRV

7   CAD Tool Process Specification

Currently, all information describing the user's process is collected through a series of previous-and-next-wizards, guiding the user through the process specification procedure. Though this model is acceptable for single stage parameterizations, it quickly becomes inadequate for specifying complex user processes. These may include several stages of parameterization, pre- and post-processing of data, archiving of data, resubmission and restarting of user programs, feedback loops to accommodate multidisciplinary optimization, etc. Currently, we are building a visual capability for complex process specification, providing an alternative to the wizard mechanism. It consists of a CAD tool for constructing a data-flow diagram describing the user's set of processes. The user creates a diagram by choosing individual process element icons from a palette and placing them in the diagram by mouse operations. Each icon represents a basic process building block, such as input file parameterization, moving, copying, or renaming files, running an executable, etc. At each node of the diagram a context-sensitive pop-up dialog queries the user for the necessary details. Internally, a directed graph representing the entire set of processes in the Experiment is created, e.g., a parameterization, followed by the execution of a simulation program, followed by the execution of post-processing program(s) and archiving. This graph is interpreted, and the required individual shell scripts are constructed from the information stored at each node. The construction process consists of assembling the required shell scripts from macros, small groups of ILab-provided shell commands that perform the requested operation.

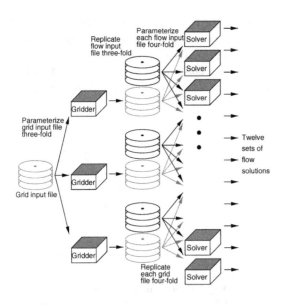

Fig. 5. Multi-stage parameterization process

Fig. 5 depicts an example of a multi-stage parameterization process. In the first stage, input to a grid generation program (Gridder) is parameterized, resulting in three input files. After running the grid generator, three grid systems have been created. These grid systems will be part of the input to a flow solver (Solver), as will a flow variables input file. It is this flow input file which is subjected to the second stage of parameterization. In the figure, a four-way parameterization has been applied. Each of these four flow input files must be replicated three times to be paired with the three grid files, and each of the grid files must be replicated four times for pairing with the flow input. The result is essentially a two-dimensional parameter study (3 × 4), but it has resulted from two independent stages of parameterization. This adds a higher degree of complexity to the user's process, and consequently, to the mechanisms required for assembling and running these jobs. It is, in part, for this reason that we are constructing a more powerful user interface mechanism for specifying and creating parameterization processes.

Summary

The needs of our user community have triggered the development of ILab, a flexible parameter study creation and job submission tool. This modern GUI implements a modular experimental workbench for programming research into local and remote job submission methods, complex user process specification technology, and for experimentation with IPG middleware. Our choice of Perl/Tk as a rapid-prototyping development language strongly facilitates experimentation and anticipated further expansion of the core user GUI capabilities. We have proven our ILab product with significant parameter study computations in a distributed environment. We are currently working closely with users whose parameter study requirements are demanding. We are adding these new capabilities to ILab using an advanced CAD-based user-interface technology.

References

1. Foster, I., Kesselman, C.: Globus: A Metacomputing Infrastructure Toolkit. Intl J. Supercomputer Applications, 11(2):115-128, 1997
2. Grimshaw, A., Ferrari, A.,Knabe, F., Humphrey, M.: Legion: An Operating System for Wide-Area Computing. Dept. of Comp. Sci., U. of Virginia, Charlottesville, Va. Available at ftp://ftp.cs.virginia.edu/pub/techreports/CS-99-12.ps.Z
3. NASA Information Power Grid:
   http://www.nas.nasa.gov/Pubs/NASnews/97/09/ipg_fig1.html and
   http://www.nas.nasa.gov/Groups/Tools/IPG/
4. Clustor (now called Enfuzion): http://www.turbolinux.com/products/enf/enfuzion.html
5. Abramson, D., Sosic, R.,Giddy, J., Hall, B.: Nimrod: A Tool for Performing Parametised Simulations using Distributed Workstations. The 4th IEEE Symposium on High Performance Distributed Computing, Virginia, August 1995
6. Henderson, R., and D. Tweten, D.: NASA Ames Portable Batch System: External Reference Specification. NASA Ames Research Center, December 1996
7. LSF: http://www.platform.com/
8. Litzkow, M., Livny, M.: Experience With The Condor Distributed Batch System. IEEE Workshop on Experimental Distributed Systems, Oct. 1990, Huntsville, Al. http://www.cs.wisc.edu/condor/publications.html
9. SpecTcl: http://dev.scriptics.com/software/spectcl
10. Bolsky, M. I., Korn, D. G.: The KornShell Command and Programming Language. Prentice Hall, 1989
11. Wissink, A. W., Meakin, R. L.: On Parallel Implementations of Dynamic Overset Grid Methods. Proceedings of SC97, High Performance Computing and Networking, San Jose, CA, Nov. 15-21, 1997

Mini-Grids: Effective Test-Beds for GRID Application

John Brooke, Martyn Foster, Stephen Pickles, Keith Taylor, and Terry Hewitt[1]

MRCCS, University of Manchester, Oxford Road, Manchester M13 9PL,
j.m.brooke@man.ac.uk,
http://www.csar.cfs.ac.uk/staff/brooke

Abstract. We describe a computing environment that we call a mini-GRID . This represents a hetereogeneous group of resources for computation, data storage, archival and visualization which can be connected via private or public networks to other resources (called guest systems) on a temporary basis as required. The mini-GRID displays the heterogeneity and some of the complexity of a full computational GRID, but in a more limited environment and can be considered to be under the control of a few organisations (or even a single organisation) making non-technical organisational issues less problematic. As such, the mini-GRID provides a flexible and controllable, but realistic test-bed for trialling GRID applications, particularly with regard to issues such as accounting and resource brokering. However, its heterogeneity, the size and complexity of the architectures involved, and its integral connection with local, national and super-national networks, prevent it from being considered as a cluster of workstations.

1 What Is a Mini-GRID?

We describe in this paper an environment that we call a "mini-GRID". This is a collection of computational and data processing resources that has a heterogeneous structure (multi-architecture, multiple levels of data storage) but is organisationally simple, e.g. under the control of a single organisation. We consider these mini-GRIDs to be of research interest in two ways. Firstly, a likely structure for the development of the world-wide GRID is the gradual connection and integration of such local GRIDs, each serving both its own hinterland and also acting as a node for wide-area applications. Secondly, because they are of sufficient complexity to test out key middle-ware components of the GRID, e.g. coupled applications, resource brokers, accounting and billing systems, without needing to address questions of local or national autonomy. We follow the line of thought developed in Chapter 1 of [1] that the development of the GRID involves the simultaneous development of local and remote links, the development of the railway infrastructure around Chicago being an example. The particular mini-GRID that we describe is based on services provided at the University of Manchester for both local and UK-wide use. The UK-wide service is called

R. Buyya and M. Baker (Eds.:) GRID 2000, LNCS 1971, pp. 158–169, 2000.

CSAR (Computing Services for Academic Research) and is provided by a consortium CfS (Computation for Science) which is a collaboration between CSC, the University of Manchester and SGI. From its very conception this service was envisaged as being multi-component and not necessarily restricted to a particular vendors hardware. It is a dynamic configuration, that can be added to by the provision of guest machines based either at Manchester or at other CfS sites (e.g. CSC Supercomputer Centre at Farnborough). However, because it is intended to be viewed as a single resource in terms of funding, an internal economy has needed to be developed that allows for the conversion and trading of resources between the various components of the service. We describe this economy further in Section 1. This economy has been operating since late 1998 and provides valuable lessons for other GRID projects since some sort of GRID economy will have to emerge to permit the sharing and inter-convertibility of resources. We show the current CSAR configuration in Figure 1, for more information about CSAR and CfS see http://www.csar.cfs.ac.uk

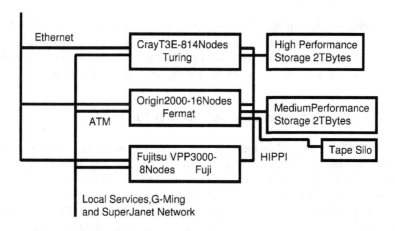

Fig. 1. The current CSAR con guration showing the multi-architectural structure. Guest systems can be added to this as required. There are three levels of data storage, high-performance attached to the T3E, medium peformance attached to the O2000 and tape-archiving via the tape silo.

Our mini-GRID also includes services provided over a local high-speed network covering the North-West of England. This originally started as a 155-Mbit/s ATM network covering the Greater Manchester area (G-MING in Figure 1). This has been extended to other sites in the North-West of England, primarily educational institutions. These networks allow local colleges, hospitals, local government offices and local businesses to access centralised facilities creating a local GRID. Since this GRID connects through the University of Manchester which is becoming a node on continental and trans-continental GRIDs, we have a route by which local access can grow to world-wide access. We briefly describe in Section 5 a project which has used the local GRID in both of these ways and we show how this could be integrated into the economy developed under the CSAR service, to allow the GRID node to recover costs from local users and give an incentive to expand its service for local access.

The plan of this research note is to present the results of ongoing experiments designed to explore the exploitation of the mini-GRID structure described above. In Section 2 we describe work on running coupled simulations across the differing components of the CSAR configuration. Section 1 describes the development of the internal mini-GRID resource economy. Section 4 describes experiments designed to test the usefulness of the Globus toolkit in this context. Section 5 describes the links over metropolitan and regional networks and how this is being extended to provide global links. Finally we draw some preliminary conclusions in Section 6 and describe some new projects which will extend the functionality of the mini-GRID.

2   Running Coupled Applications in a Mini-GRID

We describe work to utilise the core mini-GRID structure of the CSAR service (Figure 1) for running coupled applications. Since we wish to run between machines, current vendor-supplied versions of MPI cannot be used and we investigated both PVM and special MPI libraries for running across machines.

2.1   PVM - Its Continuing Role as a Grid Builder

PVM, Parallel Virtual Machine [2] first made its public appearance as Version 2, back in March 1991. Since then it has expanded and prospered, becoming available on an ever widening range of machine architectures; until, now, we have reached Version 3.4.

Being familiar, the virtues of PVM and its usefulness for GRID work is sometimes ignored. PVM lacks some of the 'sophistication' of MPI, with the latter's Derived Datatypes, and support for Cartesian mesh-based communications, for example. However, PVM's big strength remains: the fact that is was designed from the outset for connecting together collections of physically-separated heterogeneous machines, something which MPI is only beginning to address with initiatives like PACX-MPI [3] and STAMPI [4]. PVM's range of facilities may be limited to the essentials, but these provide all that is required to send data back and forth, between different computer systems, including well-defined procedures for installing the software, starting it up, and building and operating a desired configuration.

Prompted by the OCCAM [5] group's need to couple a shared-memory atmosphere model running on an SGI Origin2000 with an ocean model running on a Cray T3E-1200E, (Fermat and Turing respectively in Figure 1), we developed a demonstrator which proved the PVM concept for this application [6]. It was subsequently successfully developed to harness the two models for real production runs. Some lessons were learnt along the way.

Firstly, in order to utilise the inter-machine functionality of PVM, it was sometimes necessary to undo the carefully hand-crafted 'optimizations' which manufacturers have included (for performance reasons) in their machine specific implementations of PVM. For example, in the T3E version, only the first task, by default, communicates via the daemon, for the others `send` and `receive` are implemented on top of SHMEM. Source and target tasks are identified by non-portable processor numbers, rather than the standard task identifiers which would otherwise be allocated by the daemon. This non-standard behaviour prevents any task other than the first from seeing the outside world, completely opposing one of PVM's philosophical foundations. But, fortunately, if required, one can restore full visibility and task identifiers by setting an environment variable, `PVM_PE_LIST`, to `all`.

Secondly, bits may be missing from a particular implementation. For example, it was necessary to install the public-domain version of PVM over SGI's for the Origin2000, before we received a sensible error message which indicated the true cause of a problem we were having. It turned out that the encoding `PVMDATAINPLACE` was not implemented for `PVMFINITSEND` on SGI machines. This was absent from the documentation. Subsequent to our notifying the vendor, a documentation bug report was issued, but the omission remains.

Thirdly, PVM, like any other grid-creating system, relies heavily on the integrity of the underlying network. Our attempts to extend the demonstrator to include CSAR's 8-processor Fujitsu VPP300 (Fuji in Figure 1) were unsuccessful, for reasons still unknown. Briefly, communications between 'Fermat' and 'Fuji' were unreliable, in a non-repeatable way. They may have been affected by the level of other traffic on the ATM line connecting the two machines, and thus various internal timeouts came into play, causing 'hang-ups'.

2.2   Implications for GRID Computing

PVM already has a rudimentary way of measuring and comparing the performance of participating machines for the purpose of load-balancing. (This is made evident when one examines the list of component architectures from the 'console'.) This is a topic of considerable interest in running distributed applications over the GRID. It may be that the existing and very much alive PVM could be enhanced to encompass a more suitably refined description. The work described here is available at [6]. For a description of using PACX-MPI across a global metacomputer see [7]. Our experiments here highlight the need for reliable message passing libraries that can run across machines of different architectures and which adhere to internationally agreed standards.

3   Accounting for Resource Usage on a Mini-GRID

The University of Manchester has developed a web-based user registration system, which has been used for some years now in the administration of both local and national computing services. Features that this system provide include project management, resource allocation, and user self-registration. In 1998, the advent of the CSAR service, a privately financed initiative, saw extensive enhancements to the registration system, especially in the areas of resource management and accounting. The new facilities were developed in response to:

1. demand from the UK academic HPC community for the ability to use allocated resources in a more flexible manner, and
2. the need to account to the funding bodies.

We claim that the problems of resource management and accounting will be of increasing importance to HPC service providers, and that satisfactory solutions to these problems in the context of grid computing do not yet exist. We therefore describe our solutions in the simpler context of a mini-GRID, where the issues of cross-institutional co-operation and site autonomy do not arise. It is our thesis that many aspects of our solutions must be reflected in solutions to the general, pan-institutional problem.

When a research council approves a peer-reviewed application for computing resources on the CSAR service, a new project is set up in the registration system.

The right of a project to utilise computing resources of various types (eg. CPU time, disk and tape storage on specific machines) is represented by quantities of *specific resource tokens* of corresponding types. Tokens are valid for the lifetime of the project.

In addition to specific resource tokens, we also introduce generic service tokens. Generic service tokens have a notional cash equivalent, indicative of the expected cost of the project to the research councils.[1] In agreement with the research councils, exchange rates between generic and specific resource tokens are fixed from time to time, to reflect depreciation of the underlying asset. Table 1 shows the exchange rates currently in force.

Table 1. Resource exchange rates in the CSAR service e ective as of June 2000.

Resource Token	Value in Generic Tokens
1 T3E PE Hour	0.024
1 Gbyte-Year of T3E Disk	6.752
1 Origin 2000 CPU Hour	0.025
1 Gbyte-Year of O2000 Disk	4.292
1 Gbyte-Year of HSM/Tape	0.596
1 Fujitsu VPP CPU Hour	0.345
1 Gbyte-Year of Fujitsu Disk	4.292
1 Day training	3.000
1 Day support	11.364

The computing resources required by a project are listed on a schedule accompanying the original grant application. The schedule also lists the amount of each resource expected to be consumed in each six-month period of

---

[1] The research councils are billed periodically according to actual usage.

the life of the project. The CSAR service provides a web-based *resource calculator* `http://www.csar.cfs.ac.uk/admin/forms/calculator.shtml` to assist the principle investigator in preparing this schedule. New projects are primed with sufficient generic service tokens to meet the expected requirements. Before a project can begin to use the service, the generic tokens must be traded for specific resource tokens. The initial trade is often performed by CSAR staff, but may be performed by the principle investigator if desired. A project may subsequently trade unused resource tokens of one type for resource tokens of another type, subject to availability of the desired resource. The flexibility that this provides is one of the factors that differentiates CSAR from its predecessors in the UK.

We impose a minimum period between successive trades by any one project in order to avoid abuses such as exploitation of arbitrage opportunities arising out of possible rounding errors, or attempts to corner the market in a limited resource.

The number of specific resource tokens of any type in the trading pool at any one time is limited so as to reflect the (projected) capacity that the service can provide.

A project's cumulative usage of each resource is updated daily in batch mode. CPU time and tape storage are charged on the basis of actual consumption. Permanent disk storage is charged according to integrated disk quota, sampled daily; note however that the principle investigator is empowered to alter disk quotas freely between a lower limit of actual usage and an upper limit set by CSAR. Principal investigators are notified automatically when the project's usage of a resource first exceeds 90%, 95% and 100% of the total available; the third notification is accompanied by a withdrawal of access privileges.

It is in the interest of any HPC provider to optimize the capacity of the service to meet projected demand. Under-utilized resources are obviously undesirable. On the other hand, having insufficient resources makes it necessary to turn work away; but if the increased demand can be anticipated, it is possible to finance the purchase of additional hardware. We facilitate this by introducing a *capacity plan* for each new project, capturing the projected usage from the schedule on the original grant application, and encouraging principle investigators to review these capacity plans as their projects develop.

We believe that the regulated micro-economy embodied in our registration, trading pool, capacity planning and accountancy systems has features that most providers of pay-as-you-go supercomputing services should find desirable. We encourage grid developers to take cognizance of the considerations that have informed our approach, as these are likely to be shared by the supercomputing centres that will become the major grid nodes of the future. Although we are not advocating the introduction of resource tokens on a global scale, we think that the resource brokers of a truly ubiquitous computational grid must embrace some kind of currency to mediate negotiations, and that grid nodes must not only be able to advertise availability of resources but also to contract to a pricing policy when accepting an offered job.

4   Globus on the Mini-GRID

We describe work in progress to evaluate how Globus [8] can be adapted to serve our mini-GRID environment. We deployed Globus (1.1.2) on a variety of workstation and server machines including the Cray T3E, Origin 2000, Solaris and Linux workstations. We found no major obstacle with the installation of the software on these platforms though some scripts needed tuning to individual system requirements. All batch queue systems used were NQE/NQS based. Some questions were raised regarding the overhead of running Globus on HPC machines, these are still being studied. Our aim was to develop tools which allowed a uniform job submission interface to the different machines on the mini-GRID (see Figure 1). The requirement to make this user-friendly meant that the Globus command-line interface had to be adapted. We were able to develop software which was attractive and simpler to use than the default tools supplied by vendors with the batch system. With further effort these tools could be expanded to provide a much more flexible approach to high performance computing.

An important aspect of the Globus environment is the seamless transition between scales of computing resource. Globus comes into its own when operational practice migrates the user from the workstation through super-computing centre to specialized resource, without changing working practice significantly. However without developing a uniform job submission interface, the divide between HPC and desktop processing will remain in the near future. The job submission models supported by Globus are insufficiently sophisticated to cope with typical methods employed by the CSAR user community. There exists other software designed for job submission which overcomes some of these limitations, the UNICORE project being a key example [9]. A rapprochement of the Globus and Unicore approaches would seem to be very much in the interest of users of resources such as the mini-GRID described here.

Outside the administrative domain, Globus is found to provide the necessary infrastructure to enhance utilization of computing resources around the UK. In particular the local grid environment can be extended to encompass other major computing facilities in the UK. This activity is mainly centered upon coupling the T3E machines at Edinburgh (EPCC) and Manchester (CSAR), in order to balance the job load between the two machines. Initially the mechanism employed will be to prioritize queues on each machine for different classes of job and publishing estimates of execution time for various job specification via the MDS. In the longer term this may be replaced or complemented by a knowledge-based third party broker.

5   A Metropolitan Area GRID

The computing service at the University of Manchester has an important role in the provision of networking and high-performance services over metropolitan and regional networks. These utilise ATM at 155 Mbits/s, allowing the creation of Permanent Virtual Circuits (PVCs) giving a guarenteed networking Quality of Service (QoS). We describe here results from two projects that show in different ways how issues arising from provision of services delivered locally via the mini_GRID has implications for the development of global GRID services. In the RCNET [10] project, a collaboration between a local engineering consultancy (REL) and the University of Manchester allowed REL to move and coordinate its engineering work on a global scale. This involved connecting the company network to GMING and thus providing a route to European and global networks. This is important to REL because their mode of operation means that they typically establish working offices in areas where their services arise and these may migrate around the globe according to developments in, for example, the oil industry. These satellite offices may be very "light" in terms of equipment and so access to remote processing power is essential. Also the company's technical experts may be geographically distributed and video-conferencing and collaborative working are highly desirable.

5.1   Use of GMING

There were two ways in which access to the metropolititan-area network GMING changed the working practice of REL. Firstly, access to large servers at the University of Manchester allowed REL to run jobs which were too big for their workstations. These were run on two central machines, a Fujitsu VPX240 vector processor and an SGI Origin2000. A cost-benefit analysis was carried out to determine the savings to REL of using the local GRID in this way, rather than purchasing extra expensive workstations. This analysis is available at the RCNET WWW site [10].

Secondly the RCNET workstations were networked via an ATM switch and a link was made to a similar cluster of SG Indy workstations at UoM. The ATM technology allowed the two ATM switches linking these clusters to be connected and the two clusters were then both part of the same emulated LAN. This allowed parallel jobs to be run across the clusters and allowed the possibility of extra work from REL to be run on the UoM cluster, thus freeing REL workstations for intensive pre and post processing. LSF was used to manage the load on the UoM cluster, and account of the performance of the cluster under varying loads is given in [11].

A different use of GMING is also shown by the NOVICE project in which a large visualization server available over GMING allows hospitals throughout the Greater Manchester Conurbation to visualize medical scans from patients records. The visualization would be impossible on local equipment, since it is insufficiently powered to perform manipulation of very large datasets and to run specialist visualization software. An important feature of NOVICE is that images from the central server are sent to the remote stations using VRML. There are very delicate issues of security since private medical records are being delivered via the local GRID. These issues are all very relevant to the wider GRID, more details can be found via the NOVICE WWW site at [12].

5.2   Extension of the Local GRID to Intercontinental Networks

In the RCNET project videoconferencing experiments were carried out between the Norwegian National Point of Presence in Oslo and the University of Manchester over the pan-European JAMES ATM network. REL(Manchester) offices are close to the University and thus a means for collaborative working was established. The main aim of the experiments was to test Quality of Service networking issues by comparing the running of videoconferencing and collaborative working over two routes, the normal Internet traffic and a dedicated ATM PVC (Permanent Virtual Circuit) which established a guaranteed bandwidth of 2 Mbits/s. The qualitative results were that videoconferencing and collaborative working were much better over the ATM PVC even though the bandwidth of the Internet route was potentially greater (34 Mbits/s). Quantitative experiments were performed to ascertain the reason for this difference.

Table 2. Comparison of the mean time and standard deviation (SD) of les of various sizes. The les were transferred between Manchester and Norway between identical machines but via two routes, an ATM PVC of 2 Mbits/s and an internet shared tra c route at 34 Mbits/s.

File Size	ATM Mean	ATM SD	Internet Mean	Internet SD
1 Mbyte	198.0 kbytes/s	2.7 kbytes/s	314.6 kbytes/s	145.9 kbytes/s
5Mbyte	199.5 kbytes/s	5.5 kbytes/s	241.3 kbytes/s	69.2 kbytes/s
10Mbyte	203.3 kbytes/s	3.2 kbytes/s	251.9 kbytes/s	27.2 kbytes/s
50Mbyte	191.3 kbytes/s	0.9 kbytes/s	260.7 kbytes/s	26.1 kbytes/s

A full account of the experiments is available at [10] but the most telling were the results of sending files of different sizes via ftp. We present these results in Table 2. It will be seen that the mean rate of transfer for both methods is comparable but the standard deviation is much lower for the ATM as would be expected. The size of file transmitted makes a considerable difference to the standard deviation over the internet route. Our conjecture is that this is because the file transmission time for sending a large file is much greater than the time scale on which the shared-traffic internet route bandwith varies. We draw the analogy with turbulent fluid flow; on length and time scales greater than those of the turbulence the flow can appear to be smooth. Our qualitative and quantitative results indicate that for applications such as videoconferencing and distributed collaborative working, the effects of this "network turbulence" over shared-traffic routes needs to be taken into account.

Another important factor is latency, which is very low in an ATM PVC. To test the effect of this factor we performed tests on the startup of the Netscape browser, both locally and remotely (Figure 2). This latter involves the sending of many messages of different sizes between the two sites, it thus illustrates in a simple way some of the performance issues involved in distributed collaborative working.

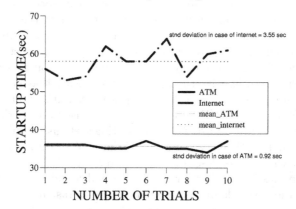

Fig. 2. Comparison of Netscape startup for ATM and Internet. The two routes are as described in Table 2

5.3   The Modular Structure of the GRID

The RCNET project was conceived before the concept of the GRID was drawn to the international community. However the whole networking and processing of RCNET is based on a modular structure, going from local to global and indicates clearly the considerations that we discuss in Sections 1 and 6. What needs to be supplied for this to be a working model, is a reliable layer of middleware that can direct jobs on the local GRIDs to centres of computational power, e.g. a resource broker. Also, there needs to be some means of "costing" this work and addressing QoS issues (for a commercial firm turnaround time may be crucial to meet their contracts). The issue of costing is taken up in Section 1. The question of a resource broker is a subject for future work.

6   Conclusion and Future Plans

As William of Occam pointed out in the 13th century, it is bad scientific practice to introduce a term unless it helps to reduce and clarify the scientific description of phenomena. An objection to the term "mini-GRID" as used here would be that there is scaling at all levels on the GRID, hence the term "mini-GRID" is meaningless. Our argument in this paper is that there is a natural structural scale for a mini-GRID, related to the wider GRID as a modular structure. Firstly the mini-GRID should relate to a particular, defined, networking complex. We suggest that a good candidate is a metropolitan area network or a node on an intercontinental GRID. Thus the mini-GRID will have an internal structure. We think that many academic supercomputing centres are likely to develop in this way. They can stabilise their funding by using their specialist expertise to attract income from local industry. In a less quantifiable fashion, by providing services to schools and civic organisations they can help to make the spending of public money more politically acceptable. An example of this sort of consideration, is the siting of large scale computing resources in regions where it is desirable to stimulate economic and social development. The Federal Swiss supercomputing centre CSCS is an example [13]. Other reasons why we predict that nodes on the computational GRID are likely to have a multi-component structure of the scale we describe here, involve the increased probability that new architectures are likely to be funded at sites that have proven expertise and a critical mass of expertise. Running a GRID node requires expertise in networking, hardware support, maintenance of infrastructure, operating systems, programming, numerical methods and particular scientific disciplines. We return to the analogy of the growth of Chicago as described in Chapter 1 of [1]. All industrialised societies develop cities on major infrastructure nodes and the development of a city involves a feedback loop. As population and infrastructure is attracted to a transportation node, more local infrastructure is needed to serve this, which attracts more population and infrastructure, in a positive feedback loop.

We believe that there is strong evidence that nodes on the GRID will need to be of a certain size and complexity to be self-sustaining. There will certainly be GRID structure below this size but it will tend to associate with a major GRID node. The GRID node can regulate an organizational regime that enables middleware, such as resource brokers, to access its resources on both sub-node and super-node scales. Between such nodes, there is a layer of political and organisational complexity and difficulty over and above the technical challenges involved.

The work we describe here on the scale of our mini-GRID is helping to clarify some of these issues, both technical and organisational. We seek to open a dialogue with other centres who recognize this mini-GRID concept as being useful. We are encouraged that the work described here is to be continued via a major European Union project, EUROGRID, which aims to connect major European sites each of which could be regarded as having the mini-GRID structure as described here. The setting up of a GRID structure across the European Union is of particular interest in the context of a global GRID, since the European Union is a federation of politically independent states with national funding councils for scientific research. There is also a strong emphasis in the EU Fifth Framework [14] on improving the quality of life for EU citizens. Thus the local aspects of the mini-GRID as described in Section 5 become very relevant.

Acknowledgements. The authors are grateful to all those who contributed to the design and development of the registration system and trading pool, especially Phil Stringer, Geoff Lane, Victoria Pennington and John Rawlins. Thanks to Fumie Costen for producing the figures.

References

1. I.Foster and C. Kesserlman, editors. *The GRID: Blueprint for a new computing infrastructure*. Morgan Kaufmann Publishers, Inc., San Francisco, California, 1998

2. For PVM details see URL http://www.epm.ornl.gov/pvm/pvm_home.html
3. Edgar Gabriel, Michael Resch, Thomas Beisel, Rainer Keller, 'Distributed Computing in a heterogenous computing environment' in Vassil Alexandrov, Jack Dongarra (Eds.) 'Recent Advances in Parallel Virtual Machine and Message Passing Interface', Lecture Notes in Computer Science, Springer, 1998, pp 180-188.
4. H. Koide, et al, *MPI based communication library for a heterogeneous parallel computer cluster, Stampi*, Japan Atomic Energy Research Institute, http://ssp.koma.jaeri.go.jp/en/stampi.html
5. The OCCAM group maintain highly-tuned models of global ocean circulation: see URL http://www.soc.soton.ac.uk/JRD/OCCAM/welcome.html
6. *Running PVM Interactively Across Turing and Fermat*, K.Taylor, CSAR Technical Report, 1999. Available at URL http://www.csar.cfs.ac.uk/sta /taylor
7. S. Pickles, F. Costen, J. Brooke, E. Gabriel, M. Müller, M. Resch, S. Ord, *The problems and the solutions of the metacomputing experiment in SC99*, in Marian Bubak, Hamideh Afsarmanesh, Roy Williams, Bob Hertzberger (Eds.) HPCN (Europe) 2000 Proceedings, Lecture Notes in Computer Science, Springer, 2000, pp 22-31
8. Details of the Globus project can be found at URL http://www.globus.org
9. Details of the Unicore project are at URL http://www.fz-juelich.de/unicore
10. J.M. Brooke and P. Jacob, editors *RCNET: Exploiting HPCN in an Engineering Consultancy Environment* Techical Reports and Papers.
    See URL: http://www.man.ac.uk/MVC/research/rcnet/
11. F. Costen, J.M. Brooke and M.A. Pettipher *Investigation to make best use of LSF with high efficency* In Proceedings of IEEE International Conference on Cluster Computing, Melbourne 1999, 211-221
12. M. Cooper, editor *Network-Oriented Visualization in the Clinical Environment* Espirit EU Project.
    see URL http://www.man.ac.uk/MVC/projects/NOVICE/
13. The C^3 Communications and Computing Camp is described at URL://www.cscs.ch (follow links for Education).
14. Details of the EU IST Call for Proposals *Information Society Technolgies Programme* at URL http://www.cordis.lu/ist/

Configuration Method of Multiple Clusters
for the Computational Grid

Pil-Sup Shin[1], Won-Kee Hong[2], Hiecheol Kim[3], and Shin-Dug Kim[2]

[1] Sungmi Telecom electronics co., LTD., Korea
psshin@sungmi.co.kr
[2] Parallel Processing Lab., Dept. of Computer Science,
Yonsei University, Seoul, Korea
{wkhong, sdkim}@kurene.yonsei.ac.kr
[3] Computer & Communication Eng., Taegu University, Korea
hckim@biho.taegu.ac.kr

Abstract. A Java-Internet cluster platform (JIP) is designed as a computing platform on the computational grid in order to utilize a large collection of computing resources on the Internet. For this goal, a basic cluster module of JIP is de ned as a cluster of heterogeneous systems connected to a high-speed network. For a scalable JIP con guration on the computational grid, the basic cluster module can be expanded into a logical set of multiple clusters. JIP is featured with a Java based programming environment, a dynamic resource management scheme, and an e cient parallel task execution mechanism. A multiple cluster con guration is applied to decrease communication time, which is a major bottleneck of performance enhancement. According to the analysis, multiple cluster con guration can enhance the performance of JIP about 2.5 ~ 3 times depending on any application chosen comparing with a single basic cluster con guration.[1]

1 Introduction

The clustering system is considered as a cost-effective system because it is constructed with a lot of commodity systems such as PCs or workstations linked with high speed network [8], [2], [3], [9]. Recently, as the Internet is provided with powerful high-performance machines and the gigabit networks, it can offer powerful infrastructure called computational grid that can solve complex problems, e.g., Legion [5], Globus [4], and Condor [9]. These make it possible to utilize the distributed computing resources on the computational grid for efficient parallel processing.

In this research, a Java-Internet cluster platform (JIP) is designed as a computing platform that makes an efficient link of several computing resources on the computational grid into a single virtual computer to support parallel processing. For this goal, a basic cluster module of JIP is defined as a cluster of

---

[1] This work was partly supported by 1997 Research Fund from Korea Research Foundation.

R. Buyya and M. Baker (Eds.:) GRID 2000, LNCS 1971, pp. 170–180, 2000.

various computer systems connected to a high-speed network. For a scalable JIP configuration, the basic cluster module can be expanded into a logical set of multiple clusters. A basic cluster module of JIP is configured as a client, a collection of computing nodes, and a cluster management system (CMS). JIP supports a shared memory system model [1] for communication between any two computing nodes. A configuration method to allow multiple clusters as a single virtual system makes the JIP scalable with ease as the number of participating clusters increases. The JIP is featured with a Java based programming environment, a dynamic resource management scheme, and an efficient parallel task execution mechanism. Based on a prototype implementation of JIP, its configuration method, effectiveness, complexity, and the performance are presented.

The JIP is designed for two primary design issues. The first one is the implementation method of JIP that is designed by Java language [6] and multithreading feature. Java enables heterogeneous clusters as well as computing nodes to be viewed as a single system image and multithreading mechanism allows a simple and effective way to manage computing resources. The second one is the design of a CMS that coordinates the supply and demand for clusters of computing resources. As the CMS plays a role of resource management and resource allocation, JIP can maintain a global view of scalable systems and construct an optimal configuration for high performance.

Simulation is performed to show how the ratio of communication causes any impact on the overall performance of JIP and how the proposed configuration method is effective. It can be shown that a reasonable speedup can be achieved for a single basic cluster module when the number of computing nodes increases especially for data parallel applications. Also the resource management method is evaluated through the numerical analysis of communication time under JIP. Simulation results show that the proposed resource management method can provide the optimal number of clusters for given application characteristics. According to the analysis, the effective number of clusters can be determined depending on the ratio of shared write accesses over the overall shared memory references. Multiple cluster configuration can enhance the performance of JIP about $2.5 \sim 3$ times depending on any application chosen comparing with a single basic cluster configuration.

2   Java-Internet Cluster Platform

Java-Internet cluster platform (JIP) is a computing environment extending previous distributed parallel computing environment into the computational grid to run parallel applications on multiple clusters at different geographical locations. JIP is designed based on the Java language for platform independence and implemented by using existing mechanisms, namely multithreading and remote method invocation (RMI) mechanisms [6] to create and manage parallelism, which provides a unified access to system resource, called a single system image.

A basic cluster module of the JIP is constructed as a *client*, and a collection of *computing nodes* connected to a high-speed network, and a cluster management

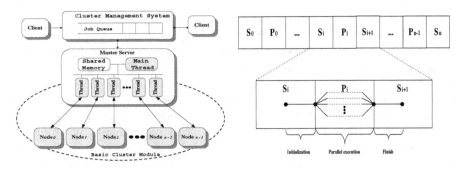

Fig. 1. Basic cluster module of JIP.   **Fig. 2.** Programming model for JIP.

system (CMS) as shown in Fig. 1. Client is a system requesting a particular job to run on the JIP and a computing node is a system that provides itself as a computing resource. A cluster is constructed as a master server (host system), and a collection of computing nodes. A master server in the cluster plays a role as a master control system, composed of a portion of shared memory for communication among computing nodes. CMS coordinates the supply and demand for computing resources and is in charge of determining a specific configuration of clusters. Because CMS also includes a job queue, multiple job requests can be processed sequentially. For a given Java application, a basic cluster module can be selected by explicit programming under configuration guideline given by the JIP. Then the CMS selects the master server as a control system to coordinate computing nodes of the selected cluster module and sends a Java parallel program. Then, the master server starts to execute a given Java application over this single virtual machine. A requested Java application is run on the top of master server and a number of threads using Java multithreading are created, where each thread is associated with one computing node. Specifically each thread is in charge of executing a block of Java code and data, called as a Java code block, on a computing node.

In the JIP, a collection of computing nodes is determined according to the proposed configuration method and its corresponding number of clusters to attain a reasonable performance gain considering communication overhead is determined. This configuration method can be expanded as a hierarchical configuration of multiple clusters to support scalability.

2.1   Effective Parallelism on JIP

As shown in Fig. 2, an application program can be represented as a set of Java code blocks under the JIP programming model, where code blocks can be divided into two types, serial code blocks (S_i) and parallel code blocks (P_i). For any chosen basic cluster module the corresponding master server will execute the serial code blocks, where parallel code blocks are executed by computing nodes within that cluster. Also the master server is in charge of controlling the overall program execution. The programmer may specify the boundary of S_i and P_i explicitly at programming time. Two code blocks, S_i and P_i, are interleaved for all i. For a given application, its corresponding system configuration is determined based on some algorithmic parameters.

In general, parallelism can be classified into function parallelism and data parallelism. A set of three code blocks, i.e., S_i, P_i, and S_{i+1}, is called as a *basic parallel module*. Specifically, applications based on function parallelism can be formed as one basic parallel module or a small number of basic parallel modules. For data parallelism, a collection of basic parallel modules is usually executed on a fixed set of computing nodes. The JIP can execute efficiently function parallelism as well as data parallelism. For those applications based on the function parallelism, the number of computing nodes can be determined by the number of independent or cooperating sub-tasks explicitly at programming time. In the case of data parallelism, programmers can specify parallelism explicitly based on a configuration method that can guide to select some system configuration parameters, i.e., the optimal number of clusters and computing nodes allocated per cluster. If the performance gain by additional parallelism is smaller than the overhead resulted from the network traffic incurred for parallel execution, the overall performance gain cannot be attained. Thus system configuration parameters should be chosen based on the trade-off between additional parallelism and the overhead incurred.

2.2   Configuration of Multiple Clusters

According to the degree of parallelism for any application, tens or hundreds of computing nodes may be used. If all computing nodes should be connected to a single master server to communicate with other computing nodes, a moderate amount of delay time will be occurred per communication and significant bottleneck problem will be caused at this centralized master server. To overcome this problem, JIP is designed for supporting multiple cluster configuration. According to the characteristics of algorithms and the patterns of shared memory references in parallel applications [7], the number of clusters is determined. Each cluster consists of one master server and multiple computing nodes.

If all the computing nodes joined for a particular job belong to several clusters, data can be classified into three types, i.e., private, locally shared, and globally shared. The private data can be accessed only by those dedicated computing nodes within a cluster. Locally shared data are shared only by a set of computing nodes belonging to a specific cluster. Globally shared data are shared among a set of chosen clusters. Thus, JIP supports a *local shared memory (LSM)* for efficient communication within a cluster. LSM is a block of shared memory allocated for each cluster and accessed by only computing nodes in the given cluster. A conventional shared memory space that can be accessed by all joined computing nodes is named as a *global shared memory (GSM)* to be distinguished from the LSM.

While one computing node is accessing its LSM to update data, other computing nodes in the same cluster should wait to access the LSM. However, the

Table 1. Variables used in numerical analysis.

Variable	Meaning	Variable	Meaning
S_{PD}	Size of Private Data	S_P	Size of a packet in unit words
S_{SD}	Size of Shared Data	N	Number of computing nodes
R_M	Ratio of SM reference instructions	G	Number of clusters
R_{MW}	Ratio of write-updates to SM references	T_{MR}	Ratio of read to SM
R_{MWL}	Ratio of LSM writes over all SM writes	R_{MWG}	Ratio of GSM writes over all SM writes
T_{SP_i}	Sequential execution time for i-th code	A	Multicasting Coefficient in master server
T_{UL}	Unit word reference time at master server	T_{UG}	Unit word reference time at CMS

other computing nodes contained in the other clusters can access their own LSM or the GSM in parallel without any delay. While a datum of GSM is updated, no computing node joined in processing can access the GSM until the current update is completed. For read-only references, LSM and GSM are accessed in the same way and all computing nodes can read the shared data independently at the same time. For write references, its procedure becomes different depending on the target, i.e., LSM or GSM. Because computing nodes in the same cluster share the LSM, only the computing nodes in the same cluster should wait until any update is completed. For the case of accessing GSM, all computing nodes should wait until the GSM is unlocked and the communication is finished to keep data coherency among GSMs in all master servers.

2.3   Global View of JIP

To accommodate a lot of users in a wide area cluster environment, CMS is very important. The CMS manages multiple clusters as one's own global virtual machine. In JIP, a client can construct a hierarchical and scalable system configuration via CMS. When a client requests a job to the CMS, the client transfers the Java parallel program with a header including the information of algorithmic characteristics, such as the degree and type of parallelism and the ratio of computation to communication. The CMS uses this information and decides the optimal number of computing nodes for achieving the optimal overall performance and eventually determines the number of clusters. For this, we must consider a programming model of JIP addressed in prior section.

As shown in Fig. 2, when T_{S_i} and T_{P_i} denote the times taken to execute the i-th sequential code block (S_i) and the i-th parallel code block (P_i) respectively in the program model, the total execution time (T) for a parallel program can be defined as the following equation:

$$T = \sum_{i=0}^{n} T_{S_i} + \sum_{i=0}^{n-1} T_{P_i}. \tag{1}$$

Sequential code blocks (S_i) are executed by the master server and parallel code blocks (P_i) are executed by computing nodes. Except both the first and last sequential code blocks, T_{S_i} is divided into the three parts, $T^G_{S_i}$, $T^D_{S_i}$, and $T^A_{S_i}$, which are the time to gather the execution results of the prior parallel code block (P_{i-1}) from the computing nodes, the time to dispatch code and data for parallel execution of the posterior parallel code block (P_i), and the time to execute remaining pure sequential code respectively. The first sequential code block (S_0) does not include the time to collect the results produced by the prior parallel code block and the last sequential code block (S_n) does not require any time to prepare for the posterior parallel code block, either. T_{P_i} is defined as the sum of $T^M_{P_i}$ and $T^E_{P_i}$, which are the times taken to execute all the shared memory reference code and the other parallel code respectively in the i-th parallel code block.

$$T_{S_i} = \begin{cases} T^A_{S_0} + T^D_{S_0}, & \text{if } i = 0 \\ T^G_{S_i} + T^A_{S_i} + T^D_{S_i}, & \text{if } 0 < i < n \\ T^G_{S_n} + T^A_{S_n}, & \text{if } i = n \end{cases}$$

$$T_{P_i} = T^M_{P_i} + T^E_{P_i}. \tag{2}$$

Thus, Eq.(1) can be changed as follows:

$$T = \sum_{i=0}^{n} T^A_{S_i} + \sum_{i=0}^{n-1} T^E_{P_i} + \sum_{i=0}^{n-1} T^C_i, \quad T^C_i = (T^D_{S_i} + T^M_{P_i} + T^G_{S_{i+1}}). \tag{3}$$

According to Eq.(3), T can be classified into the execution times of a master server and computing nodes, and the three types of communication times (T^C_i) such as dispatching time, shared memory accessing time, and gathering time. To clarify those communication times in terms of low-level communication parameters, several terms are defined as in Table 1. If data are transferred by the packet basis in the high-speed network, a burst transfer of data is preferred. $T^D_{S_i}$ and $T^G_{S_i}$ can be obtained as follows:

$$T^D_{S_i} = \left\lceil \frac{S_{PD} + S_{SD}}{S_P \cdot N} \right\rceil \cdot T_U, \quad T^G_{S_i} = \left\lceil \frac{S_{SD}}{S_P \cdot N} \right\rceil \cdot T_U. \tag{4}$$

For any P_i, the parallel code as well as the shared memory accessing code are assumed to be distributed equally among all the computing nodes for simplicity. For a given P_i, all the computing nodes can perform parallel code allocated concurrently, except for the shared memory accesses that should be processed sequentially at the master server. Thus $T^E_{P_i}$ and $T^M_{P_i}$ can be obtained as follows:

$$T^E_{P_i} = (1 - R_M) \cdot \frac{T_{SP_i}}{N},$$

$$T^M_{P_i} = R_M \cdot T_{SP_i} \cdot \left(\frac{1 - R_{MW}}{N} + R_{MW} \right) \cdot A_N. \tag{5}$$

The term of A_N in Eq.(5) is multicasting coefficient increasing according to the number of computing nodes connected to one master server, where A_N

can represent $k \cdot N$, the ratio of the time to send the same Java code block to multiple computing nodes over the time to send to a single computing node. This equation is obtained from the simulation using *smpl* and *ether* model.

For obtaining the optimal number of computing nodes (N), the execution time of parallel code block, Eq. (5), must be minimized. This equation is as follows.

$$MIN\,(T_{P_i}(N)) = MIN\,(T_{P_i}^E + T_{P_i}^M) = MIN\{(1 - R_M) \cdot \frac{T_{SP_i}}{N} $$
$$+ R_M \cdot T_{SP_i} \cdot \left(\frac{1 - R_{MW}}{N} + R_{MW}\right) \cdot A_N\}. \quad (6)$$

The execution time of parallel application according to the number of participating computing nodes (N) is varied depending on the ratio of total shared memory references and the ratio of write references among shared memory references as Eq.(6). To obtain the optimal number of computing nodes as the execution time of a parallel application, Eq.(6) is changed into equation with respect to N. The equation is differentiated by N for getting an optimal number of computing nodes. Therefore, decision function is derived as Eq.(7).

$$T'_{P_i}(N) = 0, \quad N = \sqrt{\frac{(1 - R_M) \cdot T_{SP_i}}{R_M \cdot T_{SP_i} \cdot R_{MW} \cdot k}}, \; N > 0 \;. \quad (7)$$

After the CMS determines the number of optimal computing nodes according to the information of algorithmic characteristics of application, it checks if the number of available computing nodes in multiple clusters is enough. If the number of available computing nodes in a cluster is smaller than the optimal number, the CMS constructs a multiple cluster configuration of JIP. For this, the CMS also needs to have a decision function which can decide the number of clusters for optimal performance in the multiple cluster configuration of JIP. If it is assumed that the amount of references to the LSM as well as the GSM is distributed equally among all the computing nodes, $T_{P_i}^M$ is changed as follows.

$$T_{P_I}^M = R_M \cdot T_{SP_i} \cdot \{ \left(\frac{1 - R_{MW}}{N} + \frac{R_{MW} \cdot R_{MWL}}{G}\right) \cdot \frac{A_N}{G} $$
$$+ R_{MW} \cdot R_{MWG} \cdot T_{UG} \cdot G\}. \quad (8)$$

For obtaining the optimal number of clusters (G), the execution time of parallel code block, Eq.(5), must be minimized. Thus, this equation is changed as follows.

$$MIN\,(T_{P_i}(G)) = MIN\,(T_{P_i}^E + T_{P_i}^M)$$
$$= MIN\left(R_M \cdot T_{SP_i} \cdot \{ \left(\frac{1 - R_{MW}}{N} + \frac{R_{MW} \cdot R_{MWL}}{G}\right) \cdot \frac{A_N}{G} \right.$$
$$\left. + (1 - R_M) \cdot \frac{T_{SP_i}}{N} + R_{MW} \cdot R_{MWG} \cdot T_{UG} \cdot G\}\right). \quad (9)$$

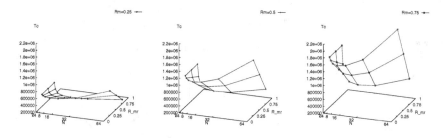

(a) Communication time (T_i^C) according to R_M.

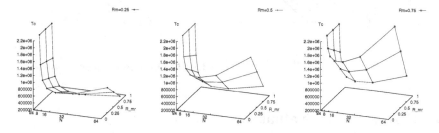

(b) Overall execution time (T_{P_i}) according to R_M.

Fig. 3. Numerical analysis of a basic cluster module of JIP.

If the Eq.(9) is arranged with respect to G and differentiated by G, we can get the optimal number of clusters. Therefore, when $T'_{P_i}(G) = 0$, decision function for the optimal number of clusters is shown in the Eq.(10).

$$A = \frac{1}{2} \cdot \left\{ \frac{2 \cdot R_{MWL} \cdot A_N}{R_{MWG} \cdot T_{UG}} \right.$$

$$\left. + \sqrt{\left(\frac{-2 \cdot R_{MWL} \cdot A_N}{R_{MWG} \cdot T_{UG}} \right)^2 + 4 \cdot \left(\frac{-(1 - R_{MW}) \cdot A_N}{3 \cdot R_{MW} \cdot R_{MWG} \cdot T_{UG} \cdot N} \right)^3} \right\},$$

$$B = \frac{1}{2} \cdot \left\{ \frac{2 \cdot R_{MWL} \cdot A_N}{R_{MWG} \cdot T_{UG}} \right.$$

$$\left. + \sqrt{\left(\frac{-2 \cdot R_{MWL} \cdot A_N}{R_{MWG} \cdot T_{UG}} \right)^2 - 4 \cdot \left(\frac{-(1 - R_{MW}) \cdot A_N}{3 \cdot R_{MW} \cdot R_{MWG} \cdot T_{UG} \cdot N} \right)^3} \right\},$$

$$G = \sqrt[3]{A} + \sqrt[3]{B}, \ G > 0 \ . \tag{10}$$

After determining the optimal number of clusters, the CMS constructs a multiple cluster configuration as many as dividing the optimal number of computing nodes into the number of clusters.

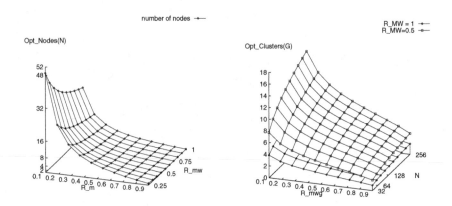

Fig. 4. Optimal number of computing nodes.

Fig. 5. Optimal number of clusters.

3   Performance Evaluation

In this section, we simulate the performance of JIP constructed with a basic cluster module or multiple clusters by using the previous equations. Fig. 3 depicts the performance of a basic cluster module of JIP using Eq.(4) and (5), when $N = 1 \sim 64$. Fig. 3 (a) shows the variation of communication time, T_i^C, according to the ratio of shared memory read references and the y-axis represents the time in milli-seconds(ms). It says that if $N \geq Opt\_N$, T_i^C does not decrease any more, but increases as the number of computing nodes increases. It is derived from the increased network contention at a master server. Fig. 3 (b) shows the variation of overall execution time, T. The ratio of performance speedup is decreased more and more as a program includes higher R_M until N becomes Opt_N, because of communication overhead that is increased suddenly, when $N \geq Opt\_N$. It means that effective parallelism and the scalability of given program vary according to R_M.

Fig. 4 depicts the optimal number of computing nodes according to characteristics of application, such as the ratio of shared memory references (R_M) and the ratio of shared memory write references (R_{MW}), obtained by using Eq.(7). According to Fig. 4, the optimal number of computing nodes, N, is decreased as R_M and R_{MW} are increased, because communication overhead occurred at a master server is increased as the R_M and R_{MW} are increased. Therefore, if the CMS constructs basic cluster module with optimal number of computing nodes by using Eq.(7), each client participating in JIP can be guaranteed by the optimal performance.

Fig. 5 depicts the optimal number of clusters according to the number of participating computing nodes (N) and the ratio of global shared memory write references (R_{MWG}), when $R_{MW} = 1$ and $R_{MW} = 0.5$, by using Eq.(10). According to Fig. 5, the optimal number of clusters, G_{OPT}, is increased as R_{MW} and

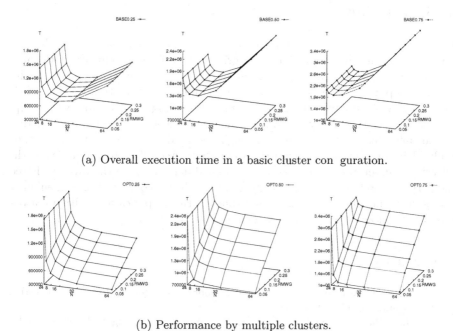

(a) Overall execution time in a basic cluster con guration.

(b) Performance by multiple clusters.

Fig. 6. Performance comparison of a basic model with scalable model.

R_{MWG} are decreased and N is increased. As R_{MWG} is increased, the overhead derived from data coherency procedure exceeds the gain by parallel memory writes and G_{OPT} becomes small. When N is increased, contention at the master server is also increased and memory latency becomes longer. It means that G_{OPT} is increased as N increases.

Fig. 6 shows the performance comparison for a basic cluster module with a multiple cluster configuration when the values of R_M are 0.25, 0.5, and 0.75. Fig. 6 shows that the performances of basic cluster module and multiple cluster configuration are depicted by comparing the OPT as a multiple cluster configuration with the BASE as the basic cluster module. The number in model, e.g., OPT0.25 indicate the value of R_M. As shown in this figure, in the case of $N = 2$, the performance of multiple cluster configuration gets worse because the preparation time and coherent time is increased. In all cases of R_M, if $N \geq 4$ and $R_{MWG} \leq 0.15$, multiple cluster configuration shows the better performance than the base cluster module and if $N \geq 64$ and $R_{MWG} \leq 0.3$, multiple cluster configuration shows the better performance than the base cluster module. In the case of $R_{MWG} = 0.05$, multiple cluster configuration can enhance the performance by 2.5 $\sim$ 3 times. The performance approaches near to the point of the basic cluster module as R_{MWG} is increased. If $R_{MWG} > 0.3$, multiple cluster configuration causes significant performance degradation. It is due to the increased overhead from the process of data coherency.

4   Conclusion

For building an efficient cluster computing platform using geographically distributed computing resources on the grid, a Java-Internet cluster platform is designed in the aspects of high programmability, efficient management for a cluster of computing nodes, system scalability, and code compatibility. The JIP is implemented with Java language and multithreading mechanisms, which supports a shared memory system with sequential consistency model. Performance of multiple clusters is evaluated through the analysis of communication time under JIP, and verified through the simulation. According to the analysis, the effective number of clusters can be determined depending on the ratio of shared memory write references. Specifically, multiple cluster configuration can enhance the performance of JIP about $2.5 \sim 3$ times in those applications with a reasonably high ratio of shared memory references.

References

1. Adve, S.V., Gharachoroloo, K.: Shared Memory Consistency Models : A Tutorial. IEEE Computer (1996) 66-76.
2. Bal, H.E., Plaat, A., Kielmann, T., et. al.: Parallel Computing on Wide-Area Clusters: the Albatross Project. Proc. of Extreme Linux Workshop (1999) 20-24.
3. Culler, D.E., Arpaci-Dusseau, A., Arpaci-Dusseau, R., Chun, B., Lumetta, S., Mainwaring, A., Martin, R., Yoshikawa, C., Wong, F.: Parallel Computing on the Berkeley NOW. Joint Symposium on Parallel Processing (1997) 30-40.
4. Foster, I., Kesselman, C.: The Globus Project: A Status Report. IPPS/SPDP'98 Heterogeneous Computing Workshop (1998) pp.4-18.
5. Grimshaw, A.S., Wulf, W.A., the Legion team: The Legion Vision of a Worldwide Virtual Computer. Communications of the ACM, Vol. 40(1) (1997).
6. Java Remote Method Invocation Speci cation. Sun Microsystems, Mountain View, California (1997).
7. Pinkston, T.M., Baylor, S.J.: Parallel Processor Memory Reference Analysis: Examining Locality and Clustering Potential. 5th SIAM Conference on Parallel Processing for Scienti c Computing (1992) 513-518.
8. Raman, A., Rajkumar, et. al.: PARDISC: A Cost E ective Model for Parallel and Distributed Computing. Proc. of Int. Conf. on High Performance Computing, IEEE Press (1996).
9. Tannenbaum, T., Litzkow, M.: The Condor Distributed Processing System. Dr.Dobbs' Journal, Vol. 20 (1995) 42-44.

A Parameter-Based Approach to Resource Discovery in Grid Computing Systems

Muthucumaru Maheswaran and Klaus Krauter

Advanced Networking Research Laboratory
Department of Computer Science
University of Manitoba
Winnipeg, MB R3T 2N2, Canada
{MAHESWAR, KRAUTER}@CS.UMANITOBA.CA

Abstract. A Grid system is essentially an infrastructure that allows location independent access to the resources and services that are provided by geographically distributed machines and networks. One of the fundamental operations needed to support location-independent computing is resource discovery. Generally, resource discovery schemes maintain and query a resource status database. Dissemination of the resource status information is one of the key operations required to keep the resource status databases consistent. This paper examines several approaches for resource status dissemination. A new concept called the Grid potential is introduced in this paper. This concept is used to control the extent of data dissemination in Grid systems.

1 Introduction

The deployment of faster networking infrastructures and the availability of powerful microprocessors have positioned network computing as a cost-effective alternative to the traditional computing approaches. The Grid is defined as a generalized, large-scale network computing system that is formed by aggregating the services provided several distributed resources [2, 6]. A Grid can potentially provide pervasive, dependable, consistent, and cost-effective access to the diverse services provided by the distributed resources and support problem solving environments that may be constructed using such resources.

One of the key motivations for constructing Grids is to provide application-level connectivity among the various machines so that resources and services supported by the individual systems can be shared in a Global fashion. To enable such sharing, it is necessary for the Grid architecture to support several services [2, 7] and resource discovery is one of them.

In a Grid system, the resource discovery service may operate in conjunction with the resource management service. When a client requests service, along with the request it presents a set of attributes that should be satisfied by a candidate resource. The resource discovery process may be responsible for generating a set of best possible candidates for the given set of attributes. The scheduling heuristics that are part of the resource management mechanism may allocate the best resource(s) from the set based on the some criterion. For example, the resource management may

R. Buyya and M. Baker (Eds.:) GRID 2000, LNCS 1971, pp. 181-190, 2000.

solicit bids from the potential candidates and select the resource with the highest bid to serve the request. Along with other services, resource discovery is necessary to support resources going off-line and coming on-line. Further, the cascaded operation of resource discovery followed by resource allocation can be efficient in an heterogeneous dynamic system such as the Grid.

Generally, resource discovery services use "status" databases that are maintained by network-wide information services to fulfill the client requests. For scalable implementations, it is essential to organize the status databases in a distributed fashion. With a distributed organization for the status databases, the queries can be executed very efficiently but the updates to the databases may be costly. Most of the update costs are caused by the communication operations performed to disseminate status information across the Grid. This paper focuses on approaches for reducing the data dissemination overhead.

In this paper, we introduce a concept called the "Grid potential" that encapsulates the relative processing capabilities of the different machines and networks that constitute the Grid. We show how the Grid potential can be used to adaptively control the extent of data dissemination in a Grid.

Section 0 proposes the idea of Grid potential that is used to adaptively to control the data dissemination overhead. Section 0 discusses the data dissemination approaches for resource discovery operation in the Grid context. Some results from simulation studies that compare the different approaches to data dissemination for resource discovery are presented in this section. Section 0 examines the related work in the research literature.

2 Grid Potential

The Grid potential concept is similar to the time-to-live idea used in the Internet [5]. Informally, the Grid potential at a point in the Grid can be considered as the computing power that can be delivered to an application at that point on the Grid. The computing power that can be delivered to an application depends on the machines that are present in the vicinity and the networks that are used to interconnect them. Consequently, a high-performance machine when connected to the Grid will induce a large Grid potential. This potential, however, will decay as the launch point of the application moves away from the point at which the machine is connected to the Grid. The rate of potential decay depends on the network link capacities. The rest of this section presents a formal definition of the Grid potential idea.

A node in the Grid has several attributes that can be categorized as rate-based attributes and non rate-based attributes. Examples of rate-based attributes include CPU speed, FLOP rating, sustained memory access rate, and sustained disk access rate. A node in a Grid can be characterized by a vector where each element of the vector is an attribute-value pair.

The Grid potential is based on the computing power or operating rate of a node. Therefore, to characterize a node for deriving the Grid potential only rate-based attributes are considered. Let $X = \langle x_0 = \alpha_0, x_1 = \alpha_1, ... \quad x_{N-1} = \alpha_{N-1} \rangle$, where x_i

is a rate-based attribute of the system and α_i its value at a given time. Let F be a set of functions $\{f_0, f_1, ..., f_{k-1}\}$, where f_i operates on the set X to return a scalar value $\lambda_i = f_i(x_0, x_1, ... x_{N-1})$. Depending on the system, different functions may be defined for it. The functions essentially form weighted sums of the attributes that can be interpreted as different types of potentials. For example, the function $\lambda_c = f_c(x_0, x_1, ... x_{N-1})$ may be interpreted as the compute potential of the system and another function $\lambda_s = f_s(x_0, x_1, ... x_{N-1})$ may be interpreted as the secondary storage potential. While the compute potential f_c may be based on attributes that relate to the processing rate of the node the storage potential f_s may be based on attributes that relate to the performance of the storage subsystem. Further, we could have functions that compute application specific potentials that could be useful if the Grid is used exclusively for particular sets of applications.

While the above functions characterize the different Grid potentials of a node in terms of its operating rates, they are not sufficient to measure the different potentials. Therefore, a suite of corresponding "benchmarking" programs are introduced to measure the different potentials.

Let Γ_i be a suite of benchmark programs meant to measure the potential that corresponds to function f_i. In the benchmark suite $\Gamma_i = \{\tau_0^i, ... \tau_{N-1}^i\}$, τ_j^i is a program specifically designed to evaluate attribute x_j of the node. Designing such programs is feasible because only rate-based attributes are considered for computing the potentials of a node. For example, one of the benchmarking programs might be measuring the rate at which arithmetic operations are being executed.

Definition 1: *Node component potential (p_j^C) with respect to attribute x_j is defined as the number of operations performed by the node in one second as measured by the benchmarking program τ_j^i.*

The performance of a node with respect to an application depends on the rate at which the basic operations required by the application can be performed by the node, i.e., the ultimate node performance depends on a weighted average of the individual node component potentials.

Definition 2: *Weighted node potential (p^W) is defined as a weighted average of the node component potentials $\{p_0^C, p_1^C, ... p_{N-1}^C\}$, i.e.,*

$$p^W = \alpha_0 p_0^C + \alpha_1 p_1^C + ... + \alpha_{N-1} p_{N-1}^C$$

The node potential as expressed by the above equation can be considered as a function of the weighting factors and the node component potentials. The weighting factors determine the relative impotance of the different component potentials. In addition to varying the weighting factors, the component potentials may be varied under certain situations.

We define the potential induced by a machine i at the point of its attachment to the Grid as the *local induced Grid potential* and is defined as $p_i^L = \mu p^W$ where $0 \le \mu \le 1$. When the machine is exclusively used for Grid computations, $\mu = 1$ and $0 \le \mu < 1$ otherwise.

Definition 3: *Grid potential* (p^G) is defined as the maximum of local induced Grid potentials. Suppose M machines are attached to a given node j, then the Grid potential at that node is given by

$$p^G = \max_{i \in [0..M]} \left\{ p_j^L(i) \right\}.$$

The Grid potential induced at the point of attachment (node) drops off as we move away from the node along the Grid. This potential drop is dependent on the network characteristics. The Grid potential induced by a machine at a node other than its point of attachment to the Grid is defined as the *remote induced Grid potential*. Consider a machine that is attached to the Grid at node i. Let p_{ij}^R denote the remote induced Grid potential of this machine at node j. The remote induced Grid potential p_{ij}^R can be considered as the effective processing power of the machine at node j.

3   Data Dissemination for Resource Discovery

3.1   Overview

Maintaining the consistency of the distributed status databases involves disseminating the status information. Based on the extent of message propagation, we can classify the data dissemination schemes into three groups.

Universal awareness: This class of data dissemination algorithms distributes the status information such that a node can learn about every other node in the Grid. For large network sizes, the approaches in this group cause significant amount of communication due to large number of message transfers.

Neighborhood awareness: The dissemination algorithms in this group propagate status information such that a node learns about the other nodes that are less than a fixed distance away from it. Although the approaches in this class limit the dissemination overhead and is scalable to very large network sizes, other components of the resource discovery mechanism should be able to handle the incomplete information in the status databases that are associated with the different nodes.

Distinctive awareness: Because the Grid is a highly heterogeneous system, various nodes on the Grid have different attributes. The nodes with distinct attributes are more significant. The extent of a node's status information propagation is controlled by the significance of the node. If all nodes are homogeneous, an algorithm in this group reduces to an algorithm in the neighborhood awareness group. In a highly heterogeneous Grid, an algorithm in this group should deliver a resource discovery efficiency close to a universal awareness type algorithm while having a communication complexity closer to the neighborhood awareness algorithm. One way of implementing distinctive awareness is to use the Grid potential idea presented in the previous section.

3.2 Data Dissemination Algorithms

Figure 1 presents the pseudo-code for the dissemination algorithm that executes on each node. This particular algorithm uses the swamping approach for dissemination. Once a message comes into the node it is validated. The validation process implements the different types of dissemination: universal awareness, neighborhood awareness, and distinctive awareness. In universal awareness, the validation process permits all incoming messages. In the neighborhood awareness, it checks the distance from the source to the current node and discards the message if it exceeds the predefined limit.

```
while (true) {
        // process incoming message
        receive messsage (X) {
                // validate the incoming message: this may depend on the local policy
                // if universal awareness this function is always true
                // if neighborhood awareness returns true only
                // if the distance to source is less than m
                // if distinctive awareness returns true only if the local Grid potential
                // is less than or equal to remote induced local Grid potential
                if (validate(X)) {
                        // update the data structures that keep awareness information in the node
                        process(X)
                }
                // if there are no incoming message then break out the loop to send messages
        } or timeout (n)

        if (currentTime > lastSentTime + n) {
        lastSentTime = currentTime
                // send to logical neighbors
                get the list of neighboring nodes Y
                foreach node in Y
                        send status update message
        }
}
```

Figure 1: Pseudo-code for flooding based data dissemination.

The distinctive awareness is implemented by the validation routine discarding the message if the remote induced Grid potential at the local node is less than the Grid potential at the node. It should be noted that the Grid potential at the local node is the maximum of all local induced potentials. Therefore, the messages arriving from remote nodes that induce less remote potential at the local node than its own potential will be discarded. This creates a "masking problem" for nodes "behind" powerful nodes in a network. For example, if a network of nodes is connected to the rest of the network via a powerful node (as explained in earlier sections, we model the Grid as a connected graph with nodes representing machines), the powerful node will drop all incoming data dissemination messages. Thus, the powerful node will block the dissemination of the status information of the "interior nodes." This masking problem is there when a flooding-based algorithm is used for data dissemination. A swamping-based algorithm that increases the neighborhood set as it discovers new nodes will be able to overcome this problem.

To reduce the high message overhead of the swamping approach, it is possible to use a random node-based approach such as the Name-dropper algorithm [3]. Using the random node-based approach instead of the flooding approach avoids the masking problem. Consider the example situation where a powerful node connects a network of less powerful nodes to the rest of the network. As part of their update messages each node will advertise their immediate neighbors to the other nodes. Therefore, the nodes behind the powerful node will be reachable.

3.3   Experimental Evaluation of the Algorithms

To evaluate the performance of the various data dissemination schemes we devised the following simulation study. In this simulation study a computational Grid is modeled by a random graph with the nodes denoting the machines. The data dissemination scheme is responsible for updating the status database that is maintained at each node. Depending on the scheme that is under consideration, we might have a complete database at each node or an incomplete database at each node. We define *data dissemination efficiency* to be 100% if the particular data dissemination algorithm creates local database that is same as an ideal global database. Higher the value the above parameter is the more accurately the local database captures the actual global status picture.

In the simulations, we "estimate" the above parameter by scheduling a stream of jobs onto the Grid using an ideal global database and local database. We use the same scheduling algorithm in both situations and the differences in the decisions taken gives a measure of the difference between the two databases. In addition to the above parameter, we also report another performance measure that is the *schedule deviation*. This parameter is, however, more dependent on the scheduling algorithm than the above parameter, i.e., it is dependent on how far the decisions taken by the scheduling algorithm is dependent on the completeness of the status information.

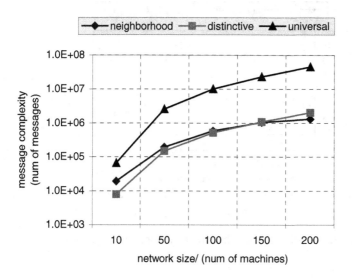

Figure 2: Variation of message complexity with network size.

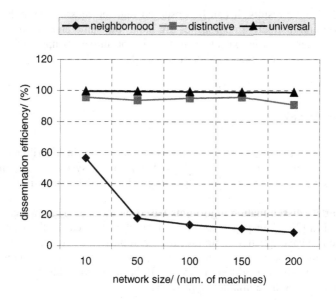

Figure 3: Variation of dissemination efficiency with network size.

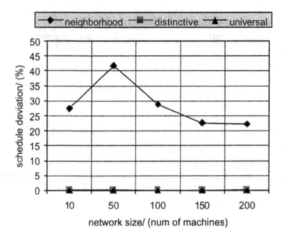

Figure 4: Variation of the schedule deviation with network size.

Figure 2 shows the variation of the message complexity with network size for the different data dissemination schemes. Figure 3 shows the variation of the efficiency of data dissemination with network size and Figure 4 shows the variation of the schedule deviation with network size.

From the above results, it can be observed that the message complexity of the neighborhood and distinctive approaches are about the same and much less than the universal approach. This is expected because in the universal approach, each node sends a message to every other node in the network.

4   Related Work

Because resource discovery is a fundamental operation in distributed computer systems it has been examined in a variety of distributed systems including: mobile computing, wireless sensor networks [4], high throughput computing [9], naming systems [1].

Several data dissemination algorithms based on the universal awareness scheme are examined in [3]. Their paper presents a new algorithm called the Name-Dropper that is proved to have a better communication complexity when compared with three other algorithms based on flooding, swamping, and random pointer jumping, respectively. Our study is different from [3] because we examine the trade-offs between various data dissemination approaches.

Matchmaking [9] is a distributed resource management mechanism developed as part of the Condor [8] project for Grid systems. The matchmaking is based on the idea that resources providing services and clients requesting service advertise their characteristics and requirements using classified advertisements (classads). A matchmaker service that may be either centralized or distributed matches the client requests to the appropriate resources. The matchmaking framework includes several components of a resource discovery mechanism.

The classad specification defines the syntax and semantic rules for specifying the evaluating the attributes associated with the characteristics and requirements. The advertising protocol lays down the rules for disseminating the advertisements. Our study differs from their work because we examine techniques for performing efficient data dissemination to support resource discovery. It may be possible to use the classad language as the specification language in the implementation of our scheme.

5 Conclusions

In this paper, we examine various strategies for data dissemination. We introduce a new class of data dissemination strategies called the distinctive awareness. This class of strategies can result in algorithms that have improved resource discovery efficiency with reduced communication overhead. We use a new concept called the Grid potential for implementing this class of algorithms. The Grid potential quantifies the relative processing powers of the different machines in a Grid.

We performed simulation studies to examine the performance trade-offs of the different data dissemination schemes. Several aspects of the Grid potential concept needs further investigation. One of them is to use application based measurement strategies for the Grid potential instead of using special benchmarks as proposed in this paper. Another one would be construct theoretical performance models for data dissemination algorithms that belong to the distinctive awareness category.

In summary, this paper introduces a new class of data dissemination for resource discovery in distributed computing systems and in particular for resource discovery in Grid systems. A novel idea called the Grid potential is also presented.

References

[1] W. Adjie-Winoto, E. Schwartz, H. Balakrishnan, and J. Lilley, "The design and implementation of an intentional naming system," *Operating System Review*, Vol. 34, No. 5, Dec. 1999, pp. 186-201.

[2] I. Foster and C. Kesselman, *The Grid: Blueprint for a New Computing Infrastructure,* Morgan Kaufmann, San Fransisco, CA, 1999.

[3] M. Harchol-Balter, T. Leighton, and D. Lewin, "Resource discovery in distributed networks," *ACM Symposium on Principles of Distributed Computing*, May 1999, pp. 229-237.

[4] W. R. Heinzelman, J. Kulik, and H. Balakrishnan, "Adaptive protocols for information dissemination in Wireless sensor networks," *ACM Mobicomm*, 1999, pp. 174-185.

[5] C. Huitema, *Routing in the Internet, Second Edition*, Prentice-Hall, Upper Saddle River, NJ, 2000.

[6] W. E. Johnston, D. Gannon, and B. Nitzberg, "Information Power Grid Implementation Plan: Research, Development, and Testbeds for High Performance, Widely Distributed, Collaborative, Computing and Information Systems Supporting Science and Engineering," NASA Ames Research Center, http://www.nas.nasa.gov/IPG, 1999.

[7] K. Krauter and M. Maheswaran, *Architecture for a Grid Operating System*, Technical Report TR-CS-00-12, Department of Computer Science, University of Manitoba, May 2000.

[8] M. J. Litzkow, M. Livny, and M. W. Mutka, "Condor - A hunter of idle workstations," *8th International Conference on Distributed Computing Systems*, 1988, pp. 104-111.

[9] R. Raman, M. Livny, and M. Solomon, "Matchmaking: Distributed resource management for high throughput computing," *7th IEEE International Symposium on High Performance Distributed Computing*, 1998, pp. 28-31.

Evaluation of Job-Scheduling Strategies for Grid Computing

Volker Hamscher[1], Uwe Schwiegelshohn[1], Achim Streit[2], and Ramin Yahyapour[1]

[1] Computer Engineering Institute, University of Dortmund, 44221 Dortmund, Germany
[2] Paderborn Center for Parallel Computing, University of Paderborn, 33095 Paderborn, Germany

Abstract. In this paper, we discuss typical scheduling structures that occur in computational grids. Scheduling algorithms and selection strategies applicable to these structures are introduced and classi ed. Simulations were used to evaluate these aspects considering combinations of di erent Job and Machine Models. Some of the results are presented in this paper and are discussed in qualitative and quantitative way. For hierarchical scheduling, a common scheduling structure, the simulation results con rmed the bene t of Back ll. Unexpected results were achieved as FCFS proves to perform better than Back ll when using a central job-pool.

1 Introduction

In recent years an increasing number of parallel computers have become part of so called computational grids or metacomputers [1], [2]. Such a grid typically contains many computers offering a variety of resources. The scheduling system is responsible to select best suitable machines in this grid for user jobs. In large grids it is very cumbersome for an individual user to select these resources manually. The management and scheduling system generates job schedules for each machine in the grid by taking static restrictions and dynamic parameters of jobs and machines into consideration.

The job scheduling for a single parallel computer significantly differs from scheduling in a metacomputer. The scheduler of a parallel machine usually arranges the submitted jobs in order to achieve a high utilization. The task of scheduling for a metacomputer is more complex as many machines are involved with mostly local scheduling policies. The metacomputing scheduler must therefore form a new level of scheduling which is implemented on top of the job schedulers. Also, it is likely that a large metacomputer may be subject to more frequent changes as individual resources may join or exit the grid at any time. Note that many users take a special advantage of a computational grid in the potential combination of many resources to solve a single very large problem. This requires the solution of various hardware and software challenges in several areas including scheduling.

R. Buyya and M. Baker (Eds.:) GRID 2000, LNCS 1971, pp. 191–202, 2000.

In this paper we discuss several architectures and scheduling policies for such a system. To this end, we are presenting a brief overview on this topic in Section 3. Next, we show a few simple scheduling algorithms for these architectures in Section 4. These algorithms are subject of the performance evaluation in Section 5 where preliminary simulation results are presented.

2   Background

The term metacomputing was established in 1987 by Smarr and Catlett [11]. The concept of connecting computing resources has been subject to many research projects. Some to be mentioned are Globus [5], Condor [10] and Legion [6].

In the area of metacomputing the topic of scheduling is an important part for building efficient infrastructures. As already mentioned, the requirements of scheduling in a metacomputing environment significantly deviate from those for scheduling of jobs on a single parallel machine. One important difference is the inclusion of network resources. Additionally, metasystems are geographical distributed and often belong to several institutions and owners. A scheduler on a single parallel machine must not cope with system boundaries and can manage the given resources independently of external restrictions.

A scheduling infrastructure in a metacomputing system must take those additional requirements into account. Therefore special mechanisms for security and fault-tolerance are needed. Also the independence of resources, especially the different ownership, requires support for the fine-tuning of scheduling policies defined by their providers.

In the next section, this paper gives an overview of common structures in metacomputing environments. The presented topologies are classified into centralized and decentralized schedulers. The structure of the scheduling infrastructure, the used algorithms and strategies are very important for the quality and performance of the system. Many of those scheduling algorithms, starting from simple FCFS strategies to improvements like backfilling [4] known from scheduling on a single parallel machine, can be adapted to the metasystem level. In this paper, we concentrate on the discussion of scheduling structures in metasystems in combination with some common scheduling algorithms.

In the following, example architectures for scheduling infrastructures are presented. Note, that this list should not be considered complete, but gives an overview on common structures in computational grids and metacomputing networks. Further we do not elaborate on the architecture of the parallel computing systems itself, but only on the logical structure of the scheduling process. First, we distinguish centralized and decentralized scheduling architectures.

2.1   Centralized Scheduling

In a centralized environment all parallel machines are scheduled by a central instance. Information on the state of all available systems must be collected here.

This concept obviously does not scale well with increasing size of the computational grid. The central scheduler may prove to be a bottleneck in some situations (e.g. if a network error cuts off the scheduler from its resources, system availability and performance may be affected). As an advantage, the scheduler is conceptually able to produce very efficient schedules, because the central instance has all necessary information on the available resources.

This scheduling paradigm is useful e.g. at a computing center, where all resources are used under the same objective. Due to this fact the lack of communication bandwidth at the central scheduling instance can be neglected.

In this scenario jobs are submitted to the central scheduler (see Figure 1). Those jobs, that cannot be started on a machine immediately after submission, are stored in a central job-queue for a later start.

We can further distinguish schedulers by the way how resources are combined for a job. This applies to centralized schedulers as well as to their decentralized alternatives that are discussed later.

Single-site scheduling. A job is executed on a single parallel machine. This means that system boundaries are not crossed. Well known scheduling algorithms for load balancing (e.g. FCFS, Backfill) can be used. The latency for the in-job-communication is often not subject to scheduling considerations due to the fact that communication inside a machine is usually very fast in comparison to distributed execution.

Multi-site scheduling. The described restriction of single-site algorithms is lifted. Now a job can be executed on more than one machine in parallel. As job-parts are running on different machines, the latency for the communication between those parts must be considered. Further, the scheduling system must guarantee that the different job-parts are started synchronously on all machines.

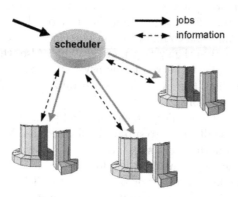

Fig. 1. Centralized Scheduling

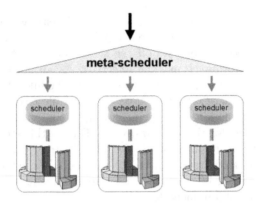

Fig. 2. Hierarchical Structure

2.2   Hierarchical Structure

A possible configuration for a computational grid is the usage of a central scheduler to which jobs are submitted, while in addition every machine uses a separate
scheduler for the local scheduling, as shown in Figure 2. Although this structure
shows properties of centralized and decentralized scheduling, we would consider it to be a centralized system as there is a single instance to which jobs are
submitted.

The main advantage is the fact that different policies can be used for local and
global job scheduling. The central scheduler is some kind of a meta-scheduler,
that redirects all submitted jobs to the local scheduling queues on the resources
based on a policy.

2.3   Decentralized Scheduling

In decentralized systems, distributed schedulers interact with each other and
commit jobs to remote systems. No central instance is responsible for the job
scheduling. Therefore, information about the state of all systems is not collected
at a single point. Thus, the communication bottleneck of centralized scheduling
is prevented which makes the system more scalable. Also, the failure of a single
component will not affect the whole metasystem. This provides better fault-
tolerance and reliability than available for centralized systems without fall-back
or high-availability solutions.

The lack of a global scheduler, which knows all job and system information at
every time instant, usually leads to sub-optimal schedules. Nevertheless, different
scheduling policies on the local sites are possible. Further, site-autonomy for
scheduling can be achieved easily as the local schedulers can be specialized on
the needs of the resource provider or the resource itself.

Unfortunately the support for multi-site applications is rather difficult to
achieve. As all parts of a parallel program must be active at the same time,

the different schedulers must synchronize the jobs and guarantee simultaneous execution which makes it more difficult to provide optimal schedules.

In the following, we present two explicit cases of decentralized architectures that were used for the evaluation shown in Section 5. Note that all jobs are submitted locally.

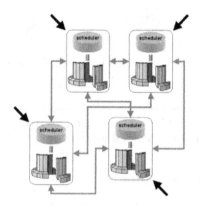

Fig. 3. Decentralized Scheduling with Direct Communication

Direct communication. The local schedulers can send/receive jobs to/from other schedulers directly (see Figure 3). Either schedulers have a list of remote schedulers they can contact or there is a directory that provides information of other systems.

If a job start is not possible on the local machine immediately, the local scheduler is searching for an alternative machine. If a system has been found, where an immediate start is possible, the job and all its data is transferred to the other machine/scheduler. In our evaluation, the execution length of the job is modified to reflect this overhead.

It can be parameterized which jobs are forwarded to another machine. Note, that this affects the local queue. This can also affect the performance of some scheduling algorithms. E.g. the backfilling algorithms (s. Section 3.2) relies on a suitable backlog.

Communication via a Central Job Pool. Jobs that cannot be executed immediately are sent to a central job pool instead of a remote machine (see Figure 4). In contrast to direct communication the local schedulers can pick suitable jobs for their schedules. In this scenario, jobs can be *pushed* into or *pulled* out of the pool. A policy is required that all jobs from the pool are executed at some time to prevent job starvation.

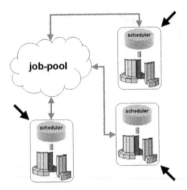

Fig. 4. Using a Job Pool in Decentralized Scheduling

This method can be modified, so that all jobs are pushed directly in the job-pool after submission. This way all small jobs requiring few resources can be used for utilizing free resources on all machines.

3   Scheduling Algorithms

The allocation process of a scheduler consists of two parts, the selection of the machine and the scheduling over time.

3.1   Selection-Strategies

We define four strategies for selecting suitable machines for a job request. In the following, M_{max} denotes all machines that are able to execute a specific job in the metacomputer. M_{free} is the subset of machines that have currently enough free resources to start the job immediately.

- *BiggestFree* takes the machine from M_{free} with the largest number of free resources. A disadvantage of this strategy is a possible delay of a wide job, as small jobs may take the critical resources necessary for the next wide job.
- *Random* chooses a machine from the sets M_{max} or M_{free} by random. On average it provides a fair distribution of the jobs on the available machines.
- *BestFit* takes the machine either from M_{max} or M_{free} that leaves the least free resources if the job is started. In comparison to *BiggestFree* this strategy does not unnecessarily fill up larger machines with smaller jobs.
- *EqualUtil* chooses the machine with the lowest utilization to balance the load on all machines [13]. Note, that this strategy does not try to keep larger machines free for larger jobs which may be a drawback.

3.2   Scheduling Algorithms

Most common algorithms in scheduling are based on list-scheduling. In the following three variants are presented that we used for our evaluation [8].

- *First-Come-First-Serve:* The scheduler starts the jobs in the order of their submission. If not enough resources are currently available, the scheduler waits until the job can be started. The other jobs in the submission queue are stalled. This strategy is known to be inefficient for many workloads as wide jobs waiting for execution can result in unnecessary idle time of some resources.
- *Random:* The next job to be scheduled is randomly selected among all jobs that are submitted but not yet started, therefore the schedule is non-deterministic. No job is preferred, but jobs submitted earlier have a higher probability to be started before a given time instant.
- *Backfill:* This is an out-of-order version of FCFS scheduling that tries to prevent the unnecessary idle time caused by wide jobs. Two common variants are EASY- and conservative-backfilling [4,9]. In case that a wide job is waiting for execution other jobs can be started under the premise that the wide job is not delayed. Note, that the performance of this algorithm relies on a sufficient backlog.

4   Evaluation

4.1   Description of the Simulation Environment

For performance evaluation of the different structures and algorithms we used a simulation environment based on discrete event simulation. It allows the evaluation of different configurations by providing results for common evaluation criteria, like schedule-length (makespan), average response-time and utilization of the machines.

Information on workload traces from the 430 node IBM RS6000/SP of the Cornell Theory Center [7] and a workload trace of the Intel PARAGON from the FZ Jülich were used to generate different *Job Sets*. Thereby the jobs contain all relevant information necessary for the scheduling.

The traces were modified to produce larger backlogs, which was done by a duplication of the jobs.

A job consists of a submission time and a requested number of resources. Also for some algorithms (backfilling) the actual or estimated execution length of a job is used.

We use a simple abstract *Machine Model* of homogeneous resources (nodes). The communication inside a machine does not prefer any specific communication patterns. Therefore, jobs can be distributed on a machine in any fashion. Every machine is capable of starting every job as long as enough resources are available. The nodes are used in an exclusive manner. After the start of a job, the subset of nodes cannot be changed and therefore no support for migration is provided here.

Some machine models used in the simulations are presented in Table 1 with information on the size of each machine and the total number of resources. The first Machine Model nrw is based on the machines available in the NRW-Metacomputing project [3].

An overview on the evaluated combinations of algorithms and selection strategies is given in Table 2. Each scheduler is simulated with different job and machine models.

4.2   Results

The different combinations of configurations, algorithms and structures produced a large amount of data. In the following, we can only discuss some of the results, while the complete listing is found in [12].

Single-Site Scheduling. First, we compare FCFS and Backfilling in the *Single-Site* scenario, see Table 3.

As expected Backfill is much more efficient than FCFS in single-site scheduling and also better than Random. Especially with the BiggestFree strategy, Backfilling is vastly superior to FCFS. As already mentioned before, large backlogs cause the Backfill scheduler to be more efficient. Note that, the simple random strategy performs only slightly worse than Backfill.

In comparison to the other selection strategies (see Section 3.1) BiggestFree performs worst, because resources are allocated without regard of wide jobs potentially submitted in near future. BestFit_Free unveils the best results in all

Table 1. Resource Con gurations

Name	Sizes of Machines	Total Resources	Number of Machine
nrw	10, 12, 16, 32,48, 192, 512, 512	1334	8
equal	256, 256, 256, 256, 256, 256, 256, 256	2048	8
4small_4big	32, 32, 32, 32, 256, 256, 256, 256	1152	8
2powN	2, 4, 8, 16, 32, 64, 128, 256	510	8

Table 2. Simulated combinations

Structure		Scheduler	Selection Strategy
Central	Single-Site	FCFS, Random, Back ll	BestFit_Free, BiggestFree, Random_Free
	Multi-Site	-	-
	Hierarchical	FCFS, Back ll	BestFit_Max, EqualUtil_Max, Random_Max
Decentral	Direct Com-munication	FCFS, Back ll	-
	Job Pool	FCFS, Back ll	-

Table 3. Exemplary results of single-site scheduling. Machine model 2powN and job model are based on trace data from CTC.

Scheduling Algorithm	Selection Strategy	Makespan	Average Response Time	Utilization
Back ll	BestFit_Free	14.878.363 s	12.445 s	66,28 %
	BiggestFree	14.878.363 s	13.060 s	66,28 %
	Random_Free	14.878.363 s	12.769 s	66,28 %
FCFS	BestFit_Free	16.361.362 s	881.155 s	60,27 %
	BiggestFree	18.086.122 s	1.806.165 s	54,52 %
	Random_Free	17.033.913 s	1.312.609 s	57,89 %
Random	BestFit_Free	14.879.165 s	13.951 s	66,27 %
	BiggestFree	15.639.085 s	40.166 s	63,05 %
	Random_Free	15.240.330 s	31.356 s	64,70 %

cases as it leaves less resources idle. Random_Free which effectively represents a mixture of both variants achieves average results.

Multi-Site Scheduling. Four computation methods are used exemplary to modify the execution length of jobs running on several machines.

1. $(1 + p)^f$
2. $\max_i[(1 + p)^{r_i}]$
3. $(1 + p) * f$
4. $\max_i[(1 + p) * r_i]$

- f specifies the number of job segments
- r_i specifies the number of requested resources by each job part i
- p denotes a unit value for the partitioning overhead

The segmentation of a job to run in parallel on several machines leads to an overhead. The size increases are described by the parameter p. Generally a larger p results in a longer average response time (ART). While the first three procedures show a monotonous behavior in this context, the last one seems not to share this trend.

An additional parameter (minJobSize) prevents a job smaller than minJob-Size from being partitioned in segments. Therefore we expect a larger makespan and a larger ART for a bigger minJobSize, but obtained different results. Further research must determine whether there is a turning point at which the originally expected correlation begins. As to be expected, multi-site scheduling does not perform as well as single-site scheduling.

Hierarchical Scheduling. The Tables 4 and 5 present the results for different selection strategies and *Machine Models*.

In both cases EqualUtil_Max performs slightly better than the Random selection strategy, nevertheless both produce fairly good results. The use of Equa-lUtil_Max proves to be advantageous if machine sizes vary. If all machines in the metasystem are equipped with the same number of resources (e.g. 8 machines with 256 resources each) the differences between both strategies are negligible.

Especially in combination with the EqualUtil strategy and heterogeneous structures, the Backfill scheduler is much more effective than FCFS as shown in Table 6.

Direct Communication. The increase of the execution length (see Sec. 2.3) leads to an expected decrease in performance (see Table 7). But it is negligible as only few jobs are affected. Overall the results for distributed structures are highly dependent on the resource configuration. In a configuration where all machines are similar in size as in set *equal*, there is no significant difference between centralized and decentralized scheduling. In an environment of machines with varying size, decentral scheduling produces much worse results.

Using a Job Pool. The scheduling depends mostly on established (fairness) policies. For instance, a job is only forwarded to the job pool, if it cannot be handled locally. Therefore, the balancing between the local and the remote queue is of major importance to prevent jobs to accumulate in one of them.

Backfill schedulers prefer the local queue for their backfilling, whereas FCFS based schedulers always use the job-pool to utilize their idle times. Therefore, FCFS has a wider variety of jobs to choose from, if enough backlog exists. Under this circumstances FCFS shows a slightly better performance than Backfill. First simulations verify this effect as presented in Table 8.

The increase of the execution length for the overhead as mentioned in Section 2.3 shows a decrease in performance as to be expected. If enough small jobs are forwarded to the central pool, the results are comparable to central scheduling.

Besides the scheduling aspect the use of a common job-pool requires certain management features. Jobs exceeding the maximum size of any resource set of the system must be rejected.

Table 4. Exemplary utilization results for each machine with di erent selection strategies in hierarchical scheduling. Machine model **equal** respectively **2powN** and job model are based on trace data from CTC.

Machine Size	256	256	256	256	256	256	256	256
Random_Max	6,85 %	6,47 %	7,27 %	8,16 %	7,53 %	7,84 %	7,38 %	6,94 %
EqualUtil_Max	7,28 %	7,35 %	7,28 %	7,35 %	7,49 %	7,30 %	7,30 %	7,30 %

Table 5. Exemplary utilization results for each machine with di erent selection strategies in hierarchical scheduling. Machine model **equal** respectively **2powN** and job model are based on trace data from CTC.

Machine Size	2	4	8	16	32	64	128	256
Random_Max	3,20 %	3,71 %	35,85 %	21,31 %	21,40 %	16,99 %	17,76 %	40,08 %
EqualUtil_Max	14,73 %	14,86 %	24,67 %	24,85 %	24,90 %	24,78 %	24,80 %	28,53 %

Table 6. Exemplary results for selection strategy EqualUtil_Free in hierarchical scheduling. Machine model 2powN and job model are based on trace data from CTC.

Scheduling Algorithm	Makespan	Average Response Time	Utilization
FCFS	120.662.772 s	32.836.642 s	8,17 %
Back ll	16.189.537 s	94.377 s	60,91 %

Table 7. Exemplary results for absolute modi cation of the execution length using Back ll-Schedulers with Direct Communication. Machine model 2powN and job model are based on trace data from CTC.

CTC

extension time of transferred jobs	Makespan	Average Response Time	Utilization
20 s	28.005.954 s	2.615.614 s	34,27 %
50 s	28.775.899 s	4.167.194 s	35,21 %

KFA

parameter p (relative length modi cation)	Makespan	Average Response Time	Utilization
0.1	23.485.345 s	26.135 s	29,31 %
0.2	23.485.635 s	26.154 s	29,31 %

Table 8. Comparing FCFS and Back ll with equal settings of parameters. Machine model nrw and job model are based on trace data from KFA.

Scheduling Algorithm	Makespan	Average Response Time	Utilization
FCFS	23.465.816 s	1.036 s	9,55 %
Back ll	23.466.498 s	1.075 s	9,54 %

5 Conclusion

In this paper, we discussed some scheduling structures that typically occur in metasystems or computational grids. As evaluating such structures highly depends on the used algorithms and strategies of the scheduling itself, a selection of them has been presented. Besides the discussion of scheduling structures, simulations were used to evaluate their run-time performance. Discrete-event simulation has been used with workload from real machine traces and sample machine configurations. The results are not meant to be complete, but give an overview on the methodology and some interesting relations. Future work will extend the studies to more architectures and include more detailed parameter and configuration variation. This is important as the current results show that the performance of the examined algorithms for the scheduling structure are highly dependent on the parameters, machine configurations and workload.

References

1. European grid forum, http://www.egrid.org.
2. The grid forum, http://www.gridforum.org.
3. C. Bitten, J. Gehring, R. Yahyapour, and U. Schwiegelshohn. The NRW-Metacomputer: Building blocks for a worldwide computational grid. In *Heterogeneous Computing Workshop 2000 at IPDPS 2000*, Cancun, Mexico, May 2000.
4. D.G. Feitelson and A.M. Weil. Utilization and Predictability in Scheduling the IBM SP2 with Back lling. In *Procedings of IPPS/SPDP 1998*, pages 542 546. IEEE Computer Society, 1998.
5. I. Foster and C. Kesselman. Globus: A metacomputing infrastructure toolkit. 11(2):115 128, 1997.
6. A. Grimshaw, A. Wulf, J. French, A Weaver, and P. Reynolds. Legion: The next logical step toward a nationwide virtual supercomputer. Technical Report CS-94-21, University of Virginia, Computer Sciences Department, 1994.
7. S. Hotovy. Workload Evolution on the Cornell Theory Center IBM SP2. In D.G. Feitelson and L. Rudolph, editors, *IPPS'96 Workshop: Job Scheduling Strategies for Parallel Processing*, pages 27 40. Springer Verlag, Lecture Notes in Computer Science LNCS 1162, 1996.
8. J. Krallmann, U. Schwiegelshohn, and R. Yahyapour. On the design and evaluation of job scheduling algorithms. In *Fifth Annual Workshop on Job Scheduling Strategies for Parallel Processing, IPPS'99; San Juan, Puerto Rico; April 1999*, Lectures Notes in Computer Science, pages 17 42, 1999.
9. D.A. Lifka. The ANL/IBM SP scheduling system. In D.G. Feitelson and L. Rudolph, editors, *IPPS'95 Workshop: Job Scheduling Strategies for Parallel Processing*, pages 295 303. Springer Verlag, Lecture Notes in Computer Science LNCS 949, 1995.
10. M. Litzkow, M. Livny, and M. Mutka. Condor - a hunter of idle workstations. In *Proceedings of the 8th Intl Conf. on Distributed Computing Systems*, pages 104 111, 1988.
11. L. Smarr and C. E. Catlett. Metacomputing. *Communications of the ACM*, 35(6):44 52, June 1992.
12. A. Streit. Evaluation of Scheduling-Algorithms for Metacomputing (in German). In *Diploma Thesis at CEI*. University of Dortmund, Germany, 1999.
13. G. D. van Albada, J. Clinckemaillie, A. H. L. Emmen, J. Gehring, O. Heinz, F. van der Linden, B. J. Overeinder, A. Reinefeld, and P. M. A. Sloot. Dynamite - blasting obstacles to parallel cluster computing. In P. M. A. Sloot, M. Bubak, A. G. Hoekstra, and L. O. Hertzberger, editors, *High-Performance Computing and Networking (HPCN Europe '99), Amsterdam, The Netherlands*, number 1593 in Lecture Notes in Computer Science, pages 300 310, Berlin, April 1999. Springer-Verlag.

Experiments with Migration of Message-Passing Tasks

K. A. Iskra[1], Z. W. Hendrikse[1], G. D. van Albada[1], B. J. Overeinder[1],
P. M. A. Sloot[1], and J. Gehring[2]

[1] Informatics Institute, Universiteit van Amsterdam,
Kruislaan 403, 1098 SJ Amsterdam, The Netherlands
{kamil,zegerh,dick,bjo,sloot}@science.uva.nl
[2] Paderborn Center for Parallel Computing,
Fürstenallee 11, 33102 Paderborn, Germany
joern@uni-paderborn.de

Abstract. The combined computing capacity of the workstations that
are present in many organisations nowadays is often under-utilised, as
the performance for parallel programs is unpredictable. Load balancing
through dynamic task re-allocation can help to obtain a more reliable
performance. The Esprit project Dynamite[1] provides such an automated
load balancing system. It can migrate tasks that are part of a parallel
program using a message passing library. Currently Dynamite supports
PVM only, but it is being extended to support MPI as well. The Dynamite package is completely transparent, *i.e.* neither system (kernel)
nor application source code need to be modi ed. Dynamite supports migration of tasks using dynamically linked libraries, open les and both
direct and indirect PVM communication. Monitors and a scheduler are
included. In this paper, we rst briefly describe the Dynamite system.
Next we describe how migration decisions are made and report on some
performance measurements.

1 Introduction

With the introduction of more powerful processors every year, and network
connections becoming both faster and cheaper, distributed computing on standard PCs and workstations of an organisation becomes more attractive and feasible. Consequently, the interest in special purpose parallel machines is declining
in favour of the clusters of workstations.

In such environments, performance optimisation and load balancing by off-
loading work to other nodes in the cluster is highly desirable. For sequential
programs, this has long been solved (*e.g.* in Condor [10,9] and Codine [17]).
For tasks in parallel programs, this still is a research issue. Dynamite [1,6,7,8]
provides a dynamic load balancing system for parallel jobs running under PVM

---

[1] Dynamite is a collaborative project, funded by the European Union as Esprit project 23499. Of the many people that have contributed, we can mention only a few:
A. Streit, F. van der Linden, J. Clinckemaillie, A. H. L. Emmen.

R. Buyya and M. Baker (Eds.:) GRID 2000, LNCS 1971, pp. 203–213, 2000.

[5] when run on clusters of workstations. The load balancing is realised through the migration of tasks.

Dynamite is an acronym for DYNAMIc Task migration Environment and is also known as DPVM [11] (Dynamic–PVM), since it is based on PVM, version 3.3.11. Dynamite currently supports PVM-based programs only, but its modular design greatly facilitates the creation of an MPI [16] version. Work on this is currently under way in cooperation with the people from Hector [12]. Various PVM variants supporting task migration have been reported, such as tmPVM [15], ChaRM [4], DAMPVM [3] and MPVM [2].

Dynamite is currently operational under Sun Solaris/UltraSparc 2.5.1 through 8 (32 bit) and Linux/i386 2.0 and 2.2[2]. It aims to provide a complete solution for dynamic load balancing, see Section 6. The strengths of Dynamite are its powerful and versatile checkpointing mechanism, its transparency, its modularity and its robustness.

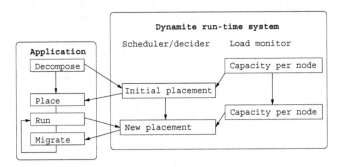

Fig. 1. Running an application with Dynamite. An application has to be decomposed into several subtasks already, and it must be linked with the Dynamite libraries. The run-time system places these on nodes in the cluster, starts execution and monitors the system. If it decides that the load is unbalanced (above a certain threshold), one or more task migrations may be performed to establish a new and more optimal load distribution.

The motivation for a continuous optimal task allocation is three-fold:

- overall performance is determined by the slowest task,
- dynamic run-time behaviour of both task (the amount of computational resources needed by a task) and node (computational resources offered by a node) may vary in time,
- computational resources used by long-running programs might be reclaimed on demand.

The Dynamite system (see Fig. 1) consists of three separate parts:

1. The load-monitoring subsystem. The load-monitor should leave the computation (almost) undisturbed.
2. The scheduler, which tries to make an optimal allocation.

---

[2] Only the libc5 and glibc2.0 libraries are currently supported.

3. The task migration software, which allows a process to checkpoint itself and to be restarted on a different host. This also has a significant impact on the message-passing libraries. An extensive and detailed description of this part of the system can be found in [8].

Dynamite is required to be as transparent to the user as possible. This implies that the checkpoint/migration mechanism must be implemented completely in user-space and no additional changes to the code of the program may be required. Indeed, the user only has to link to the Dynamite dynamic loader[3] (which contains the checkpoint/restart mechanism and is a shared library itself; it is based on the Linux ELF dynamic loader 1.9.9) and the DPVM library. From then on, the complete Dynamite functionality is available. It is also necessary to use Dynamite's infrastructure (daemons, group server, console and such) as functionality has been added and protocols have been adapted.

Users of sequential programs that do not use PVM can merely link their applications using the Dynamite dynamic loader, thus taking advantage of the checkpoint facility.

First we will describe the architecture of Dynamite in Sections 2 and 3. Thereafter quantitative results will be presented, which have been obtained with Dynamite running on a Linux cluster. These data will be compared to standard PVM runs. Subsequently, we briefly discuss the limitations of Dynamite and come to our conclusions.

2   Checkpointing Mechanism

Checkpointing a process boils down to writing the address space of a process to a file and retrieving its contents afterwards. This includes the shared libraries which may be used by the process. In addition, the contents of (some of the) processor registers must be taken care of, such as the program-counter and the stack pointer. Moreover, a proper implementation must also consider various communication channels.

In Dynamite, the checkpointing functionality was implemented in the dynamic loader, to which the following changes were made:

1. it can handle a checkpoint signal (SIGUSR1),
2. it can treat a checkpoint file just like any other executable,
3. it *wraps* certain system and library calls:
   - for open files (a.o. open, write, creat),
   - for memory allocation (mmap, munmap, mremap[4]),
4. it preserves certain cross-checkpoint data separately,
5. it provides handles for additional processing before and after checkpoints (*e.g.* for communication libaries).

---

[3] The dynamic loader can be speci ed by using the appropriate compiler option.
[4] Linux speci c.

PVM tasks communicate with each other. During the migration process, care must be taken to ensure that the communication is retained and that no messages are lost. Such tasks thus present additional difficulties. A PVM daemon must run on every node that participates in a PVM environment. The same holds true for Dynamite. The network of PVM daemons plays a central role in the communication between tasks and in initiating and co-ordinating the migration of tasks. Every PVM task has a socket connection with the local PVM daemon. This connection is used for the *indirect routing*. PVM tasks can also establish point-to-point *direct* TCP/IP communication channels with each other, to improve the performance. Task migration is mediated by the local PVM daemon, which sends the checkpoint signal to the task, and subsequently monitors the checkpointing process. After checkpointing, the daemon on the target node restarts the process. Extra care must be taken when migrating PVM tasks to ensure that they do not permanently lose the connection with the rest of the parallel application, and that the PVM message protocol is not violated.

In Dynamite robust mechanisms for address translation, connection flushing and connection (re-) establishment have been incorporated that have been demonstrated to survive thousands of consecutive migrations.

For a detailed description of the implementation, the reader is referred to [8].

3   Migration Decisions

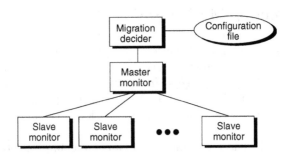

Fig. 2. Monitoring and migration decision sub-system

On each host of a Dynamite-managed resource pool there runs a small and lightweight module which we call the *slave monitor* (Fig. 2). This small program is responsible for frequently (every minute or as specified by the user) collecting status information about its host and sending it to a global *master monitor*. The master monitor therefore receives incoming messages from all hosts and uses this data for creating a history of resource consumption and availability of the complete Dynamite pool. This information is then forwarded to the *migration decider* which determines, when a migration becomes necessary, which tasks will be involved, and where they shall be moved to. Currently, the migration decider uses the following information:

N : number of PVM tasks currently managed by Dynamite

P : number of hosts in the Dynamite pool

$C_{\text{CPU}}^j, C_{\text{Mem}}^j$: relative speed and memory capacity of host j

$l_{\text{CPU}}^i, l_{\text{Mem}}^i$: CPU load and memory usage of PVM task i on a virtual host with $C_{\text{CPU}}^j = C_{\text{Mem}}^j = 1$

$L_{\text{CPU}}^j, L_{\text{Mem}}^j$: load on host j that is not under the control of Dynamite

$W_{\text{CPU}}, W_{\text{Mem}}, W_{\text{Mig}}$: relative importance of balancing CPU and memory load and minimising migrations as specified in the configuration file

H^i : host on which task i currently resides

W_{CPU}, W_{Mem}, and W_{Mig} are provided by the user whereas the remaining parameters are determined automatically by the system (except for $C_{\text{CPU}}^j, C_{\text{Mem}}^j$ which in the current implementation still have to be entered manually).

The migration decider uses two different cost functions for different types of parallel applications. Below is the default function we use for parallel applications which depend mainly on the overall performance of all of the nodes they run on. As a consequence, this cost function steers Dynamite towards an evenly loaded pool. It defines the costs of placing tasks $1, \ldots, N$ onto hosts $h^1, \ldots, h^N$ as:

$$\text{Cost}(h^1, \ldots, h^N) = W_{\text{CPU}} \sum_{j=1}^{P} \left[\underbrace{L_{\text{CPU}}^j}_{(*)} + \underbrace{\sum_{i \in \{1,\ldots,N\}, h^i = j} \frac{l_{\text{CPU}}^i}{C_{\text{CPU}}^j}}_{\text{CPU load on host } j} \right]$$

$$+ W_{\text{Mem}} \sum_{j=1}^{P} \left[\underbrace{L_{\text{Mem}}^j}_{(*)} + \underbrace{\sum_{i \in \{1,\ldots,N\}, h^i = j} \frac{l_{\text{Mem}}^i}{C_{\text{Mem}}^j}}_{\text{Memory load on host } j} \right]$$

$$+ W_{\text{Mig}} \cdot \underbrace{\text{Card} \left\{ i \in \{1, \ldots, N\} \mid h^i \neq H^i \right\}}_{\text{Necessary task migrations}}$$

This cost function has also been used for the experiments presented in Sec. 4. If tasks have to be managed that show a more synchronous behaviour, it is less important to achieve an equally balanced situation. Instead, the primary goal should then be to reduce the load of the mostly loaded host. Hence, in such a situation the user can choose to apply a second cost function in which the two sums marked with (*) are replaced by the maximum function.

The problem of mapping an arbitrary set of tasks onto a heterogeneous set of hosts is known to be NP-hard. Hence, we decided to use a simple hill climbing heuristics for the first prototype of the migration decider. Unfortunately it turned out that hill climbing failed in some very common Dynamite scenarios. Fig. 3

depicts such a case where two large tasks are running on the same host and one of these is not under the control of Dynamite. This situation represents a local minimum to hill climbing.

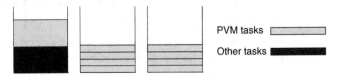

Fig. 3. A common local minimum for hill climbing

If Dynamite was to be used for managing large computing environments with hundreds or thousands of hosts, it probably would be best to use more advanced search heuristics like for instance genetic algorithms or simulated annealing. However, since the original design was made with smaller installations in mind, we decided to take a more problem oriented approach. In our target scenario it is often possible to do an exhaustive search which then results in an optimal solution and therefore avoids non-promising but still expensive migration steps.

The search algorithm that is now used in the migration decider is based on the well known branch and bound algorithm. This technique was adapted to Dynamite by two modifications:

1. The search tree is ordered in a way that increases the probability of early cut-offs. To achieve this, the current placement is made the root of the search tree. This also ensures a very rapid search, if the current situation is already balanced. Furthermore, the first levels of the tree involve placements of the heaviest tasks. As a consequence, many wrong decisions can be detected early in the search.
2. The user can specify an upper time bound for the exhaustive search. If the global optimum could not be determined in time, the algorithm will then return the best local optimum it has encountered. Due to the pre-processed search order, it is likely that the still unexplored areas of the search space contain mostly placements of small tasks and are therefore less important for the overall quality of the solution.

4   Performance Measurements

In order to prove that Dynamite delivers what it promises, a number of tests have been conducted.

Some stability testing has been done. Under Solaris, Dynamite was able to make over 2500 successful migrations of large processes (over 20 MB of memory image size) of a commercial PVM application Pam-Crash [19] using direct connections, after which the application finished normally. Similar results have been obtained under Linux.

A series of performance measurements was made on the selected nodes of the DAS cluster [18], which run Linux kernel 2.0 and 2.2 on PentiumPro 200 MHz

CPUs. The scientific application Grail [13,14], a FEM simulation program, has been used as the test application.

Table 1. Execution time of the Grail application, in seconds.

	Parallel environment	Execution time
1	PVM	1854
2	DPVM	1880
3	DPVM + sched.	1914
4	DPVM + load	3286
5	DPVM + sched. + load	2564

Table 1 presents the results of these tests, obtained using the internal timing routines of Grail. Each test has been performed a number of times and an average of the wall clock execution times of the master process (in seconds) has been taken. The parallel application consisted of 3 tasks (1 master and 2 slaves) running on 4 nodes. To obtain the best performance, when using plain PVM, it would be typical to use a number of nodes equal to the number of processes of the parallel application. In this example, for DPVM, one node is left idle (DPVM chooses to put the group server there, but this uses only a minimal amount of CPU time). Such a decomposition would be wasteful for standard PVM.

In the first set of tests presented in Table 1, standard PVM 3.3.11 has been used as the parallel environment.

In the second row, PVM has been replaced by DPVM. A slight deterioration in performance (1.5%) can be observed. This is mostly the result of the fact that migration is not allowed while executing some parts of the DPVM code. These *critical sections* must be protected, and the overhead stems from the *locking* used. Moreover, all messages exchanged by the application processes have an additional, short (8 byte) DPVM fragment header.

In the test presented in the third row, the complete Dynamite environment has been started: in addition to using DPVM, the monitoring and scheduling subsystem is running. Because in this case the initial mapping of the application processes onto the nodes is optimal, and no external load is applied, no migrations are actually performed. Therefore, all of the observed slowdown (approx. 2%) can be interpreted as the monitoring overhead.

In the fourth set of tests an artificial, external load has been applied. This has been achieved by running a single, CPU-intensive process for 600 seconds on each node in turn, in a cycle. Since the monitoring and scheduling subsystem was not running, no migrations could take place. A considerable slowdown of about 75% can be observed.

The final, fifth set of tests is the combination of the two previous tests: the complete Dynamite environment is running, and the external load is applied. Dynamite clearly shows its value: by migrating the application tasks away from the overloaded nodes, it manages to reduce the slowdown from 75% to 34%. The following factors contribute to the remaining slowdown:

– it takes some time for the monitor to notice that the load on the node has
  increased and to make the migration decision,
– the cost of the migration itself,
– the master task, which is started directly from the terminal window, is not
  migrated; when the external load procedure was modified to skip the node
  with the master task, the slowdown decreased by a further 10%.

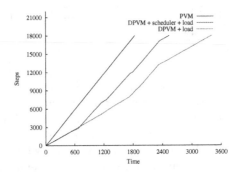

Fig. 4. Execution progress of Grail for three cases. Note that the plain PVM run was
made without an external load, whereas both DPVM runs were done with such a load
(see text).

Figure 4 presents the execution progress of Grail for three of the five cases.
For the standard PVM with no load applied this is a straight, steep line. The
other two lines represent DPVM with load applied, with and without the monitoring subsystem running. Initially, they both progress much slower than PVM –
because the load is initially applied to the node with the master task, no migrations take place. After approximately 600 seconds the load moves on to another
node. Subsequently, in the case with the monitoring subsystem running, the mi-
grator moves the application task out of the overloaded node, and the progress
improves significantly, coming close to the one of the standard PVM. In the case
with no monitoring subsystem running, there is no observable change at this
point. However, it does improve between 1800 and 2400 seconds from the start:
that is when the idle node is overloaded. After 2400 seconds from the start, the
node with the master task is overloaded again, so the performance deteriorates
in both DPVM cases.

Experiments presented in [7] demonstrate that Dynamite works best for programs with a moderate to high computation to communication ratio and moderate task sizes.

Initial experiments using the Dynamite scheduler for cluster management
are inconclusive: it functions for small to medium number of tasks, but when
the number of tasks significantly exceeds the number of available nodes, the
scheduler doesn't seem to be able to balance them properly.

5   Limitations

The Dynamite system has a number of limitations, most of which are the limitations of the checkpointing mechanism itself. The checkpointer is designed to preserve the memory image of the process and its open files, but nothing more than that. For example, processes that use any of the following features will not be migrated properly:

- pipes,
- sockets,
- System V IPC, like shared memory,
- kernel supported threads,
- mmapping/opening of special files, like /dev/..., /proc/..., etc.

Some of these, like sockets, might eventually be supported, but supporting shared memory is practically unsolvable in general.

Another limitation, specific to the DPVM subsystem, is an inability to migrate the master PVM task if it is started from the terminal window. Such a task checkpoints correctly, but in order to restart properly, it would have to be restarted manually from a terminal window, whereas it is started by the PVM daemon on the destination host, without standard input and with redirected standard output/error streams. Because of these limitations, the restarted process hangs.

As regards the scheduler, we find that sub-optimal decisions are sometimes made in complex situations. Further research into scheduling methods for dynamic task re-allocation is needed.

6   Conclusions and Future Prospects

Concluding, task migration in parallel programs has been shown to provide a viable solution to the load-balancing problem. We have succeeded in implementing such a system completely in user space. Since the system is stable now, it can now be used as a research and production tool.

It has also been demonstrated that Dynamite can realise an optimal utilisation of system resources for long-running jobs (a couple of hours and more).

The mean system load is not always a good criterion for load balancing. Future experiments will include the maximum load criterion and possible others.

Dynamite is transparent (existing object files can be relinked to create a Dynamite-enabled executable). Its checkpointing mechanism is easily portable to other operating systems using the ELF binary format.

Dynamite aims to provide a complete integrated solution for dynamic load balancing. In order to accomplish this, the following challenges are still to be solved:

- support for MPI,
- generic support for the migration of the TCP/IP sockets,
- support for Linux GNU libc 2.1 library.

Meanwhile, Dynamite will be used as a research tool, in order to do experiments on dynamic task scheduling, which is an area of active research. Currently, attempts are being made to assess the usefulness of Dynamite as a cluster-management type software. The results of these experiments will be presented in the future.

References

1. Albada, G.D. van, Clinckemaillie, J., Emmen, A.H.L., Gehring, J., Heinz, O., Linden, F. van der, Overeinder, B.J., Reinefeld, A., Sloot, P.M.A.: Dynamite blasting obstacles to parallel cluster computing. in Sloot, P.M.A., Bubak, M., Hoekstra, A.G., Hertzberger, L.O., editors, High-Performance Computing and Networking (HPCN Europe '99), LNCS **1593** 300 310
2. Casas, J., Clark, D.L., Konuru, R., Otto, S.W., Prouty, R.M., Walpole, J.: MPVM A Migration Transparant Version of PVM. Computer Systems **8 nr 2** (1995) 171 216
3. Czarnul, P., Krawczyk, H.: Dynamic Allocation with Process Migration in Distributed Environments. in Dongarra, J.J., Luque, E., Margalef, T., editors, Recent Advances in Parallel Virtual Machine and Message Passing Interface: 6th European PVM/MPI Users' Group Meeting, LNCS **1697** (1999) 509 516
4. Dan, P., Dongsheng, W., Youhui, Z., Meiming, S.: Quasi-asynchronous Migration: A Novel Migration Protocol for PVM Tasks. Operating Systems Review **33 nr 2** (1999) 5 14
5. Geist, A., Beguelin, A., Dongarra, J., Jiang, W., Mancheck, R., Sunderam, V.: PVM: Parallel Virtual Machine. A Users' Guide and Tutorial for Networked Parallel Computing. MIT Press, Cambridge, Massachusetts (1994) http://www.epm.ornl.gov/pvm/
6. Iskra, K.A., Hendrikse, Z.W., Albada, G.D. van, Overeinder, B.J., Sloot, P.M.A.: Experiments with Migration of PVM Tasks. in ISThmus 2000, Research and Development for the Information Society, Conference Proceedings, Poznan, Poland (2000) 295 304
7. Iskra, K.A., Hendrikse, Z.W., Albada, G.D. van, Overeinder, B.J., Sloot, P.M.A.: Performance Measurements on Dynamite/DPVM. in Dongarra, J., Kacsuk, P., Podhorszki, N., editors, Recent Advances in PVM and MPI. 7th European PVM/MPI User's Group Meeting, LNCS **1908** (2000) (in press)
8. Iskra, K.A., Linden, F. van der, Hendrikse, Z.W., Albada, G.D. van, Overeinder, B.J., Sloot, P.M.A.: The implementation of Dynamite an environment for migrating PVM tasks. Operating Systems Review **nr 3** (2000) 40 55
9. Litzkow, M., Tannenbaum, T., Basney, J., Livny, M.: Checkpoint and migration of Unix processes in the Condor distributed processing system. Technical Report 1346, University of Wisconsin, WI, USA (1997)
10. Livny, M., Pruyne, J.: Managing Checkpoints for Parallel Programs, in Rudolph, L., Feitelson, D. G. editors: Proceedings IPPS Second Workshop on Job Scheduling Strategies for Parallel Processing, LNCS **1162** (1996) 140 154
11. Overeinder, B.J., Sloot, P.M.A., Heederik, R.N., Hertzberger, L.O.: A dynamic load balancing system for parallel cluster computing. Future Generation Computer Systems **12** (1996) 101 115
12. Robinson, J., Russ, S.H., Flachs, B., Heckel, B.: A task migration implementation of the Message Passing Interface. Proceedings of the 5th IEEE international symposium on high performance distributed computing (1996) 61 68

13. Ronde, J.F. de, Albada, G.D. van, Sloot, P.M.A.: High Performance Simulation of Gravitational Radiation Antennas, in L.O. Hertzberger, P.M.A. Sloot, editors, High Performance Computing and Networking, LNCS **1225** (1997) 200 212

14. Ronde, J.F. de, Albada, G.D. van, Sloot, P.M.A.: Simulation of Gravitational Wave Detectors. Computers in Physics, **11 nr 5** (1997) 484 497

15. Tan, C.P., Wong, W.F., Yuen, C.K.: tmPVM   Task Migratable PVM. Proceedings of the 2nd Merged Symposium IPPS/SPDP. (1999) 196 202

16. MPI: A Message-Passing Interface Standard, Version 1.1. Technical Report, University of Tennessee, Knoxville (1995) `http://www-unix.mcs.anl.gov/mpi/`

17. `http://www.genias.de/products/codine/`

18. The Distributed ASCI Supercomputer (DAS).
    `http://www.cs.vu.nl/das/`

19. `http://www.esi.fr/products/crash/`

Adaptive Scheduling for Master-Worker Applications on the Computational Grid

Elisa Heymann[1], Miquel A. Senar[1], Emilio Luque[1], and Miron Livny[2]

[1] Unitat d'Arquitectura d'Ordinadors i Sistemes Operatius
Universitat Autònoma de Barcelona
Barcelona, Spain
{e.heymann, m.a.senar, e.luque}@cc.uab.es

[2] Department of Computer Sciences
University of Wisconsin– Madison
Wisconsin, USA
miron@cs.wisc.edu

Abstract[*]. We address the problem of how many workers should be allocated for executing a distributed application that follows the master-worker paradigm, and how to assign tasks to workers in order to maximize resource efficiency and minimize application execution time. We propose a simple but effective scheduling strategy that dynamically measures the execution times of tasks and uses this information to dynamically adjust the number of workers to achieve a desirable efficiency, minimizing the impact in loss of speedup. The scheduling strategy has been implemented using an extended version of MW, a runtime library that allows quick and easy development of master-worker computations on a computational grid. We report on an initial set of experiments that we have conducted on a Condor pool using our extended version of MW to evaluate the effectiveness of the scheduling strategy.

1. Introduction

In the last years, Grid computing [1] has become a real alternative to traditional supercomputing environments for developing parallel applications that harness massive computational resources. However, by its definition, the complexity incurred in building such parallel Grid-aware applications is higher than in traditional parallel computing environments. Users must address issues such as resource discovery, heterogeneity, fault tolerance and task scheduling. Thus, several high-level programming frameworks have been proposed to simplify the development of large parallel applications for Computational Grids (for instance, Netsolve [2], Nimrod/G [3], MW [4]).

Several programming paradigms are commonly used to develop parallel programs on distributed clusters, for instance, Master-Worker, Single Program Multiple Data (SPMD), Data Pipelining, Divide and Conquer, and Speculative Parallelism [5]. From

---

[*] This work was supported by the CICYT (contract TIC98-0433) and by the Commission for Cultural, Educational and Scientific Exchange between the USA and Spain (project 99186).

R. Buyya and M. Baker (Eds.:) GRID 2000, LNCS 1971, pp. 214-227, 2000.
© Springer-Verlag Berlin Heidelberg 2000

the previously mentioned paradigms, the Master-Worker paradigm (also known as task farming) is especially attractive because it can be easily adapted to run on a Grid platform. The Master-Worker paradigm consists of two entities: a master and multiple workers. The master is responsible for decomposing the problem into small tasks (and distributes these tasks among a farm of worker processes), as well as for gathering the partial results in order to produce the final result of the computation. The worker processes execute in a very simple cycle: receive a message from the master with the next task, process the task, and send back the result to the master. Usually, the communication takes place only between the master and the workers at the beginning and at the end of the processing of each task. This means that, master-worker applications usually exhibit a weak synchronization between the master and the workers, they are not communication intensive and they can be run without significant loss of performance in a Grid environment.

Due to these characteristics, this paradigm can respond quite well to an opportunistic environment like the Grid. The number of workers can be adapted dynamically to the number of available resources so that, if new resources appear they are incorporated as new workers in the application. When a resource is reclaimed by its owner, the task that was computed by the corresponding worker may be reallocated to another worker.

In evaluating a Master-Worker application, two performance measures of particular interest are *speedup* and *efficiency*. Speedup is defined, for each number of processors n, as the ratio of the execution time when executing a program on a single processor to the execution time when n processors are used. Ideally we would expect that the larger the number of workers assigned to the application the better the speedup achieved. Efficiency measures how good is the utilization of the n allocated processors. It is defined as the ratio of the time that n processors spent doing useful work to the time those processors would be able to do work. Efficiency will be a value in the interval [0,1]. If efficiency is becoming closer to 1 as processors are added, we have linear speedup. This is the ideal case, where all the allocated workers can be kept usefully busy.

In general, the performance of master-worker applications will depend on the temporal characteristics of the tasks as well as on the dynamic allocation and scheduling of processors to the application. In this work, we consider the problem of maximizing the speedup and the efficiency of a master-worker application through both the allocation of the number of processors on which it runs and the scheduling of tasks to workers at runtime.

We address this goal by first proposing a generalized master-worker framework, which allows adaptive and reliable management and scheduling of master-worker applications running in a computing environment composed of opportunistic resources. Secondly, we propose and evaluate experimentally an adaptive scheduling strategy that dynamically measures application efficiency and task execution times, and uses this information to dynamically adjust the number of processors and to control the assignment of tasks to workers.

The rest of the paper is organized as follows. Section 2 reviews related work in which the scheduling of master-worker applications on Grid environments was studied. Section 3 presents the generalized Master-Worker paradigm. Section 4 presents a definition of the scheduling problem and outlines our adaptive scheduling strategy for master-worker applications. Section 5 describes the prototype implementation of the scheduling strategy and section 6 shows some experimental data obtained when the proposed scheduling strategy was applied to some synthetic applications on a real grid environment. Section 7 summarizes the main results presented in this paper and outlines our future research directions.

2. Related Work

One group of studies has considered the problem of scheduling master-worker applications with a single set of tasks on computational grids. They include AppLeS [6], NetSolve [7] and Nimrod/G [3].

The AppLeS (Application-Level Scheduling) system focuses on the development of scheduling agents for parallel metacomputing applications. Each agent is written in a case-by-case basis and each agent will perform the mapping of the user's parallel application [8]. To determine schedules, the agent must consider the requirements of the application and the predicted load and availability of the system resources at scheduling time. Agents use the services offered by the NWS (Network Weather Service) [9] to monitor the varying performance of available resources.

NetSolve [2] is a client-agent-server system, which enables the user to solve complex scientific problems remotely. The NetSolve agent does the scheduling by searching for those resources that offer the best performance in a network. The applications need to be built using one of the API's provided by NetSolve to perform RPC-like computations. There is an API for creating task farms [7] but it is targeted to very simple farming applications that can be decomposed by a single bag of tasks.

Nimrod/G [3] is a resource management and scheduling system that focuses on the management of computations over dynamic resources scattered geographically over wide-area networks. It is targeted to scientific applications based on the "exploration of a range of parameterized scenarios" which is similar to our definition of master-worker applications, but our definition allows a more generalized scheme of farming applications. The scheduling schemes under development in Nimrod/G are based on the concept of computational economy developed in the previous implementation of Nimrod, where the system tries to complete the assigned work within a given deadline and cost. The deadline represents a time which the user requires the result and the cost represents an abstract measure of what the user is willing to pay if the system completes the job within the deadline. Artificial costs are used in its current implementation to find sufficient resources to meet the user's deadline.

A second group of researchers has studied the use of parallel application characteristics by processor schedulers of multiprogrammed multiprocessor systems, typically with the goal of minimizing average response time [10, 11]. However, the results from these studies are not applicable in our case because they were focussed basically on the allocation of jobs in shared memory multiprocessors in which the computing resources are homogeneous and available during all the computation. Moreover, most of these studies assume the availability of accurate historical performance data, provided to the scheduler simultaneously with the job submission. They also focus on overall system performance, as opposed to the performance of individual applications, and they only deal with the problem of processor allocation, without considering the problem of task scheduling within a fixed number of processors as we do in our strategy.

3. A Generalized Master-Worker Paradigm

In this work, we focus on the study of applications that follow a generalized Master-Worker paradigm because it is used by many scientific and engineering applications like software testing, sensitivity analysis, training of neural-networks and stochastic optimization among others. In contrast to the simple master-worker model in which the master solves one single set of tasks, the generalized master-worker model can be used to solve of problems that require the execution of several batches of tasks. Figure 1 shows an algorithmic view of this paradigm.

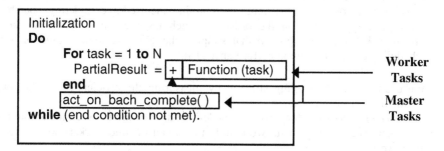

Fig. 1. Generalized Master-Worker algorithm

A Master process will solve the N tasks of a given batch by looking for Worker processes that can run them. The Master process passes a description (input) of the task to each Worker process. Upon the completion of a task, the Worker passes the result (output) of the task back to the Master. The Master process may carry out some intermediate computation with the results obtained from each Worker as well as some final computation when all the tasks of a given batch are completed. After that a new batch of tasks is assigned to the Master and this process is repeated several times until completion of the problem, that is, K cycles (which are later refereed as *iterations*).

The generalized Master-Worker paradigm is very easy to program. All algorithm control is done by one process, the Master, and having this central control point facilitates the collection of job's statistics, a fact that is used by our scheduling mechanism. Furthermore, a significant number of problems can be mapped naturally to this paradigm. N-body simulations [12], genetic algorithms [13], Monte Carlo simulations [14] and materials science simulations [15] are just a few examples of natural computations that fit in our generalized master-worker paradigm.

4. Challenges for Scheduling of Master-Worker Applications

In this section, we give a more precise definition of the scheduling problem for master-worker applications and we introduce our scheduling policy.

4.1. Motivations and Background

Efficient scheduling of a master-worker application in a cluster of distributively owned resources should provide answers to the following questions:

How many workers should be allocated to the application? A simple approach would consist of allocating as many workers as tasks are generated by the application at each iteration. However, this policy will incur, in general, in poor resource utilization because some workers may be idle if they are assigned a short task while other workers may be busy if they are assigned long tasks.

How to assign tasks to the workers? When the execution time incurred by the tasks of a single iteration is not the same, the total time incurred in completing a batch of tasks strongly depends on the order in which tasks are assigned to workers. Theoretical works have proved that simple scheduling strategies based on list-scheduling can achieve good performance [16].

We evaluate our scheduling strategy by measuring the efficiency and the total execution time of the application.

Resource efficiency (*E*) for *n* workers is defined as the ratio between the amount of time workers spent doing useful work and the amount of time workers were able to perform work.

$$E = \frac{\sum_{i=1}^{n} T_{work,i}}{\sum_{i=1}^{n} T_{up,i} - \sum_{i=1}^{n} T_{susp,i}}$$

n: Number of workers.

$T_{work,i}$: Amount of time that worker i spent doing useful work.

$T_{up,i}$: Time elapsed since worker i is alive until it ends.

$T_{susp,i}$: Amount of time that worker i is suspended, that is, when it cannot do any work.

Execution Time (ET$_n$) is defined as the time elapsed since the application begins its execution until it finishes, using *n* workers.

$$ET = T_{finish,n} - T_{begin,n}$$

$T_{finish,n}$: Time of the ending of the application when using *n* workers.

$T_{begin,n}$: Time of the beginning of the application workers.

As [17] we view efficiency as an indication of benefit (the higher the efficiency, the higher the benefit), and execution time as an indication of cost (the higher the execution time, the higher the cost). The implied system objective is to achieve efficient usage of each processor, while taking into account the cost to users. It is important to know, or at least to estimate the number of processors that yield the point at which the ratio between efficiency to execution time is maximized. This would represent the desired allocation of processors to each job.

4.2. Proposed Scheduling Policy

We have considered a group of master-worker applications with an iterative behavior. In these iterative parallel applications a batch of parallel tasks is executed K times (iterations). The completion of a given batch induces a synchronization point in the iteration loop, followed by the execution of a sequential body. This kind of applications has a high degree of predictability, therefore it is possible to take advantage of it to decide both the use of the available resources and the allocation of tasks to workers.

Empirical evidence has shown that the execution of each task in successive iterations tends to behave similarly, so that the measurements taken for a particular iteration are good predictors of near future behavior [15]. As a consequence, our current implementation of adaptive scheduling employs a heuristic-based method that uses historical data about the behavior of the application, together with some parameters that have been fixed according to results obtained by simulation.

In particular, our adaptive scheduling strategy collects statistics dynamically about the average execution time of each task and uses this information to determine the number of processors to be allocated and the order in which tasks are assigned to processors. Tasks are sorted in decreasing order of their average execution time. Then, they are assigned to workers according to that order. At the beginning of the application execution, no data is available regarding the average execution time of tasks. Therefore, tasks are assigned randomly. We call this adaptive strategy *Random and Average* for obvious reasons.

Initially as many workers as tasks per iteration (N) are allocated for the application. We first ask for that maximum number of workers because getting machines in an opportunistic environment is time-consuming. Once we get the maximum number of machines at the start of an application, we release machines if needed, instead of getting a lower number of machines and asking for more.

Then, at the end of each iteration, the adequate number of workers for the application is determined in a two-step approach. The first step quickly reduces the number of workers trying to approach the number of workers to the optimal value. The second step carries out a fine correction of that number. If the application exhibits a regular behavior the number of workers obtained by the first step in the initial iterations will not change, and only small corrections will be done by the second step.

The first step determines the number of workers according to the workload exhibited by the application. Table 1 is an experimental table that has been obtained from simulation studies. In these simulations we have evaluated the performance of different strategies (including *Random and Average* policy) to schedule tasks of master-worker applications. We tested the influence of several factors: the variance of tasks execution times among iterations, the balance degree of work among tasks, the number of iterations and the number of workers used [18].

Table 1 shows the number of workers needed to get efficiency greater than 80% and execution time less than 1.1 the execution time when using N workers. These values would correspond to a situation in which resources are busy most of the time while the execution time is not degraded significantly.

Table 1. Percentage of workers with respect to the number of tasks.

Workload	<30%	30%	40%	50%	60%	70%	80%	90%
%workers (largest tasks similar size)	Ntask	70%	55%	45%	40%	35%	30%	25%
%workers (largest tasks diff. size)	60%	45%	35%	30%	25%	20%	20%	20%

The first row contains the *workload*, defined as the work percentage done when executing the largest 20% tasks. The second and third rows contain the workers percentage with respect to the number of tasks for a given workload in the cases that the 20% largest tasks have similar and different executions times respectively.

For example, if the 20% largest tasks have carried out 40% of the total work then the number of workers to allocate will be either $N*0,55$ or $N*0,35$. The former value will be used if the largest tasks are similar, otherwise the later value is applied. According to our simulation results the largest tasks are considered to be similar if their execution time differences are not greater than 20%.

The fine correction step is carried out at the end of each iteration when the workload between iterations remains constant and the ratio between the last iteration execution time and the execution time with the current number of workers given by table 1 is less than 1.1. This correction consists of diminishing by one the number of workers if efficiency is less than 0.8, and observing the effects on the execution time. If it gets worse a worker is added, but never surpassing the value given by table 1. The complete algorithm is shown in figure 2.

```
1.  In the first iteration Nworkers = Ntasks

    Next steps are executed at the end of each iteration i.

2.  Compute Efficiency, Execution Time, Workload and the Differences of the execution times of the
    20% largest tasks.
3.  if (i == 2)
            Set Nworkers = NinitWorkers according to Workload and Differences of Table 1.
    else
            if (Workload of iteration i != Workload of iteration i-1)
                Set Nworkers = NinitWorkers according to Workload and Differences of  Table 1
            else
                if (Execution Time of it. i DIV Execution Time of it. 2 (with NinitWorkers) <= 1.1)
                    if (Efficiency of iteration i < 0.8)
                            Nworkers = Nworkers – 1
            else
                Nworkers = Nworkers + 1
```

Fig. 2. Algorithm to determine *Nworkers*.

5. Current Implementation

To evaluate both the proposed scheduling algorithm and the technique to adjust the number of workers we have run experiments on a Grid environment using MW library as a Grid middleware. First, we will briefly review the main characteristics of MW and then we will summarize the extensions included to support both our generalized master-worker paradigm and the adaptive scheduling policy.

5.1. Overview of MW

MW is a runtime library that allows quick and easy development of master-worker computations on a computational grid [4]. It handles the communication between master and workers, asks for available processors and performs fault-detection. An application in MW has three base components: Driver, Tasks and Workers. The Driver is the master, who manages a set of user-defined tasks and a pool of workers. The Workers execute Tasks. To create a parallel application the programmer needs to implement some pure virtual functions for each component.

Driver: This is a layer that sits above the program's resource management and message passing mechanisms. (Condor [19] and PVM [20], respectively, in the implementation we have used). The Driver uses Condor services for getting machines to execute the workers and to get information about the state of those machines. It creates the tasks to be executed by the workers, sends tasks to workers and receives the results. It handles workers joining and leaving the computation and rematches running tasks when workers are lost. To create the Driver, the user needs to implement the following pure virtual functions:

get_userinfo(): Processes arguments and does initial setup.

setup_initial_tasks(): Creates the tasks to be executed by the workers.

pack_worker_init_data(): Packs the initial data to be sent to the worker upon startup.

act_on_completed_task(): This is called every time a task finishes.

Task: This is the unit of work to be done. It contains the data describing the tasks (inputs) and the results (outputs) computed by the worker. The programmer needs to implement functions for sending and receiving this data between the master and the worker.

Worker: This executes the tasks sent to it by the master. The programmer needs to implement the following functions:

unpack_init_data(): Unpacks the initialization data passed in the Driver pack_worker_init_data() function.

execute_task(): Computes the results for a given task.

5.2. Extended Version of MW

In its original implementation, MW supported one master controlling only one set of tasks. Therefore we have extended the MW API to support our programming model, the *Random and Average* scheduling policy and to collect useful information to adjust the number of workers.

To create the master process the user needs to implement another pure virtual function: **global_task_setup**. There are also some changes in the functionality of some others pure virtual functions:

global_task_setup(): It initializes the data structures needed to keep the tasks results the user want to record. This is called once, before the execution of the first iteration.

setup_initial_tasks (iterationNumber): The set of tasks created depends on the iteration number. So, there are new tasks for each iteration, and these tasks could depend on values returned by the execution of previous tasks. This function is called before each iteration begins, and creates the tasks to be executed in the *iterationNumber* iteration.

get_userinfo(): The functionality of this function remains the same, but the user needs to call the following initialization functions there:

- **set_iteration_number (n)**: This is used to set the number of times tasks will be created and executed, that is, the number of iterations. If **INFINITY** is used to set the iterations number, then tasks will be created and executed until an end condition is achieved. This condition needs to be set in the function **end_condition()**.

- **set_Ntasks (n)**: This is used to set the number of tasks to be executed per iteration.

- **set_task_retrive_mode (mode)**: This function allows the user to select the scheduling policy. It can be FIFO (**GET_FROM_BEGIN**), based on a user key (**GET_FROM_KEY**), random (**GET_RANDOM**) or random and average (**GET_RAND_AVG**).

- **printresults (iterationNumber)**: It allows the results of the *iterationNumber* iteration to be printed.

In addition to the above changes, the MW*Driver* collects statistics about tasks execution time, workers' state (when they are alive, working and suspended), and about iteration beginning and ending.

At the end of each iteration, function **UpdateWorkersNumber()** is called to adjust the number of workers accordingly with regard to the algorithm explained in the previous section.

6. Experimental Study in a Grid Platform

In this section we report the preliminary set of results obtained with the aim of testing the effectiveness of the proposed scheduling strategy. We have executed some synthetic master-worker applications that could serve as representative examples of the generalized master-workers paradigm. We run the applications on a grid platform and we have evaluated the ability of our scheduling strategy to dynamically adapt the number of workers without any *a priori* knowledge about the behavior of the applications.

We have conducted experiments using a grid platform composed of a dedicated Linux cluster running Condor, and a Condor pool of workstations at the University of Wisconsin. The total number of available machines was around 700 although we restrict our experiments to machines with Linux architecture (both from the dedicated cluster and the Condor pool). The execution of our application was carried out using the grid services provided by Condor for resource requesting and detecting, determining information about resources and fault detecting. The execution of our application was carried out with a set of processors that do not exhibit significant differences in performance, so that the platform could be considered to be homogeneous.

Our applications executed 28 synthetic tasks at each iteration. The number of iterations was fixed to 35 so that the application was running in a steady state most of the time. Each synthetic task performed the computation of a Fibonacci series. The length of the series computed by each task was randomly fixed at each iteration in such a way that the variation of the execution time of a given task in successive iterations was 30%. We carried out experiments with two synthetic applications that exhibited a workload distribution of 30% and 50% approximately. In the former case, all large tasks exhibited a similar execution time. In the latter case, the execution time of larger tasks exhibited significant differences. These two synthetic programs can be representative examples for master-worker applications with a highly balanced distribution of workload and medium balanced distribution of workload between tasks, respectively. Figure 3 shows, for instance, the average and the standard deviation time for each of the 28 tasks in the master-worker with a 50% workload.

Different runs on the same programs generally produced slightly different final execution times and efficiency results due to the changing conditions in the grid environment. Hence, average-case results are reported for sets of three runs.

Tables 2 and 3 show the efficiency, the execution time (in seconds) and the speedup obtained by the execution of the master-worker application with 50% workload and 30% workload, respectively. The results obtained by our adaptive scheduling are shown in bold in both tables. In addition to these results, we show the results obtained when a fixed number of processors were used during the whole execution of the application. In particular, we tested a fixed number of processors of n=28, n=25, n=20, n=15, n=10, n=5 and n=1. In all cases the order of execution was carried out according to the sorted list of average execution time (as described in previous section for the *Random and Average* policy). The execution time for n=1 was used to compute the speedup of the other cases. It is worth pointing out that the number of processors allocated by our adaptive strategy was obtained basically through table 1. Only in the case of 30% workload, did the fine adjustment carry out the additional reduction of the number of processors.

The first results shown in tables 2 and 3 are encouraging as they prove that an adaptive scheduling policy like *Random and Average* was able, in general, to achieve a high efficiency in the use of resources while the speedup was not degraded significantly. The improvement in efficiency can be explained because our adaptive strategy tends to use a small number of resources with the aim of avoiding idle time in workers that compute short tasks. In general, the larger the number of processors the larger the idle times incurred by workers in each iteration. This situation is also more remarkable when the workload of the application is more unevenly distributed among tasks. Therefore, for a given number of processors the largest loss of efficiency was obtained normally in the application with a 50% workload.

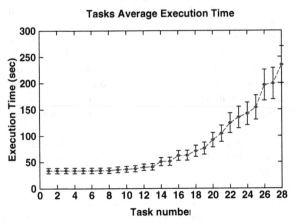

Fig. 3. Tasks execution times.

Table 2. Experimental results in the execution of a master-worker application with 50% workload using the *Random and Average* policy.

#Workers	1	5	8	10	15	20	25	28
Efficiency	1	0,94	**0,80**	0,65	0,43	0,33	0,28	0,22
Exec. Time	80192	16669,5	**12351**	12365	13025	12003	12300,5	12701
Speedup	1	4,81	**6,49**	6,49	6,16	6,68	6,52	6,31

Table 3. Experimental results in the execution of a master-worker application with 30% workload using the *Random and Average* policy.

#Workers	1	5	10	15	**18**	20	25	28
Efficiency	1	0,85	0,85	0,87	**0,78**	0,72	0,59	0,55
Exec. Time	36102	9269	4255	3027	**2459**	2710	2794	2434
Speedup	1	3,89	8,48	11,93	**14,68**	13,32	12,92	14,83

It can also be observed in both tables that the adaptive scheduling strategy obtained in general an execution time that was similar or even better than the execution time obtained with a larger number of processors. This result basically reflects the opportunistic nature of the resources that were used in our experiments. The larger the number of processors allocated, the larger the number of task suspensions and reallocations incurred at run time. The need to terminate a task prematurely when the user claimed back the processor prevented normally the benefits in execution time obtained by the use of additional processors. Therefore, from our results, we conclude that, the reduction in the number of processors allocated to an application running in an opportunistic environment is good not only because it improves overall efficiency, but it also avoids side effects on the execution time due to suspensions and reallocations of tasks.

As is perhaps to be expected, the best performance was normally obtained when the largest number of machines were used, although better machine efficiencies were obtained when a smaller number of machines were used. These results may seem to be obvious, but it should be stressed that they have been obtained from a real test-bed, in which resources were obtained from a total pool of non-dedicated 700 machines. In this test-bed our adaptive scheduler used only statistics information collected at runtime, and the execution of our applications should copse with the effects of resource obtaining, local suspension of tasks, task reassume and dynamic redistribution of load.

We carried out an additional set of experiments in order to evaluate the influence in the order of task assignment. Due to time constraints, this article only contains the results obtained when a master-worker application with 50% workload was scheduled using a *Random* policy. In this policy, when a worker becomes idle, a random task from the list of pending tasks is chosen and assigned to it. As can be seen when tables 2 and 4 are compared, the order in which tasks are assigned has a significant impact when a small number of workers is used. For less than 15 processors the *Random and Average* policy performs significantly better than the *Random* policy, both in efficiency and in execution time. When 15 or more processors are used, differences between both policies were nearly negligible. This fact can be explained because when the *Random* policy has a large number of available processors, the probability to assign a large task at the beginning is also large. Therefore, in these situations the assignments carried out by both polices are likely to follow a similar order. Only in the case of 20 processors, was *Random's* performance significantly worse than *Random & Average*. However, this could be explained because the tests of the Random policy with 20 processors suffered from many task suspensions and reallocations during their execution.

Table 4. Experimental results for Random scheduling with a master-worker application with 50% workload.

#Workers	1	5	10	15	20	25	28
Efficiency	1	0,80	0,56	0,40	0,34	0,26	0,26
Exec. Time	80192	20055	14121	13273	13153	12109	12716
Speedup	1	4,00	5,68	6,04	6,10	6,62	6,31

7. Conclusions and Future Work

In this paper, we have discussed the problem of scheduling master-worker applications on the computational grid. We have presented a framework for master-worker applications that allow the development of a tailored scheduling strategy. We have proposed a scheduling strategy that is both simple an adaptive and takes into account the measurements taken during the execution of the master-worker application. This information is usually a good predictor of near future behavior of the application. Our strategy tries to allocate and schedule the minimum number of processors that guarantees a good speedup by keeping the processors as busy as possible and avoiding situations in which processors sit idle waiting for work to be done. The strategy allocates the suitable number of processors by using the runtime information obtained from the application, together with the information contained in an empirical table that has been obtained by simulation. Later, the number of processors would eventually be adapted dynamically if the scheduling algorithm detects that the efficiency of the application can be improved without significant losses in performance.

We have built our scheduling strategy using MW as a Grid middleware. And we tested the scheduling strategy on a Grid environment made of several pools of machines, the resources of which were provided by Condor. The preliminary set of tests with synthetic applications allowed us to validate the effectiveness of our scheduling strategy. In general, our adaptive scheduling strategy achieved an efficiency in the use of processors close to 80% while the speedup up of the application was close to the speedup achieved with the maximum number of processors. Moreover, we have observed that our algorithm quickly achieves a stable situation with a fixed number of processors.

There are some ways in which this work can be extended. We have tested our strategy on a homogeneous Grid platform where the resources were relatively closed and the influence of the network latency was negligible. A first extension will adapt the proposed scheduling strategy to handle a heterogeneous set of resources. In order to carry this out, a normalizing factor should be applied to the average execution times to index table 1. Another extension will focus on the inclusion of additional mechanisms that can be used when the distance between resources is significant (for instance, by packing more than one task to a distant worker in order to compensate network delays). A second extension will be oriented to the extension of the scheduling strategy to be applied for applications that are not iterative or that exhibit different behaviors at different phases of the execution. This extension would be useful for applications that follow, for instance, a Divide and Conquer paradigm or a Speculative Parallelism paradigm.

8. References

1. I. Foster and C. Kesselman, "The Grid: Blueprint for a New Computing Infraestructure", Morgan-Kaufmann, 1999.
2. H. Casanova and J. Dongarra, "NetSolve: Network enabled solvers", IEEE Computational Science and Engineering, 5(3) pp. 57-67, 1998.
3. D. Abramson, J. Giddy, and L. Kotler, "High Performance Parametric Modeling with Nimrod/G: Killer Application for the Global Grid?", in Proc. of IPPS/SPDP'2000, 2000.
4. J.-P. Goux, S. Kulkarni, J. Linderoth, M. Yoder, "An enabling framework for master-worker applications on the computational grid", Tech. Report, University of Wisconsin – Madison, March, 2000.
5. L. M. Silva and R. Buyya, "Parallel programming models and paradigms", in R. Buyya (ed.), "High Performance Cluster Computing: Architectures and Systems: Volume 2", Prentice Hall PTR, NJ, USA, 1999.
6. F. Berman, R. Wolski, S. Figueira, J. Schopf and G. Shao, "Application-Level Scheduling on Distributed Heterogeneous Networks", Proc. of Supercomputing'96.

7. H. Casanova, M. Kim, J. S. Plank and J. Dongarra, "Adaptive scheduling for task farming with Grid middleware", International Journal of Supercomputer Applications and High-Performance Computing, pp. 231-240, Volume 13, Number 3, Fall 1999.

8. G. Shao, R. Wolski and F. Berman, "Performance effects of scheduling strategies for Master/Slave distributed applications", Technical Report TR-CS98-598, University of California, San Diego, September 1998.

9. R. Wolski, N. T. Spring and J. Hayes, "The Network Weather Service: a distributed resource performance forecasting service for metacomputing", Journal of Future Generation Computing Systems", Vol. 15, October, 1999.

10. T. B. Brecht and K. Guha, "Using parallel program characteristics in dynamic processor allocation policies", Performance Evaluation, Vol. 27 and 28, pp. 519-539, 1996.

11. T. D. Nguyen, R. Vaswani and J. Zahorjan, "Maximizing speedup through self-tuning of processor allocation", in Proc. of the Int. Par. Proces. Symp. (IPPS'96), 1996.

12. V. Govindan and M. Franklin, "Application Load Imbalance on Parallel Processors", in Proc. of the Int. Paral. Proc. Symposium (IPPS'96), 1996.

13. E. Cantu-Paz, "Designing efficient master-slave parallel genetic algorithms", in J. Koza, W. Banzhaf, K. Chellapilla, K. Deb, M. Dorigo, D. Fogel, M. Garzon D. E. Goldberg, H. Iba and R. Riolo, editors, Genetic Programming: Proceeding of the Third Annual Conference, San Francisco, Morgan Kaufmann, 1998.

14. J. Basney, B. Raman and M. Livny, "High throughput Monte Carlo", Proceedings of the Ninth SIAM Conference on Parallel Processing for Scientific Computing, San Antonio Texas, 1999.

15. J. Pruyne and M. Livny, "Interfacing Condor and PVM to harness the cycles of workstation clusters", Journal on Future Generations of Computer Systems, Vol. 12, 1996.

16. L. A. Hall, "Aproximation algorithms for scheduling", in Dorit S. Hochbaum (ed.), "Approximation algorithms for NP-hard problems", PWS Publishing Company, 1997.

17. D. L. Eager, J. Zahorjan and E. D. Lazowska, "Speedup versus efficiency in parallel systems", IEEE Transactions on Computers, vol. 38, pp. 408-423, 1989.

18. E. Heymann, M. Senar, E. Luque, M. Livny. "Evaluation of an Adaptive Scheduling Strategy for Master-Worker Applications on Clusters of Workstations". Proceedings of 7th Int. Conf. on High Performance Computing (HiPC'2000) (to appear).

19. M. Livny, J. Basney, R. Raman and T. Tannenbaum, "Mechanisms for high throughput computing", SPEEDUP, 11, 1997.

20. A. Geist, A. Beguelin, J. Dongarra, W. Jiang, R. Manchek and V. Sunderam, "PVM: Parallel Virtual Machine A User's Guide and Tutorial for Networked Parallel Computing", MIT Press, 1994.

Authors Index

Lecture Notes in Computer Science

For information about Vols. 1–1882
please contact your bookseller or Springer-Verlag